Horror recollected in tranquillity

MEMORIES OF THE WATERLOO CAMPAIGN

Horror recollected in tranquillity

MEMORIES OF THE WATERLOO CAMPAIGN

Related in letters to his grandchildren
by
Frederick Hope Pattison
(Formerly Captain, 33rd (Duke of Wellington's) Regiment)

Edited by S Monick

Published by
The Naval & Military Press Ltd
PO Box 61, Dallington
Heathfield, East Sussex TN21 9ZS

Text © 2001 S. Monick
This edition © The Naval & Military Press Ltd 2001

First published in 2001 by
The Naval & Military Press Ltd
PO Box 61, Dallington
Heathfield, East Sussex TN21 9ZS

All rights reserved. No part of this book may be reproduced, stored in a retrieval system, or transmitted in any form or by any means without the prior written permission of the publisher, nor be otherwise circulated in any form of binding or cover other that that which it is published and without a similar condition being inposed on the subsequent publisher.

Designed and produced by Well House Publishing

CONTENTS

PART I
Introduction 1
Editorial approach 40

PART II
The Letters 45
Appendices 75

PART III
Notes 81
Biographical note on editor 169
Index 170

Horror recollected in tranquillity

PART I

Introduction

Frederick Hope Pattison's memoirs of the Waterloo campaign were privately printed in Glasgow in 1870, and bear the title *Personal recollections of the Waterloo campaign; in a series of letters to his grandchildren*. The work is certainly modest in its dimensions; a mere 48 pages in its original published form (comprising a series of five letters and appendices). The work's unpretentious character accords with the author's modest role in the battle (as a senior lieutenant and company commander).

We have very little biographical information relating to the author. We know, on the basis of the concluding line of the work, that the author was in excess of 80 years of age when he compiled the *Letters*. The *Waterloo Roll Call* (London: William Clowes & Sons, 1890, p.133) informs us that he served in the rank of lieutenant at Waterloo. The *Army List* informs us that he attained the rank of captain in 1817 and this source further informs us that Pattison was placed on half-pay, in the rank of captain (ie he had retired from the active list) on 2 December 1821. He last appears in the *Army List* of 1830 as a half-pay captain.

Despite this paucity of information, however, we are enabled to derive the impression of a tough, resourceful officer. Two reference in the *Letters* enable us to form such a conclusion. First, we are informed that he was a company commander and, in this role, commanded a key tactical unit within the battalion, at the forefront of the battle (see below). Second, in **Letter V** Pattison alludes to his having been a lieutenant in a grenadier company. The term 'grenadier' should not be confused within this context with the Grenadier Guards. In the 18th century the grenadier companies were the equivalent of today's shock troops. Grenadiers were especially trained troops adroit at hurling grenades, or small bombs (the primitive ancestors of the modern hand grenade). Hence the device of a flaming grenade to denote such a unit. In 1686 King James II had introduced grenadier companies into each line regiment. As the duty of this type of soldier was dangerous and demanded special qualities (similar to those required of a modern commando serving in the Royal Marines or Special Air Service Regiment), the grenadier was regarded as a member of an elite unit. By the latter part of the 18th Century the grenade had been discontinued, but the term 'grenadier' continued to bestow special distinction. (Thus, the First Regiment of Foot Guards was named Grenadiers as an honour after their distinguished service at Waterloo). His membership of such a unit further suggests that Pattison was a physically powerful individual.

We are also informed by Pattison that he was a battle-seasoned soldier. In **Letter I** Pattison states, in a footnote, that he had served in the abortive assault upon Bergen-op-Zoom in Holland, in March 1814. In this theatre of operations Pattison also served at Mexem, (as we are informed in a footnote in **Letter IV**), forming part of the offensive designed to capture Antwerp (in which the British forces co-operated with Bulow's Prussian army). Moreover, a footnote contained in

Letter V indicates that he had served in India, for he refers to having been garrisoned at Seringapatam in 1810. Brig B W Webb-Carter informs us that Pattison purchased an ensign's commission in 1810, joining the 33rd Regiment when it was stationed at Seringapatam. [Webb-Carter, B W (ed). A line regiment at Waterloo. *Journal of Army Historical Research*, Vol 43 (1965), pp 60-66]. We also know, on the basis of a footnote contained in **Letter IV**, that Pattison came to England in 1812, as a member of the headquarters company of the 33rd Regiment, which returned from India in that year.

Pattison also alludes, in a footnote contained in **Letter I**, to his father, and informs us that the family was domiciled in Scotland (specifically, Glasgow, which appears to be the family's continued base throughout the 19th Century, judging from various references to that city dispersed throughout the text). His father appears to have played a prominent role in local politics, being of a liberal persuasion and inflamed sectarian passions in the process. We are also informed in **Letter III** that his brother, Alexander, was an officer of note, having served throughout the Peninsular War with distinction, and as an ADC on Picton's staff at Salamanca (1812).

Important aspects of Pattison's personality clearly emerge in the *Letters*. First, we gain the distinct impression of an educated, cultivated mind. It is apparent that he was fluent in French; whilst the reference to the neo-classical sculptor Canova, in **Letter V**, evinces an interest in the arts. Moreover, it is clear that he was of an intellectual cast of mind. This is demonstrated by his reference to the Swiss philosopher Lavater, in **Letter V**. Second, his thought was profoundly shaped by a religious framework. Metaphorical references of a religious character are prolific; often to a suffocating extent. Religious imagery suffuses Pattison's account. An obvious illustration of this characteristic occurs in **Letter II**; in which the downpour of rain that descended on the field of Waterloo, on the day prior to the battle, is transmuted into Elijah's breaking of the drought that had plagued Israel.

The *Letters*

The principal power of the *Letters* derive from their narrowly individualized approach; ie the preponderant value placed upon the highly personalized response. The title makes the reader immediately aware of this approach (Personal recollections...) and it is reiterated in the following comment (Letter III):

> 'It would manifestly be impossible for one who held so narrow and circumscribed a position as I did in the battle, being merely an officer commanding a company of infantry, to attempt a detailed account of the stupendous incidents which transpired during this momentous day. To do so adequately would have required ubiquity of body or omniscience of mind. To avoid, therefore, all risk of misinterpretation, I shall confine myself entirely to incidents which occurred in my immediate neighbourhood, and fell directly under my own observation.'

The approach to the narrative, as a consequence of this highly individualized response, is impressionistic. One may quote as an illustration the following passage from Letter I:

'Captain Haigh, perceiving that the front of the square facing the artillery was bending inwards, left his place much excited, and, flourishing his sword, called aloud, vehemently with an oath, "Keep up, keep up; I say keep up". The words were vibrating on his lips, when a cannon-ball hit him on the abdomen, and cut him nearly in twain. He fell on his back; the separation between soul and body was most appalling. His eyes strained as if they would leap from their sockets and the quiver of the lip with the strong convulsion of his whole frame, showed unquestionably how unwilling his spirit was to be driven in this ruthless way from her clay tenement.'

Pattison, therefore, does not merely drily comment that the square formed by the 33rd Regiment was savaged by artillery fire. He highlights this vulnerability of the square to cannon by narrating a vivid individual example of the slaughter created. In this respect, the tactics and weapons technology of the period are presented to the reader through the prism of the writer's personal experience. Similarly, in reflecting upon the carnage created by the battle of Waterloo, Pattison states in **Letter V**:

'The shooting rays from the east, which heralded the birth of another day, spread light over a series of blood and desolation unparalleled in modern warfare...the passions that govern men in life are fixed, so that even the cold hand of death cannot remove them from his countenance. Here indeed was a large field of contemplation; and among the dead around me, one instance was so illustrative of the truth of this statement that I cannot resist giving it. A French gunner, whose back had been placed in an erect position against the wheel of a broken-gun carriage, was an expression so life-like it required almost minute examination to realize that the vital spark had fled. His shako, which lay at his right side, had fallen from his head, and completely exposed his face. His large blue eyes seemed fixed on *me*, and wore even in death a living expression. His right hand was raised as if under great excitement, and for a second I imagined him to be yet alive, and in the act of enthusiastically exclaiming, "Vive l'Empereur".'

The vivid and dramatic pen portrait of the dead French gunner projects the intensity of a Goya painting. The two passages quoted above exemplify a vital element in the atmospheric effects created by the writer; viz their visual quality. The writer's personal narrative of the Waterloo campaign evokes the impression of a series of graphic sketches in which the reader's eye is the dominant faculty which responds. Two further illustrations underscore this facet. In **Letter I** Pattison relates the death of an officer of the grenadier company, one Lt Arthur Gore:

'At this juncture Lieutenant Arthur Gore of the Grenadier Company, who was standing close by me (an exceedingly handsome young man; like Saul, from his shoulders and upwards he was higher than any of his compatriots), was hit by a cannon ball, and his brains bespattered the shakos of the officers near him.'

In **Letter V** Pattison relates the death of a further member of his battalion:

> 'My right hand man, a brave fellow, was at this instant shot right through the head. He leaned on me in falling; the ball entered his left temple, and I can never forget the impression of his countenance in the momentary transition from life to death.'

The writing of history assumes many forms. At one level the reader encounters the detailed analytical study of the military historian. However, such analyses invariably lack the immediacy and power of the atmosphere created by conflict. In recording his vivid impressions of the battles in which he was engaged, cast in a largely visual mould, Pattison reminds us that this dimension of felt experience is an equally valid aspect of the writing of military history. If the objective military historian suggests the wide angled lens of the photographer, seeking to encompass an all-embracing approach, Pattison's letters exemplify the sharply angled, close up focus. Indeed, the vigour and freshness communicated to the reader via Pattison's personalized impressions relegate the marked lack of historical veracity to a subordinate consideration. An immediate illustration of this facet occurs in a footnote appended to **Letter IV**. The charming anecdote detailing the presence of the Duke of Clarence (the future William IV) at Antwerp greatly detracts from the error concerning the Duke's relationship to Queen Victoria. Such anecdotes further convey a certain connotation of eccentricity (as in the outlandish comparison of the Duke of Clarence with King Charles XII of Sweden).

One thus gains the distinct and powerful impression, in these letters, of a sharply individual timbre and intonations speaking directly, after more than a century, of deeply felt experience borne of the heat of battle. Pattison certainly displays remarkable powers of recall in relating events that he had witnessed, and actively participated in, 55 years previously. Memory is obviously the key to access to this narration (as opposed to diaries or journals). He acknowledges the predominant role played by this faculty in the opening paragraph:

> 'It is an axiom, that events which occur in childhood or youth leave an imperishable impression on the memory; whereas those which take place in declining years, "when the keepers of the house tremble", may be likened to characters written on the sea-shore, perfectly legible when executed, but only remaining so until the receding tide returns to obliterate them for ever.'

[It may be incidentally noted that this opening paragraph introduces a dominant element in the style of the letters; viz the role of metaphor, which invariably produces hyperbole through the straining of this desire for effect. This aspect of Pattison's style is immediately apparent in the description of Capt Haigh's death, quoted above, and is discussed below, within the context of the literary dimension of the work]. One need not doubt the authenticity of this reconstruction. Such recall of vivid and minutely detailed events is not unknown in the literature of war. [An immediate example that suggests itself is Henry Williamson's series of autobiographical novels relating to the Western Front of 1914-1918 (*A test to destruction*, *Fox under my cloak*, *Love and the loveless*, and *The golden virgin*, which bear the generic title, *Chronicles of ancient sunlight*). Written some 40 years after the events which they describe, the novels feature the hero, Philip Madison, with whom the author totally identified. As with Williamson's work - although obviously on a minuscule scale in comparison - Pattison's memoirs, related over half a century after the events described occurred - convey an accumulated sense of 'felt life', and the reader is saturated with the atmospheric effects created by the writer.

The narrowly circumscribed scope of the work lends a strong sense of compactness to the work. As a result, it does not become unbalanced through being subject to wearying digressions involved in a detailed study of strategy or tactics, for example. (Where the writer does deal with such topics, they are woven into the movements of his battalion and always related with a conciseness which is never subject to vague generalities). The author is, admittedly, deflected at numerous points from the main flow of his narrative, often encapsulated in footnotes. However, such interpolations add to the charm of the work; for they reinforce the impression of spoken communication (digressions being a feature of orally communicated history). These footnotes often exemplify afterthoughts, so to speak, careering at a tangent from the main stream of the writer's thought; a characteristic feature of orally transmitted reminiscences. A notable illustration of this facet is evidenced in **Letter III**, in a postscript ('Memorandum') in which the author relates the hospitality accorded him by a French veteran of Napoleon's army, in the course of the march which followed the battle of Waterloo. It is noteworthy that such afterthoughts embody a common aspect of memory; viz the recollection of finer detail juxtaposed with confusion over more general points. To return to the example furnished in the footnote appended to **Letter IV**, Pattison evinces a detailed recollection of Carnot's frustration of the British attempt to destroy the French ships in Antwerp; whilst mistaking King William IV as the father, instead of the uncle, of Queen Victoria. A major characteristic of the work is the numerous biographical details but these do not disrupt the narrative continuity as they are introduced on the basis of having been personal acquaintances of the writer (a further illustration of the Letters' vivid recapture of orally transmitted testimony); as in the case of Maj Gen Cooke, Lt Col Elphinstone, Lt James Furlong (who furnish footnotes in **Letter I**); Capt James Drummond Elphinstone and Lt Pagan (footnotes in **Letter III**). Moreover, whilst unobtrusively presented, such biographical details lend a certain depth to the characters presented, who are humanized in the process (as in the case of Capt Haigh, whose death is related in **Letter I**; cf above). Personalities such as the captain would otherwise be presented as mere stereotypes, lacking colour and form. It is also noteworthy that the personal reminiscences contained in the footnotes form a skilful device whereby the history of the 33rd Regiment is interwoven with the narrative of the Waterloo campaign. Thus, in the footnote contained in **Letter I**, relating to the OC of the 33rd Regiment, Lt Col Elphinstone, we are informed of the regiment's service at Bergen-op-Zoom (1814). Similarly, in the footnote concerning Maj Gen Cooke (also contained in **Letter I**), the regiment's service at Bergen-op-Zoom is reiterated. In a similar manner, the footnote relating to the family background of the Haigh brothers recalls the 33rd Regiment's service at Seringapatam, in which their father gained a quartermaster's commission.

It is apparent from the foregoing observations that the *Letters* certainly repay publication (thus affording opportunities for further study). However, in order to provide a detailed critique of the work, it is necessary to analyse its major facets, which operate on two levels. The first is the literary dimension - relating to form and style - and the second is the historical-military context.

THE LITERARY DIMENSION

Form: The letter in the English literary tradition

One is immediately struck by a question relating to the form of the memoirs. For Pattison to encapsulate his memoirs in a series of five letters may perhaps appear a somewhat incongruous form to the modern reader. However, one should bear in mind that this form (the letter as a vehicle of argument, reminiscence, biography, instruction, etc) exemplifies an important skein in the English literary tradition.

The Augustan tradition: The 18th Century witnessed the apotheosis of the art of letter writing. There are numerous illustrations of this process whereby the Augustans cultivated the art of letter writing to a highly sophisticated literary form. One important illustration is the epistolary novel (ie a work of fiction projected in the form of letters). Samuel Richardson's novels (*Pamela, Clarissa Harlowe* and *Sir Charles Grandison*) immediately spring to mind within this context. A second important illustration is contained in the works of 1st Viscount Henry St John Bolingbroke. His work, *A letter to Sir William Wyndham* (written in 1717, but published only in 1753), concerning the Jacobite question, is persuasively written and of interest for Bolingbroke's comments upon his former colleagues, as well as for his description of the court of the Old Pretender (ie James Edward Stuart, the son of the exiled King James II). Bolingbroke's *Letters on the study and use of history* (written in 1735 and published in 1752) argues that England should follow the example of her European neighbours and produce written histories. The book was widely read, and not only in England, for Voltaire acknowledged its influence. In 1736 Bolingbroke also wrote *A letter on the spirit of patriotism*, regarding his future conception of the Tory party (published in 1749). An especially famous series of 18th Century letters was compiled by Philip Dormer Stanhope, 4th Earl of Chesterfield, whose *Letters to his son, Philip Stanhope ...* was published in 1774.

The Romantic tradition: However, the Augustan tradition of the literary letter underwent a marked transformation during the succeeding century. The heavily classical orientation of the 18th Century letter - with its preponderant emphasis upon correct form and highly polished style - yielded during the 19th Century to a far more subjective and personal approach; attaining its apotheosis in the letters of Byron, and especially those of Keats, whose 200 letters were composed within the brief span of only four years. The practice of both letter writing and journal compilation considerably expanded towards the end of the 18th Century and the process continued into the 19th Century. Indeed, the Napoleonic Wars furnish a powerful illustration of this process. Pattison was in actual fact adopting a literary form that had been widely used during the 19th Century as a vehicle for reminiscences and observations relating to the Napoleonic Wars. (The Peninsular War proved to be a prolific source of letters in this regard). The most significant of such letters included those written by: Brig Gen Catlin Craufurd; Lt Gen Thomas Dyneley (covering the period 1806-1815); Sir Augustus Frazer; Maj Edward Griffith; Commissary General Havilland Le Mesurier and his son, Col Havilland Le Mesurier (covering the French Revolutionary Wars and the Peninsular War); Robert Bullard (a general of cavalry); the Pakenham family (spanning the period 1806-1815; Maj Gen Sir F P Robinson); Lt Rice Jones, RE; Ralph Heathcote (entitled *Letters of a young diplomat and soldier during the time of Napoleon*); Arthur Shakespeare; William Warre; the Duke of Wellington (letters written to his brother, William Wellesley); Henry, William and Charles Booth; William Bell, 89th Foot (covering the period 1808-1810); Marshal Beresford (letters written to his wife, Lady Anne Beresford); Lt and Capt George Bowles; Lt William Brereton, RHA; Rev Samuel Briscall; Lt John Carss. (It is the intention of this introduction to seek to prove that the letters of Frederick Hope Pattison embody a worthy addition to this corpus of literature).

The 19th Century witnessed two major breaks with the Augustan tradition of letter writing. The first was the extension of the practice beyond the confines of 'polite society'. This process was obviously intimately related to the increasing affluence of the middle classes, resulting in increased leisure (especially for women); combined with vastly improved communications and postal services (an especially marked feature of the second half of the century). The letters of the 19th Century were directed at a far broader social sector than their 18th Century predecessors. (Pattison's letters are a case in point. Although officially focused upon his grandchildren, the very fact that they were published bespeaks of the author's intention to reach a far wider audience, as he himself acknowledges). Second, one notes the disregard for the highly structured, polished style implicit in the classical canons of Augustan taste. [Samuel Richardson, in point of fact, was a major influence in propagating a far more idiomatic style in his novelettish letters, and, to this context, greatly contributed to the erosion of the Augustan classical tradition in English literature]. Third, one has the dimension of subjectivity; the letter emerging as an emotional liberating force. This expression of emotion was synonymous with what might be termed the feminization of society; not in the sense only that there were to be far more women writers in the course of the 19th Century but - of greater significance - the concept that the release of feminine modes of feeling were an essential component of general human experience. The emotional responses were thus enormously heightened in Romantic literature; in contrast with the Augustan ideal of the narrowly reasoned and tightly imposed control of emotional life. This freedom of emotional expression is a peculiar trait of the Romantic 'sensibility' and is clearly evidenced in Pattison's memoirs. For example, he writes of his reactions to the battle of Quatre Bras in the following terms (**Letter I**):

> 'The multitudinous thoughts which arose and passed through my mind in quick succession, after the termination of this bloody conflict, were so complex and anomalous, that to attempt an analysis of them were altogether vain. The most prominent of these thoughts, however, was a deep sense of gratitude and thankfulness to the God of battles, who gives the victory to whom He pleases for shielding me from those winged messengers of death that had cut down so many of my comrades on my right hand and on my left. summoning them with all their imperfections to his dread tribunal; and for vouchsafing to me the composure and presence of mind to enable me, I trust, to fulfil my duty on that trying occasion.'

In a similar vein of emotional release, he writes in **Letter II**, in relation to the battle of Quatre Bras:

> 'Now that the fierce and cruel passions engendered by war had been softened down, the heart must have been hard indeed which would contemplate without deep emotion and poignant regret, those foul deeds of blood and devastation perpetrated the day before, and forced on our attention by the all-revealing light of another morning. Wives made widows, children fatherless, plighted vows broken, maidens' hearts desolated, these were the remoter associations of the scene. The immediate ghastly and revolting picture that lay before our eyes was made up of a beautiful country, bearing in its bosom the rich fruits of an approaching harvest, trodden under foot, polluted with the blood of our bretheren and strewn with their corpses; cuirassiers dead, still cased in their armour; wounded sufferers fevered; war-horses, artillery-carriages, muskets, pistols, swords, innumerable refuse of cartridges and other implements of war, promiscuously mingled together. O, War! War! offspring of hell and sin, disguise and mingle the cup, as thou wilt, thou art yet indeed a bitter draught.'

Certainly, Pattison is very far indeed from conforming to the popular stereotyped image of the taciturn officer, whose emotions are rigidly controlled (the 'stiff upper lip'). This element of Romantic sensibility precludes any glorification of, or exultancy in, battle. The reader's overriding response to such passages is one of a deeply felt sense of pathos. The sense of profound pathos which the author thus evokes is perhaps most powerfully realized in Pattison's heart rending evocation of the mutilated cavalry mount, standing on only three legs amidst the carnage of the battlefield (**Letter V**). We instantly share with him the deep sense of regret felt at having no recourse to a pistol with which to terminate the poor creature's suffering. One must, of course, acknowledge that the Romantic movement - represented by Wordsworth, Keats, Shelley and other writers - had reached its height in the 1830s, a generation before the letters of Pattison were compiled; and, during the final quarter of the 19th Century, had entered upon a phase of decadence. Nevertheless, the Romantic school had attained its climax at a point in time which coincided with Pattison's youth and middle age and, in this respect, were formative influences in his reading. (We should, however, take note of the fact that we have no idea of assessing the extent to which the letters were the creation of Pattison's assistant, the Rev Hugh Macmillan, whom he acknowledges at the close of his final letter as his interlocutor. The frequent pulpit-type invocations, which are discussed below, might possibly suggest this assistant's intervention. It is feasible, in the light of his advanced years, that Pattison related his reminiscences orally and they were then translated into a literary form by the Rev Macmillan, who thus functioned as a 'ghost writer'. Ultimately, we can only base our critique solely upon the final printed form of the letters).

Style

If one were to attempt to seek the stylistic model of Pattison's letters, one would unhesitatingly present the works of Thomas Carlyle (1795-1881). Carlyle achieved a reputation and position in his lifetime which may be equated with the status of Dr Johnson in the Augustan age. However, the comparison ceases at that juncture; for, in place of the wit, poise and logic - characteristically Augustan qualities - that characterize Johnson's style, Carlyle exudes urgency, compulsion and passion. Carlyle's monumental work, *History of the French Revolution* (1837) firmly established him as a celebrated figure in English letters. He managed to present history as a living, dynamic force in a study which spans the period from the death of Louis XV in 1774 to Napoleon's suppression of the Paris insurrection in 1795. The key to Carlyle's approach was the evocation of vivid portraiture and the presentation of stirring events which bore the strong impress of the poetic imagination. He believed that:

'Reality, if rightly interpreted, is grander than fiction'

and that

'History is the true poetry'.

Thus, in recreating the past and enabling his readers to relive the events that he so graphically describes, he adopted an elaborate rhetorical style: rich in metaphor; abounding in biblical and Shakespearean echoes; redolent with pulpit declarations; infused with probing appeals designed to evoke the responses of the emotions and imaginations. (It is characteristic of the power of the work that *The French Revolution* inspired Dickens to write *A tale of two cities*). The work of Carlyle exemplifies, to a large extent, the impress of the Romantic movement upon the writing of history; an aspect which clearly reinforces the argument of Carlyle's impact upon Pattison.

Carlyle popularized a strident, heavily rhetorical style in Victorian narrative literature. The impress of that influence upon Pattison's style is immediately discernible; and is evidenced in the extracts from his letters quoted above. In the extract commencing,'Now that the fierce and cruel passions engendered by war...' the Shakespearean echo strikes the reader's ear ('foul deeds of blood and devastation...Wives made widows, children fatherless, plighted vows broken, maidens' hearts desolated [evoking clear echoes of *Henry V*] ... O, War! War! offspring of war and sin'). The attempt to activate the imagination is readily apparent in the description of the dead French gunner, referred to above, in which the staring eyes of the corpse remain deeply impressed upon the mind's eye. Throughout, as has been intimated above, one has the profusion of strained metaphor, as in the description of Capt Haigh's death.

The pulpit-type invocations, which are a marked feature of Carlyle's work (he had originally intended to enter the Ministry, having been educated at Edinburgh University) finds clear expression at several points in Pattison's letters. For example, in **Letter V**, in the course of recounting how a musket ball had grazed his skull, he writes:

> 'When a lieutenant in the Grenadier company, I often wished that in stature I had been two inches higher. "Vain man would be wise, though man be born like a wild ass's colt". This miraculous escape ought to have told me the truth of this scriptural declaration, and kept my soul humble and trustful on Him who alone holds in his hands the issues of life and death.'

The declaration from the pulpit resounds in the reader's ears when we read in **Letter V**:

> 'Preparations were soon set on foot to bury the dead by digging large trenches, into which they were thrown promiscuously - friend and foe alike - there to rest in PEACE until the resurrection trumpet shall, by a large blast, awake them from long sleep'.

Summary of literary dimension of Pattison's work

If one were to summarise the purely literary dimension of Pattison's work, one might state that it clearly illustrates the role of the letter in the English literary tradition. During the 19th Century the Augustan tradition in this form - characterised by the highly structured form (conforming to classical canons of taste) and the highly select audience - had undergone a radical transformation under the impact of the Romantic movement. Pattison's letters clearly reflect that transition in terms of taste and style; especially with regard to might be termed the 'feminization' of literature (ie the acceptance of the release of emotion as a legitimate response on the part of the writer), combined with literature's 'democratization' (ie the appeal to a far more broadly based audience). The element of feminization generated that concept of 'sensibility' which a modern audience might well mistake for sentimentality. In projecting this essentially Romantic response to felt experience, Pattison admits of a humane and sensitive approach to war. The work's narrowly personalized approach embodies a welcome addition to our body of personal memoirs relating to the battles of Quatre Bras and Waterloo; a value which owes a great deal to the writer's powerful evocation of atmosphere and visual detail. Ultimately, Pattison's letters project a series of cameo portraits indelibly impressed upon the mind's eye: exampled in the portrayal of the dead

French gunner, his eyes staring fixedly at the writer (and the reader); of Pattison's comrade dropping dead beside him in the square, his blood spattering the shakos of his fellow soldiers; of the mutilated horse standing on three legs in the midst of the battlefield (almost dumbly pleading for an end to his misery); of the wounded French soldier, responding with an incredible stoical silence whilst a ball is extracted from his breast; of the 33rd's square being mercilessly swept by cannon fire, decimating its defenders. One of the most striking features of the work is the capture of the tempo of the campaign. The periods of compulsive urgency are successfully interlocked with the inevitable lulls; largely through the medium of the reflective passages conjoining with the narration of battle scenes.

The military/historical context

Pattison is writing of a campaign which exemplifies a military technology vastly distanced from our own time. In order to bridge this distance, it is necessary to recapture the spirit and tempo of the military context which forms the vital background to Pattison's work. This process of reconstruction must centre upon:
- The social complexion of Wellington's army.
- The organisational structure of that army.
- The organisational structure of the British infantry, the most decisive arm of that force and, obviously, that in which Pattison was most intimately concerned.
- The tactics and drill of the period.

By analysing these central themes of the military-historical background it is hoped to absorb the military and social environment in which Pattison served. A two-fold purpose is served thereby. First, we are made aware of the tensions and pressures of a military scenario which, although obviously archaic in modern terms, was intensely meaningful to its participants. Pattison does not feel it necessary to elucidate such terms as 'line' and 'square', which were fundamental to British tactical manoeuvres at the time of the Waterloo campaign. However, such concepts are alien to the non-specialist reader. By being made fully aware of their implications, we gain access to Pattison's world, and more fully appreciate his role on the battlefield; specifically, the complex pattern of control that he was required to impose upon his company's movements. Further, we gain greater insight into the tactical manoeuvres which he so lucidly and succinctly recounts; as in the case of Sir John Colborn's tactics, which overwhelmed the Imperial Guard. By understanding the conventional tactics of the period we are enabled to understand the character of Sir John's movement when his 52nd Light Infantry advanced in column of companies. Second, it is a truism that character and personality are moulded by environment. By examining the social facets of the British Army during the early decades of the 19th Century, we are made aware of important dimensions of Pattison's personality; especially the ethos shaping the behaviour and attitudes of the officer class. We also gain further insight into the relationship between Pattison and his subordinates in the rank-and-file. Moreover, this process of historical reconstruction enables us to assess the impact of certain events upon the imaginations of the participants. An immediate example is the loss of one of the Colours, which is related in **Letter I**. We gain access to a heightened awareness of the significance of this event if we recognize the profound emotional significance of the Colours in the regiment's collective imagination.

The social character of Wellington's army

'Scum of the earth': At the time of Pattison's service the Catholic-Irish peasantry had dominated the ranks since the first quarter of the 18th Century, when the restriction upon the recruitment of this social and geographical sector had been abolished; whilst most of the remainder had entered the service through desperate force of circumstances. Within this context, Corelli Barnett writes [1]:

> 'The British Army did not reflect the balance of British society. Since the restrictions on the recruitment of Catholic peasants had been removed in the 1780s, there had been a flood of Irish peasants - to the extent that the Commander-in-Chief hesitated to send troops to Ireland in 1797 to put down the feared rebellion because whole regiments were full of Irish. Although the Irish were hardy and brave, they were also ignorant, mad for drink, violent and without self-discipline. The jails of England continued to yield their army of drunks, felons, debtors and psychopaths. There was a leavening of intelligent and "respectable" men in the ranks who had enlisted because of some single social lapse, like a getting girl with child, and of men who chose a soldier's life either for the bounty or delusions of military glory, or for some other reason not readily apparent.'

John Stevenson, who had served in the 3rd Regiment of Foot Guards, in his book *A soldier in time of war* (London, 1841), comments, on p 153, of the social calibre of the British Army, during the first quarter of the 19th Century, in the following terms:

> '... of those who voluntarily enlist, some few are driven by poverty ... but some have disgraced themselves in their situation or employment, many have committed misdemeanours which expose themselves to the penalties of the law of the land, and many are confirmed drunkards - in fact generally speaking such as have been the pests of their neighbourhoods, the annoyance of all respectable persons, the plague of magistracy, and the trouble of the parish soldiers.' [2]

Wellington certainly shared this view. He stated:

> 'I have often been inclined to attribute the frequency and enormity of the crimes committed by the soldiers to our having so many men who left their families to starve, for the inducement of a few guineas to get drunk'.

The Duke further remarked that:

> 'English soldiers are fellows who have enlisted for drink - that is the plain fact - they have all enlisted for drink'.

He argued that if the British Army were to match the French military machine:

'we must compose our army of soldiers drawn from all classes of the population of the country; from the good and middling, as well as in rank as in education, as from the bad, and not, as we in particular do, from the bad only.'

His reference to 'the scum of the earth', however, has been notoriously misinterpreted; for it refers, not to the trained troops (whom he described in a frequently omitted addition as 'the fine fellows they are') but to newly enlisted recruits.

There was thus very little inducement for 'respectable' men to serve in the Army, to which such a social taint was attached. (Indeed, the soldier continued - in the eyes of the general public - to be viewed in the light of anti-social beast, until the appalling conditions to which he was subject were publicized in the reportage of the Crimean War of 1854-1856). There are, however, three important qualifications to this depressing scenario. First, merit displayed in the ranks was recognized by the military authorities and the army offered prospects of a career to individuals whose lack of education would have imposed severe disabilities in civil life. A case in point was John Biddle who, at the time of Waterloo, was 27 year old Colour Sergeant in the light company of the 2nd Battalion of the Coldstream Guards. (The rank of Colour Sergeant was instituted in July 1813 as a means of recognizing the most meritorious NCOs). Biddle was a former labourer from Little Selsey, Worcestershire. He was wounded in the action which took place in the region of Hougoumont and left the regiment in 1825, following 19 years service, with an impeccable record. Within this context, one should note that the British Army was certainly not a closed caste system, and men in the rank-and-file were certainly not excluded from the officer establishment. It is important to bear in mind that a comparatively large number of commissioned officers (5,4% or one officer out of every 20) derived from the ranks. Paradoxically, the British Army was surprisingly democratic in its selection of officers, as Michael Glover attests in examining the extremely variegated social background of British officers during the Napoleonic Wars [3]:

'The fathers of regimental officers covered a wide social range, from the Duke of Beaufort, who had five sons and two grandsons on the active list, to Private Babington Nolan, Thirteenth Light Dragoons, whose son was given an ensigncy in the Sixty First Foot (and whose grandson was to carry the order that launched the Light Brigade at Balaclava). The morganatic son of HRH the Duke of Sussex was a lieutenant in the Royal Fusiliers. The son of a sergeant major in the Royal Scots died commanding the Scots Greys at Waterloo. Lieutenant Edward Fox Fitzgerald, Tenth Hussars, was the son of Lord Edward Fitzgerald, the Irish rebel; and Colonel John Elley, Royal Horse Guards, was the son of an eating house keeper in Holborn.'

One notes that Capt Haigh's father had been commissioned from the ranks (**Letter I**)). The last reference in the above quoted extract does indeed attest to a remarkably democratic spirit in the British Army of the period. For the Royal Horse Guards was one of the (then) three cavalry regiments which formed the Household Cavalry (the mounted branch of the Household Division, forming the personal escort of the Sovereign); the other two regiments being the 1st and 2nd Life Guards. The Household Division (which encompassed the (then) three regiments of Foot Guards) represented the most elitist regiments in the British Army, and were mainly the receptacle of the aristocracy. Commissions were invariably awarded to men in the ranks for long and steady service. Some, however, were granted as a reward for specific acts of gallantry (eg Sgt John Masterson, of the 87th Regiment, who captured a French eagle at Barossa in 1811, is a case in point. A further example is furnished by Sgt William Newman, who rallied a knot of stragglers during the retreat to Corunna in 1808. It was the common practice for men commissioned from the ranks to receive a grant of £50 for their initial expenses from the Royal Patriotic Fund. It is apparent that those officers commissioned from the ranks were older than those who had joined directly from school. There were, however, notable exceptions; as in the case of Sgt John Fraser (of the 71st Regiment), who was commissioned at the age of 24.

Second, there was a large influx of recruits from the Militia; in the first five years of the Peninsular War (1809-1813) some 55 000 recruits enlisted in the Regular Army from this source [4]. This development exercised a marked impact on the social calibre of the British Army during the Napoleonic Wars, the overall character of the enlisted man improving as a result. For the Militia was drawn from a broader social base than the Regular Army, conscription playing a major role in its composition. To a certain degree, therefore, it leavened the ranks of the Regular Army in the sense that Wellington desired. Moreover, such recruits entered the Regular Army with experience of drill and arms, and experience of discipline (an asset obviously shared by former Militia officers).

Third, the introduction of short service engagements of seven years in 1807 (as opposed to life) introduced a higher calibre of recruit into the Regular Army.

Public hostility: Dislike of, and antagonism towards, the standing army was a marked characteristic of such social attitudes within all 'respectable' levels of society. One authority states [5]:

> 'Dislike of the military was not confined entirely to radical spokesmen and writers. Major Edward Mcready recalled that the reception accorded to the 30th on its return from Waterloo was anything but cordial. "We were barbarously treated at Ramsgate, overcharged by an innkeeper at Margate, drenched to the skin every day, and looked crossly on by everyone but the waiters at the inns. As to the peasantry, a civil word could not be extracted from them."' [6]

Low social status: The lowly social status of the other ranks was accented by the extremely poor educational standards. The following figures relating to the rank and file of the British Army in 1857 - 42 years after Waterloo - are most revealing. The percentage unable to read and write was estimated to be 20.5%; the percentage able to read but not write, and barely able to sign their name, was 18.5%; the percentage able to read and write a little was 56%; and those with a 'superior degree of education' was 4.7%. [7]

No less than in the Navy of the period, the harshest possible discipline, exemplified by the practice of flogging, was considered to be essential to enforce obedience to the military code; the resort to which was confirmed (in the eyes of the military authorities) by the generally low social level of the recruits and their corresponding susceptibility to indiscipline, alcohol abuse, etc. The Duke of Wellington possessed implicit faith in the value of flogging as the main antidote to the army dissolving into a criminal mob. While there were, admittedly, senior commanders who dissented from such attitudes - Lt Gen Sir John Moore being an obvious example - even the more humane methods which they advocated yielded to the lash in times of crisis. Brig Gen Robert Craufurd - a notorious exponent of the efficacy of flogging - prevented his units from disintegrating during the terrible retreat to Corunna by the extensive use of the cat-o-nine tails. Only the light infantry regiments (in which Moore had been trained) and in the Rifle Corps does one observe the application of less severe discipline. This factor probably derived from the extremely high *esprit de corps* which prevailed within the 95th Rifles, or Experimental Corps of Riflemen, as it was first designated. This aspect of the military life of the period is clearly evoked in the memoirs of Sgt John Douglas, of the 1st Regiment (The Royals) (later the Royal Scots). [8] His battalion commander, Lt Col Hay, was clearly a firm adherent to this school of thought. After sentencing a man to 800 lashes (of which 775 were delivered), he states:

> 'Now, Sir, I would sooner flog you for giving insolence to a lance corporal than for striking an officer, for that is the link in the chain by which the whole army is fastened.'

It was not uncommon for officers to mete out sentences of 1 000 lashes or more. Whilst, to the contemporary reader, such practices bespeak of a fearsome cruelty, one must bear in mind that the social complexion of institutions (notable among which are, of course, the armed forces) reflect the climate of society in which they are rooted. Until the 1830s, some 200 crimes involved the death sentence. (Pattison refers to this savage code in a footnote contained within **Letter I**, when he states that, during his father's time, the theft of half-a-crown invoked the death penalty). There was a further reason for the widespread belief in the efficacy of the lash. The tactics of the period (cf below) placed an overwhelming emphasis upon automatic and unthinking obedience to pre-determined drills. With the exception of the Rifle Corps and light infantry regiments (cf below), individual enterprise and initiative formed extremely low priorities. Such a climate of control would be synonymous with the most draconian incentives to inflexible obedience.

Social cohesiveness: As has oft been remarked, a marked feature of the British Army at Waterloo was the remarkable degree of inner cohesiveness displayed by the British troops in the battle; manifested in the steadfastness of the British squares, exemplifying an extremely high level of discipline. This cohesiveness, and the discipline of which it is symptomatic, forms a continual undercurrent in Pattison's narration of the battle scenes (although it is never explicitly remarked upon, suggesting that it was a feature of British military life taken for granted). The sole occasion of lack of steadfastness on the part of the British soldiery is the attempt of the former apprentice hairdresser to be permitted to withdraw from the line; a cameo scene that enhances the narration with a powerful sense of social realism.

To what one may attribute this overwhelming disciplinary control? In his book, *Wellington's army in the Peninsula 1808-1814*, Michael Glover approaches this question when he writes (9):

> 'The officers had one virtue equal to their gallantry. They seem, without exception, to have understood the art of leadership. How else could they have welded the drunken plundering collection of social misfits into "the most complete machine for its numbers now existing in Europe"?'

Whilst not attempting to attenuate this undeniable quality, it is suggested that the answer to the question posed in the final sentence resides in a more complex interaction of social pressures. The answer, it may be justifiably argued, resided in a social-psychological process that balanced coercive with conditioned power. Coercive power consists essentially of control through force (ie the deterrent of savage punishment, as discussed above). However, it is a misleading over-simplification to imagine that this was the sole source of control. Conditioned power (ie the willing consent of the ruled) was of equal, if not greater significance. There were three major factors in the operation of conditioned power in Wellington's army. The first was the almost universal sanction accorded to autocratic patterns of government which characterized British government and society at that time. The second factor, as Michael Glover states in the above quoted extract, was the peculiar quality of leadership provided by the British officer establishment. At the core of that leadership was the uniquely British code of the gentlemen, modelled upon the social morality instilled by the governing elite of aristocracy and landed gentry. The third was the almost tribalistic loyalty generated by the regimental tradition.

[The terms 'autocratic' and 'authoritarian' may justifiably be applied to British political society at the time of Waterloo, as the rule of the governing elite was untempered by any popular voice in government. The vast majority of the British population were excluded from the franchise, which was then based upon property qualifications. The first great movement marking the erosion of the monopoly of political control enjoyed by the traditional patrician class (the nature of which is defined below) was the First Reform Bill of 1832, which devolved a far greater degree of political power upon the industrial and mercantile classes; greatly enhanced in economic and social power by the Industrial Revolution of the late 18th Century]. Comment has been made above regarding the manner in which the widespread practice of flogging reflected the savage criminal code then in operation. (To retiterate, Pattison refers to this code in a footnote contained in **Letter I**, when he states that, during his father's time, the theft of half-a-crown constituted a hanging offence).

During the Napoleonic Wars political and social control of British society was firmly vested in that minute social echelon defined as the patrician classes. The fundamental source of its economic power (and thus overwhelming social prestige) was landed property. The aristocracy formed the apex of this social class, which was defined by the five ranks of the peerage (Prince, Earl, Duke, Marquess and Viscount), recognized as the hereditary nobility and holding privileges denied to commoners. Ranking next to the peers in the order of precedence were the baronets. This also was a legally established title, a hereditary knighthood. The third layer of status within the patrician class consisted of the landed gentry. Unlike the peers and baronets the landed gentry (which features so prominently in the novels of Jane Austen, contemporaneous with the Napoleonic Wars) possessed no hereditary titles nor legal privileges. The distinction was totally irrelevant, however, for it was obvious to contemporaries that for all practical purposes the landed gentry were the equivalent of continental nobles, characterized by hereditary estates, a leisured life style, their social pre-eminence and armorial bearings. This elite possessed the overwhelming amount of the land of the British Isles. Individually the majority owned estates of at least 1 000 acres. At the lower end of the scale of land ownership there was the squire, the commanding personage in rural society and politics. (During the 18th Century the squirearchy had increasingly distanced itself from the 'lesser' ranks in the rural population, and the squire's son no longer shared the education of the village children).

Conditioned power underscored the control of the aristocracy and landed gentry. David Cannadine writes within this context [10]:

'... this position as the power elite also rested on popular sanction. For the first three-quarters of the nineteenth century, the majority of the population unquestioningly accepted the patricians' right to rule. Landowners had leisure, confidence, expertise: they had time to govern. The business of businessmen was business, the business of landowners was government. For generations, and in some cases for centuries, the same gentry and noble families had sent representatives into Parliament. Dynasties like the Derbys, the Bedfords, the Devonshires, and the Salisbury's were generally recognized to constitute the great governing families of the realm. To most people this was the natural order of things: it had been ever thus. As such, these gentry and grandees possessed that most indispensable of all characteristics of a dominant group - the sense shared, not only by themselves, but by the populace, that their claim to govern was legitimate. They were not only the lords of the earth and stars of the firmament: they were also the makers of history.'

There are several manifestations of the translation of this popular attitude towards the governing class from the civilian world into the ranks of the British Army. It is significant that the savage coercive power which underpinned the control of the officer establishment did not generally lead to a sense of alienation or revolt on the part of the rank-and-file. It is perhaps significant that the implicit faith in the efficacy of the lash possessed by many officers was strongly shared by men of good character in the rank and file. James Anton, who served as Quartermaster-Sergeant of the 42nd Highlanders, remarked [11]:

'Philanthropists who decry the lash ought to consider in what manner the good men - the deserving exemplary soldiers - are to be protected; if coercive measures are to be resorted to in purpose to prevent ruthless ruffians from insulting with impunity the temperate, the well-inclined and the orderly disposed, the good must be left to the mercy of the worthless.'

It is, perhaps, further significant that when John Douglas, of the 1st Royal Scots, in his memoirs (12), records the flogging of a man who received 775 lashes (cf above), he makes no comment upon the matter (although he is certainly far from inhibited in speaking his mind) and does not appear to be outraged in any sense. It is further noteworthy that one of the most powerful adherents of the need for flogging, Brig Gen Craufurd (popularly known as 'Black Bob' to the troops) enjoyed a high level of popularity with the troops under his command who, indeed, virtually idolised him (although his uncontrollable rages rendered him unpopular with his officers). When Craufurd died Rifleman Harris wrote in his memoirs (*The recollections of Rifleman Harris*):

'I do not think I ever admired any man who wore the British uniform more than I did General Crauford [sic].'

It would appear that 'Black Bob's' positively savage approach to discipline was resented more by his officers than the men upon whom it was inflicted.

With regard to the second central factor underpinning the social cohesiveness of Wellington's army - the peculiar nature of the leadership provided by the officer class - the key to such leadership was the social morality instilled by the governing classes. This elite had established a social ethos which furnished the essential social code required of commissioned officers. That code is embodied in the concept of the 'gentleman'. The concept embodies a complex system of ethics which successively defies definition. However, the key to the ideal of the gentleman may be interpreted in terms of 'disinterestness'. It is a dominant theme in the novels of Jane Austen (which furnish an most incisive commentary upon the society of her time) and in these works our conception of the 'gentleman' may be most clearly formed. Within this context one critic writes (13):

'... it is inevitable that this society should have placed particular emphasis on the individual's obligations to recognize the needs of others and to strive to meet these needs. And, indeed, the right of the landed gentleman to rule resided finally in the belief that he was better situated than members of other groups to live up to such obligations. The banker and merchant might have had incomes as large as the landowners, but they had to work for theirs. The landowner's wealth, on the other hand, was unearned, and this meant that he had leisure. In the eighteenth century, leisure was not equated with idleness. On the contrary, it "was the ideal at which the whole society aimed" [Perkin, H. *The origin of modern English society 1780-1880*. London: Routledge & Kegan Paul, 1969, p 55] because, without it, it was considered unlikely that the individual could develop the level of disinterestness necessary if he were to place the general welfare above his earnings. The man who had to earn his living, it was believed, tended either to be completely caught up in the business of survival, or, even worse, to regard the making of money as an end in itself.'

The governing elite thus furnished society with its moral leadership. The middle classes were expected simply to follow the example thus established by the aristocracy and gentry. The heart of the gentlemen's code thus encompassed sensitivity towards, and awareness of, the needs of others; a powerful feeling of obligation towards those less privileged and fortunate than oneself. Polite behaviour was deemed to be a fundamental component of that sense of obligation. Within this context Edmund Burke writes [*First Letter on a Regicide Peace*. Works, Vol VIII, p 172]:

> 'Manners are of more importance than laws. Upon them, in a great measure, the laws depend. The law touches us but here and there, and now and then. Manners are what vex and soothe, corrupt or pacify, exalt or debase, barbarize or refine us...They give their whole form and colour to our lives. According to their quality, they and morals, supply them or they totally destroy them.'

Men of lower rank had an added incentive to aspire to such an ideal, as they had little patronage to dispense. Only through the medium of good manners could men and women in the lower social echelons hope to fulfil the ideals established by the landed gentleman. The health of the society, therefore, was felt to depend above all upon an infinite number of minute rituals of concern, each one of which contributed to harmonious relationships between ranks, and within families and communities. When he speaks of 'manners' Burke is not, of course, referring merely to delineated questions of etiquette; but, rather, to that entire complex of gestures – both of speech and body – by which one individual acknowledges his/her existence of another. It is in his/her more formal contacts that the quality of an individual's polite performance is most severely tested. In this respect, the officers' mess formed a microcosm of the larger society beyond its confines.

In Wellington's army, therefore, one finds the officer establishment aspiring to a code of gentlemanly behaviour modelled upon the social ethos established by the governing elite. This concept of the code of the gentleman is captured in the following extract from the *Regulations for the Rifle Corps*, which prescribes the ideal relations between officers and other ranks, and which was practiced in that and many other of the finer regiments:

> 'Every inferior, whether officer or soldier, shall receive the lawful commands of his senior with deference and respect, and shall execute them to the best of his power. Every superior, in his turn, whether he be an officer or a non-commissioned officer, shall give his orders in the language of moderation and of regard to the feelings of the individual under his command; abuse, bad language and blows being positively forbid in the regiment.'

The above quoted passage exemplifies two vital facets of the gentleman's ethos; viz the sense of mutual obligation ('shall give his orders in the language of moderation...and of regard to the feelings of the individual under his command') and polite behaviour ('bad language and blows being positively forbid...').

If one wishes to conceive of Pattison's social exterior – his deportment and relationships with both his fellow officers and other ranks – one may conceive of it in terms of characters who feature in Jane Austen's novels (Mr Darcy in *Pride and Prejudice*, or Edward Ferrars in *Sense and Sensibility*). There is, in point of fact, a charming evocation of this social code in the scene portrayed in **Letter III**, when Pattison blends so amiably with the family of the French veteran. He treats his host and hostess with the deepest respect and consideration, totally uncontaminated by any sense of patronisation or felt social superiority.

Within this context, it is germane to the argument that the worst abuses created by the purchase system had been eliminated towards the end of the 18th Century; and as a result the quality of the officer establishment (and thus its leadership capability) had been considerably enhanced. The rationale of the purchase system of recruitment and promotion was that officers should be men 'of high social position, holding large possessions and attached to the Protestant succession.' The *raison d'etre* underlying the system was the exclusion of the professional military careerist, introduced by Cromwell into the British Army. Cromwell's Parliamentary army had been so hated by the establishment during the English Civil War of 1642-1649 and the subsequent period of the Commonwealth (1649-1660) that the purchase system had been created following the restoration of Charles II in 1660 specifically to militate against a military meritocracy, which could conceivably threaten the patrician governing class (as it had done during the Cromwellian Interregnum). The prices of commissions were fixed by the commander-in-chief. These varied enormously, being obviously far higher in the elitest, most prestigious regiments (ie the Foot Guards, Household Cavalry and line cavalry). An ensigncy (the most junior officer) in a 'marching regiment of foot' might cost £400. However, an ensigncy in the Foot Guards was priced at £600 and a cornetcy (the most junior commissioned rank in a cavalry regiment) of dragoons £735. In the Royal Horse Guards (the 'Blues') a cornetcy was valued at £1050 and in the Life Guards (in which the most junior commissioned rank was 'cornet and sub-brigadier') the price was £1 600.

The worst abuses of the commission system had involved 'commission brokers', who had secured majorities for teenage youths in regiments which possessed a mere skeletal form. Anybody with money or credit was enabled to purchase any rank that he pleased. Andrew Gammell, for example, was appointed an ensign on 24 December 1793; on 18 September 1794 he had risen to be lieutenant colonel of the 104th Foot. Nor was there any minimum age. Ensigns aged seven years of age are reported; whilst Francis Hastings Doyle became a captain in the 106th Regiment of Foot one month before his 12th birthday.

The Duke of York, the commander-in-chief, had removed the excesses to which the system lent itself. (He commenced this operation by relegating the majority of over-promoted children and teenagers to half-pay, in which status some remained a charge on the taxpayers for the ensuing 60 years). He would probably have preferred to abolish the existing system but could not do so, as his predecessor, Sir George Yonge, had sold so many commissions for a vastly increased number of regiments whose strength mainly existed on paper. Nevertheless, he tried to ensure that the existing system operated as equably as possible. In pursuit of this aim, he introduced a number of important measures. First, new candidates for commissions were required to produce recommendations by a field officer. Second, no man could purchase the rank of captain until he had performed two years successful service as a subaltern, while purchase of the rank of major was dependent on six years service as a captain. Third, the abuse of infant officers was ended by establishing the minimum age of purchase at 16 years. Fourth, a system of periodic confidential reports for officers was introduced. Fifth, officers who lacked the necessary financial resources would be advanced on the basis of a list from which the commander-in-chief could select officers for commands to which purchase did not apply. Certainly, there is no evidence to suggest that officers who had procured their commissions by purchase served less creditably than their counterparts who had not followed this avenue to officer status. [During the Peninsular War purchase accounted for less than one in five of first commissions (19.5%). In line infantry regiments the proportion was less than 17%. Purchase was, however, a major factor in the cavalry regiments (accounting for 47%) and in the Foot Guards 44%].

With regard to the strength of the regimental tradition, it should be noted that the regiment represented the dominant form of military organization within the British Army during the greater part of the 19th Century. The specialized corps (eg the Army Service Corps, Army Ordnance Corps, etc) were controlled by civilian departments until the final decades of the 19th Century. It has oft, with considerable justification, been remarked that there has never been a 'Royal Army', as there has been a Royal Navy and Royal Air Force. The development of the British Army has been characterized by a diversity and heterogenous character that has extended from the regimental level to the most senior dimensions of control. The regimental structure has manifested an almost tribal separatism; the regiment being the focus upon which the infantryman (and cavalryman) has concentrated his loyalties. It is more accurate to state, however, that the battalion was the self-contained entity which was the focus of fierce loyalties and independence. The regiment invariably contained several battalions, each one of which operated independently, and only by the wildest of coincidences did two battalions of the same regiment operate in unison. (The 33rd Regiment proved to be the exception to the rule in this regard, however, being a single-battalion regiment).

Lord Wavell captured the essence of the regiment when he wrote, a few months before his death [14]:

> 'A regiment is more than a mere organization; it is in faith a family, with its descendants, its pride and its possessions, and through all its vicissitudes a community and continuity.'

This concept is reaffirmed in the following statement [15]:

> 'The history of a regiment is the history of an inner faith and its transmission from man to man, and from generation to generation. A regiment's success or failure in war turns in the last resort on that faith.'

A key element in regimental tradition is ritual, and the permanent impress which it exercises upon the collective imagination. Ritual plays a central role in the formulation of the unit's traditional fabric. Within a specific military context, ritual may be defined as the reverence and highly formalized protocol attached to the symbolic manifestations of the regiment's history. The objects of ritual - whatever form they may assume - encapsulate the shared experience of successive generations that have served the unit (the essence of its history). To cite but one example, which features in Pattison's memoirs (**Letter I**), the Battle Honours emblazoned on the Regimental Colour embody the experience of the regiment's members in key battles and campaigns in which the battalion has been involved. The Regimental Colour thus exemplifies the symbolic projection of the unit's service. The role of collective awareness, rooted in ritual, is pivotal to the process whereby a regiment's past service inspirits and motivates the contemporary serving members of the unit. For the symbolic manifestations of that consciousness - enshrined in a highly formalized protocol - impress themselves upon the imagination of those successive generations who, obviously, have not personally been involved in those central experiences that have shaped the regiment's history. The ritualized character of these manifestations (the Regimental Colour and badges) attach a hallowed significance to these symbols which tend to firmly anchor their message in the consciousness of successive generations involved in the service of the regiment.

The role of tradition in inculcating what has been termed a collective awareness is most succinctly and lucidly stated in a source which is, admittedly, remote from military history; viz T S Eliot, in an essay entitled *After strange gods* (1934) [16]:

> 'Tradition is not solely, or even primarily, the maintenance of certain dogmatic beliefs; these beliefs have come to take their living form in the course of the formation of a tradition. What I mean by tradition involves all those habitual actions, habits and customs, from the most significant religious rite to our conventional way of greeting a stranger, which represents the blood kinship of "the same people living in the same place."'

Tradition may thus be defined in terms of a combination of these symbolic manifestations and their veneration through the medium of ritualized observances. Precedent is the key factor in both processes. The essence of precedent is a model that is unerringly adhered to (be that model a parade, an item of uniform, or the enactment of a ceremony, as in the presentation of a Colour). Precedent is an integral aspect of ritual (which, in turn, underpins regimental tradition) in so far as the continual recapitulation of its manifestations exemplifies a reaffirmation of central themes or messages that it symbolizes. Its effect is to reassert the significance of the events enshrined in these ritualistic observances within the collective consciousness of the participants.

In elucidating this concept of collective awareness ('blood kinship'), rooted in the regimental tradition which, in turn, is founded upon ritual and reaffirmed through precedent, we arrive at the core of the process whereby the regimental structure of the British infantry was a key factor in underpinning discipline during the Napoleonic Wars. The inculcation of the new 'blood kinship' generated by the concept of the regiment (in essence a form of extended family, in so far as it possesses a hereditary memory) overrules and submerges the individual consciousness (which must inevitably encompass fear within the full gamut of emotions that it experiences) and substitutes in its place the mutually reinforcing collective awareness (and deep sense of mutual responsibility) implicit in a single, co-ordinated organism. Indeed, Pattison's letters testify to the manner in which the regiment formed a continuous skein in individual family histories. In **Letter I** he refers to the two generations which served the 33rd Regiment, in the form of the Haigh family. In the same letter we are also informed, in a further footnote, of the Gore brothers, both of whom served in the Waterloo campaign; and whose family had been associated with the regiment since the unit's foundation.

One must, of course, admit that the tradition of discipline within the British army was sometimes grievously sullied. An immediate example is the terrible licence manifested by British troops following the fall of Badajoz (1812) in the course of the Peninsular War. It is, perhaps, significant, that such occasions occurred when the enemy was absent, and the need for this mutually reinforcing power, noted above, lacking.

The tradition of steadfast discipline which is embodied in the British square at Waterloo enjoyed a remarkably long tenure. It is, indeed, a key factor in the survival of the British Army during World War I; when the terrible depredations of the Western Front generated mutinies in the French, Russian and German armies.

The organization of the British Army

Dual control: As discussed above, within the context of the regimental tradition, the heterogenous character implicit in that tradition was reflected also in the senior levels of control, characterized by diversity and lack of unity. These characteristics emerged in their most extreme form during the 18th Century, and were clearly visible at Waterloo, where there was not one British Army but two; embodying a dual control. The first force was under the command of the Commander-in-Chief, with his office at the Horse Guards in London; comprising the cavalry and infantry. His duties of administering this force was shared with the Secretary at War, whose office was located at the War Office and who, among a curious miscellany of duties, was responsible to Parliament for the financial expenditure of the army. The Commander-in-Chief was not, however, responsible to the Secretary at War; being answerable only to the Sovereign. [This curious, if not eccentric, organisational structure survived until the second half of the 19th Century. The Secretary at War's position and responsibilities was integrated into that of the Secretary for War as the result of the scandalous state of affairs revealed by the Crimean War of 1854-1856. In 1870 the Commander-in-Chief fell under the political control of the Secretary of State; and in 1904 the post was abolished, to be superseded by that of the Chief of the Imperial General Staff]. The second Regular Army was controlled and directed by the Master General of the Ordnance (MGO) who, in addition to serving as the Minister of Supply, was responsible for the artillery and engineers. Normally a member of the cabinet, the MGO was one of the great officers of state. This ascendancy is clearly reflected in the fact that, when in 1763 the Marquess of Granby was offered the post of either Commander-in-Chief or Master General of the Ordnance, he unhesitatingly chose the latter. The headquarters of the MGO remained physically and administratively totally distinct from either the War Office or Horse Guards.

When a force was despatched on active service, the Commander-in-Chief 'requisitioned' the MGO for the required units of artillery and engineers. Whilst they then came under the operational control of the force commander, the direct (if distant) control exercised by the MGO was maintained for the purposes of personnel administration, promotion, posting, etc. (The Navy maintained a similar system of dual control at this period, exemplified by the co-existence of the Navy Board and Admiralty). The existence of two parallel armies inevitably generated tension and friction, which resulted in the bizarre scenario of duplicated units being established to perform essentially the same function. In 1800, for example, the Commander-in-Chief created his own corps of engineers (the Royal Staff Corps) as a result of being exasperated by a system under which the engineers were controlled by the MGO.

The situation was rendered even more complex by yet another level of control, critical to the army's success. This was represented by the Commissariat, controlled by the Commissary General and a staff of assistants, serving with every division and brigade. This was a civilian department (the remote ancestor of the Army Service Corps) responsible for the provision of rations and the procurement of all local produce.

Brigades and divisions: Prior to 1809 the highest formation in the British Army had been the brigade, comprising normally three battalions. After that date the army was organized on the basis of 'divisions'; permanent formations incorporating several infantry brigades with their supporting artillery and other services. This organisational pattern first emerged during the Copenhagen expedition of 1807, when the permanently organized divisions were each commanded by a regularly appointed lieutenant general.

The army which landed in the Peninsula in 1808 (commanded by Sir Arthur Wellesley, later the Duke of Wellington) basically operated on a brigade level until Sir John Moore assumed command; when the troops were formed into four divisions (each consisting of two infantry brigades with a cavalry brigade). Upon Wellesley re-assuming command in 1809 the system reverted to the brigade organisational pattern until 18 June of that year, when a General Order instituted the divisional system that was maintained for the remainder of the war. A cavalry division (comprising three brigades) was included. Initially four divisions were formed, but the number had been increased to nine by 1812 (eight British and one Portuguese). The British divisions were numbered 1-7 and the eighth (the most renowned) simply designated the Light Division. Each brigade comprised three infantry battalions (although occasionally a fourth might be added).

The Light Division embodied Wellington's response to the deployment of French light troops (the *Tirailleurs* and *Voltigeurs*) who acted as skirmishers, harrassing and undermining the battle line in preparation for the attack by French columns. This tactic was countered by the role of British light infantry and riflemen, who would halt the French skirmishers well short of Wellington's main position (cf endnote [17]). As a first step towards achieving this object, the Light Division was created; the function of which was to screen the army when both stationary and mobile. The Light Division consisted of only two small brigades, each containing a battalion of Cacadores (Portuguese light infantry); four companies of riflemen derived from the 95th Rifles (later increased when the 2nd and 3rd battalions of that regiment joined the army); and a British light infantry battalion (which included the 43rd and 52nd Regiments). The 7th Division also included a heavy component of light infantry. It possessed two light infantry brigade of the King's German Legion and nine rifle companies of the Brunswick-Oels Jagers; in addition to the two newly trained British light infantry battalions (the 51st and 68th Regiments). The presence of the King's German Legion and the Brunswick-Oels Jagers points to the heavily cosmopolitan character of the 7th Division, which was further accented by a Portuguese brigade and a battalion originally recruited from French *emigres* and deserters (the *Chasseurs Britanniques*); the latter of which became noted for the alacrity with which they deserted. The division (probably because of the diversity of the ethnic groups represented) never enjoyed much favour and in 1813 it reverted to a more formal divisional organization; the light infantry battalions drawn from the King's German Legion being transferred to the 1st Division.

As stated above, British brigades normally consisted of three line battalions. However, this number might fluctuate considerably, as a result of sickness or casualties. To reiterate, a fourth might occasionally be added. Since a Guards battalion was invariably of greater strength than their line infantry counterparts, a Guards brigade normally consisted of two battalions.

The organization of the British infantry

During the 19th Century the infantry of the British Army comprised four distinct types of foot soldier, which have featured at various points in the foregoing discussion. However, it is considered necessary to recapitulate their main features under the above heading.

The Foot Guards: At the time of Waterloo, the Foot Guards comprised three regiments: the 1st (designated the Grenadier Guards following Waterloo); the 2nd (Coldstream Guards); and the 3rd (Scots Guards). [Two further regiments of Foot Guards - the 4th (Irish Guards) and 5th (Welsh Guards) - were formed in 1900 and 1915 respectively]. To reiterate, the Foot Guards formed the infantry component of the Household Division, forming the personal escort of the Sovereign. [Since 1968 the two regiments of Household Cavalry and five regiments of Foot Guards have been known collectively as the Household Division; the Foot Guards (formerly designated the Brigade of Guards) being thenceforth termed the Guards Division].

The line infantry: Ranking in precedence below the Foot Guards were the regiments of the line (prior to 1881 the numbered regiments of foot). These comprised the heavy infantry and light infantry.

The heavy infantry

The heavy infantry had their origins in the traditional tactics of the British Army, developed during Marlborough's time; ie the early decades of the 18th Century. These tactics centred upon the highly disciplined fire in volleys, at extremely short range, in line or square formation (to which the nature of the muzzle loading smooth bore musket - characterized by its extremely short range - naturally lend itself). At the beginning of the 19th Century each battalion consisted of a small headquarters company (basically administrative personnel) and ten companies. Of these eight were designated 'battalion' or 'centre' companies (signifying their position when the battalions were assembled in line; cf below) and two 'flank companies'. Of these two latter companies the right (comprising the physically most powerful and stalwart members) consisted of grenadiers (essentially shock assault troops); whilst the left flank company was formed, supposedly, from the lightest and most agile troops, performing the functions of light infantry. However, the use of light infantry companies by these infantry regiments was rendered largely superfluous through the practice (which became widespread during the Peninsular War) of attaching rifle companies to each battalion; cf above.

Within each company two junior officers served under a captain; these two officers being in theory a lieutenant and an ensign. Pattison's immediate superior, therefore, would have been a captain. A battalion at full strength would be commanded by a lieutenant colonel. Serving under him would be two majors, 10 captains, 20 lieutenants or ensigns, the adjutant (generally a lieutenant) and the quartermaster; an assistant surgeon was usually attached. General Sir David Dundas who drastically revised and standardised the system of line infantry tactics, envisaged the strength of each company as consisting of three officers, two sergeants, three corporals, one drummer and 30 privates. This represented the peace-time establishment. When embarking for the Peninsula, companies might number almost 100; including a pay sergeant, perhaps four other sergeants and six corporals. A battalion which could field 700 men in the field was considered to be strong; and many fell considerably below this figure. Indeed, due to the absorption of many soldiers into duties such as baggage-guards, storemen, etc and those who were sick or absentee, a company could probably not deploy more than 55 men in the field. For administrative purposes, each company was divided into two platoons.

At the time of Waterloo the British line infantry regiments comprised 104 numbered regiments. Prior to 1752 the infantry regiments had been named after their colonel but, after that date, they were assigned a number. The number allocated to a regiment signified its seniority; based upon the date of their first being absorbed into the regular army establishment (not, it should be noted, upon the date that the unit originated). After 1782 a territorial designation was added (ie a county with which the unit was associated; eg the 77th (East Middlesex) Regiment). Some units, however, had no territorial designations; ie the 41st, 89th, 98th, 102nd and 103rd); whilst others possessed titles (eg the 33rd (1st Yorkshire West Riding) Regiment, the 7th Royal Fusiliers, 60th Royal Americans, 97th Queen's Germans) which did not reflect any territorial associations.

The light infantry

To reiterate, the essence of light infantry was a reaction to the formalized line-of-battle tactics adopted by conventional heavy infantry. The former were highly mobile, fast moving troops who were skilled in scouting and operating in 'open order'; covering the flanks, rear and van of the army. The British Army had gained great experience in light infantry tactics as a result of its campaigns on the North American continent (in the wars against the French, the Red Indians and the rebellious American colonists; the last named during the American War of Independence (1776-1783). By the end of the 18th Century, however, the efficiency of the light infantry companies operating within conventional heavy infantry regiments had significantly declined. Much of the credit for the creation of the light infantry arm has (with justice) been accorded to Lt Gen Sir John Moore, who perfected the system of training at his camp at Shorncliffe at the very beginning of the 19th Century. (He had written of light infantry tactics and practiced the drill in Ireland, in 1798-1799).

The first light infantry regiment to be raised was the 90th Perthshire Volunteers, raised in 1794 by the francophobic Sir Thomas Graham of Balgowan (whose detestation of the French was largely based upon their desecration of his wife's coffin, whilst he was accompanying it through France during the French Revolution). The second regiment to be officially converted was the 43rd (Monmouthshire) Regiment of Foot, in 1803. The other light infantry regiments were: the 51st (2nd West Riding) (converted to light infantry in 1809); the 68th (Durham) (converted in 1808); the 71st Highlanders (converted to Highland Light Infantry in 1808); the 85th (Bucks Volunteers) (converted to light infantry in 1808).

Rifle regiments

The second major innovation in the British Army of the 19th Century was the advent of rifle regiments. These also had their origins in the North American campaigns of the 18th Century; in which the efficiency of the rifle, as deployed by colonial militia units, fighting in the dense forests and utilizing open order and camouflage, had made a significant impression. The essence of the rifle regiments' distinction from other formations of the British Army during the early 19th Century was, as their name implies, the role of the rifle, as opposed to the conventional musket. At that time the rifle's main characteristic was the grooved barrel; affording a twist to the trajectory of the ball which afforded far greater range and accuracy. These attributes compensated for the far slower rate of loading. The method of ignition, it should be noted, was identical to that of the musket (the flintlock). The weapon adopted by the rifle regiments during the Napoleonic Wars was the Baker rifle; probably the finest mass produced weapon of the era. (It should be noted that the rifle could be fired from the lying position, which was impossible to execute with the musket). [By the last quarter of the 19th Century the distinction between the rifle regiments on the basis of type of weapon had disappeared, with the demise of the smooth bore musket; and all regiments of the British Army were equipped with the same basic pattern rifle; eg Martini Henry, Schneider, Lee Enfield].

The first rifle corps to be raised in the British Army was the 5th Battalion of the 60th (Royal American) Regiment, founded in 1797 (in which the serving members were preponderantly German). The second rifle corps to be raised was the 95th Rifles, which originated in the Experimental Corps of Riflemen, formed in 1800. The unit continued to be designated the Experimental Corps of Riflemen until 1802, when it was retitled the 95th Rifles (Rifle Regiment). So outstanding was its performance during the Peninsular War, during the years 1808-1814, that, following the end of the Napoleonic Wars, it was withdrawn from the line and retitled the Rifle Brigade (1816); an enormous enhancement in its status. In accordance with their unique role - that of the most advanced skirmishers - demanding the maximum utilization of concealment and cover, the rifle battalions were the first to adopt camouflage uniforms. The 5th/60th Battalion was the first green uniformed regiment in the British Army (although the entire regiment - the ancestor of the modern King's Royal Rifle Corps - was not clothed in green (symbolizing the forests of the regiment's North American homeland) until 1814. The 95th Rifles followed this precedent. The Brunswick-Oel Jagers, on the other hand, wore the black uniform characteristic of their sister units in the Brunswick force, symbolizing their mourning for the 'rape' of their homeland. The Portuguese Cacadore regiments all wore brown (possibly the first antecedent of khaki).

Tactics and drill

To reiterate, the military technology that shaped the battles of the Napoleonic Wars - climaxed at Quatre Bras and Waterloo - was hugely distant from that of our own time; and, indeed, had become obsolete in Pattison's later life; such being the phenomenal development of military science in the author's own lifetime. Pattison's narrative vividly captures the tempo and atmosphere of Quatre Bras and Waterloo. We gain access to that world thus evoked through a detailed knowledge of the tactics and drill in which his narrative is anchored.

Since the dawn of the 18th Century, the infantry had emerged as the queen of the battlefield, proving to be the most decisive arm. The three major tactical formations which shaped the movements of the British infantry during the Peninsular campaign of 1808-1814 and the Waterloo campaign were: column of route, line and square. Column of route formed the approach march to the area of conflict. Line and square were the most common tactical formations adopted in contact with the enemy. These formations were based on the Regulations formulated by Gen Sir David Dundas in his manual, *Rules and regulations for the field formation exercise of movements of His Majesty's Forces* (first published in 1792). The formations prescribed were largely based upon those currently followed by the Prussian army. Although heavily condemned as being intolerably dogmatic and inflexible, the manual possessed the major advantage of furnishing a sound tactical doctrine for the infantry.

Column of route: Column of route was adopted for all movements where there was no immediate threat of contact with the enemy. The column, if formed two deep, comprised four men abreast; six abreast if formed three deep. The length of a column of route had to equal the frontage of the same unit when deployed in line; on the grounds that marching men required double the space occupied by the men when stationary. Dundas emphasized that this length should not be exceeded. This march discipline prevailed within the British Army until the 1930s, when a greater degree of dispersal and more open formations were necessitated by the threat of air attack. Battalions commenced their march from the camping grounds with arms at the slope or shoulder and bands playing. After a short distance had been travelled the men were permitted to break step and march at ease. At every hour of the clock there was a short break to permit the men to rest and adjust their equipment. Prior to this hourly halt and immediately following it, men marched to attention and in step for a few minutes. The same drill was followed when the troops arrived at their destination or were required to exercise a manoeuvre.

Line: The most common tactical formation adopted by Wellington when engaging the enemy was the line. When contact with the enemy appeared a distinct possibility, column of route was transformed into line. A battalion, when fighting in line formation, positioned all its companies side by side; each company being formed in two ranks, one man standing behind the other. The companies were numbered or lettered, standing in their pre-arranged order from left to right. Soldiers were permitted a distance of 21 inches (53 cm) from each other in the ranks. Intervals between the front and rear ranks varied. One had close column, which might involve only seven paces between the front and rear ranks of each company. Open column was far more common when the line was mobile. In this formation the distance between the front and rear ranks of each company was equal to its frontage. The reason for adopting open column was that with such intervals between the two lines the battalion could form line facing left or right very quickly indeed; as each company needed to do no more than execute a right or left wheel for the entire battalion to be 'dressed' in line. [Dundas divided the battalion into eight equal divisions. (The term 'division' in this context should not be confused with the higher military formation, absorbing two brigades). These divisions roughly corresponded to the eight line companies should the grenadier and light companies be excluded; whilst, if they were present, he allowed the number of divisions to be increased to 10. (In actual fact, it was rare for the light company to serve in the battle line; its normal task being to screen the front or flanks of the battalion or brigade).]

One can readily imagine the complexity and precision of manoeuvre required to convert the column of route to column of line formation; especially where the obstacles of broken ground were compounded by the assaults of enemy cannon and musketry. The leading company/division normally halted to allow the companies following to reach their positions. The rear company/division might therefore find that it had some 200 yards to traverse. (This distance would be tripled should the entire brigade be advancing in column of companies/divisions).

Dundas was a rigid proponent of the three-rank line, stating in his *Rules and regulations* ... that:

> 'The fundamental order of the infantry, in which they should always form and act, and in which all their various operations are calculated, is in three ranks: the formation in two ranks is to be regarded as an occasional exception, that may be made from it, when an extended or covered front is to be occupied, or when an irregular enemy, who deals only in fire [ie skirmishers] is to be opposed...In no sense is the fire and consistency of the third rank given up; it serves to fill up the vacancies made in the others in action; without it the battalion would soon be in single rank.'

In the above passage Dundas is pointing to a significant defect implicit in the two-rank line; viz the 'shrinkage' that occurred in combat as breaches in the foremost line were filled by the rear line, closing in towards the centre.

However, the two-deep line gained increasing favour within the British military establishment and in 1801 received official approval. The two-deep line had proved far more effective against the French columnar attacks as it could deliver a greater intensity of fire than the three-deep formation. By forming a two-deep line more muskets could be brought to bear upon the flanks of the attacking column. For example, a French battalion of approximately 850 men, comprising six companies (each company with a frontage of 45 men), advancing on a two-company front, could deploy a maximum frontal firepower of 180 muskets. (Obviously, only the troops at the head of the column could fire). Opposing them in the two-deep line, 500 men of a British battalion could discharge between six and 10 shots per minute; a lethal onslaught of fire when directed at the comparatively small target formed by the head of the column. The firing would occur whilst the front rank knelt and the second remained standing. The normal practice was for volleys to be fired by platoons, thereby producing a ripple effect. When the fire of the latter platoons commenced the muskets of the earlier platoons would have been reloaded, thereby producing a continuous volley. Counteracting the charges of 'shrinkage' referred to by Dundas, the two-deep line was capable of exhibiting a decisive flexibility; as was clearly illustrated at the battle of Alexandria (1801), when the rear rank of the 28th Regiment faced-about to repel an attack from the rear. With regard to Dundas' objection that, in the case of a two-rank formation, there was no third line from which to fill the gaps created by casualties, this problem was overcome by the line closing on the centre (or in certain instances to a flank) as breaches in the line appeared.

It is apparent that the two-depth formation embodied a compromise between Dundas' tactical doctrine and current military practice during the Napoleonic Wars. Whilst refuting the three-depth formation in favour of the two-depth line, Wellington adhered to Dundas' prescription for the tightly packed formation. (This attained its apotheosis when the line was converted into square; cf below). The major factor determining the closely knit line was, as intimated above, density of fire, which counteracted the latent deficiencies of the flintlock smooth bore musket in terms of shortness of range and inaccuracy. The collective fusillade at short range overcome such defects [17].

If the column was of brigade strength (ie normally incorporating three battalions) one would have three two-line formations advancing. The senior battalion was positioned on the right, the next senior on the left, and the junior in the centre. Assuming a front rank of 280 men (on the basis of the average strength of the battalion being 560 men), the frontage of a battalion would be approximately 200 yards. In the case of a column comprising a brigade (ie three battalions) the average frontage of a brigade column advancing in line would be some 600 yards. If the two line formation continued to advance, the marching pace would be extremely slow, in order to ensure the alignment of the troops. Obviously the efficacy of such a system demanded the strictest ingrained discipline. For infantrymen to break ranks in the line could prove disastrous, as the cavalry might then swoop into the breach thus created and take the troops in the flank. Similarly, a bulge which might occur when the men advanced forward of the line could expose the infantry to fire from either side, whilst they were deprived of the supporting fire of their comrades. When advancing the men on the flanks maintained their alignment by dressing on the Colours, positioned on the centre. If a brigade advanced in line, the Colour parties had to align themselves with the Colours of the particular battalion that had been assigned to determine pace and direction (ie the senior battalion). The Colours were positioned in the centre with the colonel (mounted) six paces behind. The senior major and adjutant (also mounted) took up their positions behind the third/fourth companies and sixth/seventh companies respectively. The company commanders (dismounted) took up a position on the front rank of their company; with a sergeant covering them in the rear rank. The remaining officers and sergeants, drummers, pioneers and other supernumeraries, formed a third line; their orders, to quote Dundas, being 'to keep the others closed up to the front during the attack and prevent any break beginning in the rear.'

Square: This formation developed from the line. With No 1 company/division positioned on the right and No 8 on the left, the procedure was as follows: The fourth and fifth companies/divisions maintained their positions; the second and third formed a line at right angles to No 4 company/division; whilst the sixth and eighth companies/divisions closed the square and faced the rear. It is necessary to bear in mind that the square did not always incorporate the two-rank formation characteristic of the line. It could assume several forms, involving many other drills. For example, it could be formed of four ranks, intended to cushion the impact of a cavalry assault and furnish replacements for casualties incurred in the forward lines. Further, on occasions two battalions might unite. Both types of squares were present at Waterloo. When two or more squares were formed, they would be deployed in echelon, in order that the fire of one could sweep the face of another.

The officers and colour parties took up their positions in the centre of the square, the former exultantly waving their swords in the air whenever a volley was fired. Dundas recommended that the troops be aligned in close order. In such a formation each man:

'must feel with his elbow the touch of his neighbour ... nor in any situation of movement in front, must he ever relinquish such touch, which becomes in action the principal direction of his order.'

Troops were invariably aligned in such close order, the ranks positioned one pace apart. Two paces distance was reserved for parade ground exercises. The order was even more confined

'when the body was halted and is to fire'.

The term 'square' is in fact a misnomer, for it would present an oblong shape, with three companies formed on each of two sides and two on the other sides.

The square invariably adopted a four line formation (as opposed to the two-depth formation of the line); as indicated by Pattison. This necessitated some contraction of the company frontage compared with the two-depth line. When the front rank fired, kneeling on one knee, the musket was angled upwards to present a fearsome hedgehog of bayonets at the height of the horse's breast. The square was hollow, the centre occupied by officers, musicians, Colour parties, etc.

Forming square required as much precision and discipline as the conversion of route into line (cf above). Timing was essential. The 42nd Regiment at Quatre Bras teetered on the edge of destruction when French cavalry entered the square before it was completed. However, the rear face was coolly closed and the French intruders trapped within killed. Pattison refers to this peril when he writes of the plight of the 69th Regiment at Quatre Bras (**Letter I**), which was attacked by cuirassiers before it had properly formed square; with the result that three of its companies were sabred and its Colours lost.

The square was proof against attack from the most determined cavalry assaults, including those of lancers. The formation was impenetrable to cavalry, faced with the terrifying barrier of bayonets. The lancers enjoyed some advantage as they could spear the infantry whilst remaining beyond the reach of the bayonets. However, they proved extremely vulnerable to the volley fire directed from the faces of the squares. On very rare occasions squares were broken by cavalry; as when the infantry panicked, were unable to fire due to their flintlocks having been subjected to torrential rain; or when a cavalry horse fell dead into one face of the square, crashing a hole in the formation. The latter occurrence distinguished the battle of Garcia Hernandez (1812), when Brock's Dragoons, of the King's German Legion, broke into a regiment of French infantry securely positioned in square and delivering fire. The source of this remarkable cavalry success was an event so unique and uncommon in contemporary warfare that it helps to explain why the event had no counterpart at Waterloo. One of the dragoon horses, moving on a true course and at some speed, was killed in mid-stride, together with its rider. The charge was automatically continued for several paces, the momentum being maintained; dead rider and steed not collapsing until directly above the bayonets of the front rank. The latter fell beneath the weight, creating a breach through which the remainder of the regiment poured. The dead horse and its rider had thus achieved what living flesh and blood could not; ie to act as a giant projectile with which to batter a hole in the face of the square.

The ideal disposition of a number of battalions in square was in a pattern of alternate 'chequerboards'. Such a disposition produced an interlocking and mutually-supporting fields of fire; whilst precluding the possibility of their fire striking one another. This disposition was a feature at Waterloo, resulting in a scenario in which the French cavalry rode impotently around and between the squares, being shot down in devastating numbers, but unable to respond. Terrain did not always permit such a disposition of squares. The key to the British victory at Waterloo, as is well known, was the futile assaults launched by the French cavalry against the squares, unsupported by horse artillery or infantry. Although the square proved invulnerable against such unsupported cavalry assaults, in the face of co-ordinated attacks deploying cavalry in conjunction with infantry and artillery/horse artillery, it could be destroyed. Its vulnerability to artillery fire (to which Wellington had scant recourse) was a marked feature at Quatre Bras, as Pattison clearly attests.

The square proved a vital tactical formation during the Napoleonic wars, in the light of the line's vulnerability to cavalry. Admittedly, there were occasions on which line formations could repulse cavalry assaults; but such infantry successes depended upon the flanks being secure, as at El Bodon (1812) or Sabugal (1811). The dire peril faced by British infantry when undefended by the square formation was graphically demonstrated at Albuera (1811). Colborne's brigade hurried forward, in line formation, to stabilize the allied right flank. Lacking any support to secure its flank, the brigade was masked by an immense hail storm, and failed to notice the French 2nd Hussars and Polish 1st Lancers of the Vistula Legion. The French and Polish cavalry fell upon the British brigade, which was destroyed with terrifying rapidity. The battalion farthest from the point of contact (the 1st/31st) managed to form square and repel the tail-end of the charge. However, its sister regiments suffered appalling casualties: the 1st/3rd lost 643 men out of a total of 755; the 2nd/48th 343 out of 452; and the 2nd/66th 272 out of 441. No engagement demonstrated more vividly the necessity of the square in the face of cavalry attack.

Conclusion

The object of the foregoing detailed introduction has been to enable the reader to gain intimate access to the inner and public worlds of Frederick Hope Pattison. This two-fold purpose has shaped the structure of this introductory essay. The inner world encapsulates the writer's emotional responses, which have been projected onto the reader's consciousness through the medium of the letters. This aspect of the work has been discussed via the approach to the literary form adopted (ie the letters). The public world, in which Pattison fulfilled a role predetermined by the collective organism (the British Army) of which he was a member, has been analyzed through the medium of the military-historical context, which has sought to recapture the tempo and pulse, so to speak, of the battle scenario which is the central theme of the letters. The essence of the military officer in any army is the curtailment of private feeling in the execution of duty. In this sense, the letters may well have fulfilled the Romantic movement's imperative of emotional release in a fundamental sense. For these feelings - the inner world of the writer that was of necessity repressed during his service - attained perhaps a much sought for liberation through the medium of the letters. In this respect their retrospective character, embodying memories extending back over half a century, may well point to a lifetime's suppression; the result of a traumatic response to the terrifying experience that he had lived through at Quatre Bras and Waterloo. (As is well known, repression is an invariable consequence of trauma). That Pattison possessed a highly sensitive personality is an inescapable conclusion to be drawn from the letters. To cite but one example, the image of the mutilated horse remains indelibly impressed upon the mind's eye, with the intensity of Picasso's painting *Guernica* (in which a dead horse forms an unforgettable and terrifying image of war).

The element of romance thus plays no role in Pattison's memoirs. His account clearly breaks with the tradition discussed by John Keegan in his work, *The face of battle: a study of Agincourt, Waterloo and the Somme.* (18) Keegan defines this tradition in terms of the 'ritually dramatic approach'. (The adjective 'ritually' underscores the element of conventional posture). The essence of this tradition was the dominant motif of epic romance, which shaped the interpretation of the battle by both eye-witness participants and distant observers. He writes (19):

'Waterloo, it seemed to contemporaries, had reversed the tide of European history ... official thanksgiving determined ... that the style writers adopted should be heroic and declamatory from the outset ... Even the French, by some strange translatory process, managed to make an epic out of the defeat. And the two most distinguished literary figures whose imaginations were captured by Waterloo - Byron and Victor Hugo - turned their feelings into poetry.

Remarkably the results - *Childe Harold* and *Les Chatiments* are still thrillingly readable. But the cumulative effect of treating the battle as a drama seen and felt as such by the participants in the heat of combat, has been to cover the human experience and military facts with a thick sedimentary deposit of romance ... The visual imagination of writer and reader was meanwhile fed by an outpouring of brightly covered canvases from the studios of successful salon painters - Dighton, Philoppoteaux, Raffet, Bellange, Caton Woodville - paintings which by their combination of photographic observation of detail with defiance of physical laws anticipate the work of the Surrealists. Much of the prose imagery in the constantly retold story of Waterloo - flashing sabres, dissolving squares and torrents of horseflesh - has its counterparts often, one suspects, its origins in the vision of artists who saw the battlefield, if at all, only as tourists.'

It is the abiding quality of Pattison's memoirs that, despite the undoubted distaste which is evoked in the modern reader by his strident rhetorical style, infused with hyperbolic metaphors, the 'sedimentary deposit of romance' is incisively eliminated, to reveal the profound pathos and insensate inhumanity of war. To pursue Keegan's analogy of writers of Waterloo with their counterparts in contemporary art, Pattison's memoirs have far more in common with Goya than the stylized conventional heroism implicit in the works of Lady Butler or Vereker M Hamilton.

Paradoxically, the personality which could present such an image of war co-existed with a tough, martial spirit, as his service clearly attests. Ultimately, the letters may have been an essentially therapeutic exercise in resolving such a contradiction. It perhaps required the tranquillity generated by the passage of years and old age for the horror to be lucidly recollected.

In any event, the editor sincerely hopes that he has persuaded readers of the relevance of acquainting themselves with this long neglected work.

S Monick
July 1997

Endnotes/Bibliographical Sources

(1) Barnett, Corelli. *Britain and her army 1509 - 1970*. Harmondsworth (Middlesex): Penguin, 1984, p 241.

(2) Quoted by: Monick, S. The memoirs of Sergeant John Douglas, late of the 3rd Battalion, 1st Royal Scots. Pt II. *Military History Journal* (Johannesburg, South Africa), Vol No 2, December 1995, p 48.

(3) Glover, Michael. *Wellington's army in the Peninsula 1808 - 1814*. Newton Abbot (etc): David & Charles, 1977, p 36-37. (Historic Armies and Navies).

(4) The Militia in its recognizable form dates from the Restoration of Charles II in 1660. It was the home defence force, comprising a series of infantry battalions formed on a county basis. It was customary for the Militia to be formed ('embodied') only in time of war; although the machinery for its assembly remained in place throughout. The Militia was unique with regard to the British military tradition in so far as it involved a certain degree of conscription. Each county was allocated a 'quota' of men to be recruited in wartime, according to the population of the county. Consequently, small counties might form very small battalions whilst Yorkshire, for example, possessed several full strength battalions. Recruitment was based upon two methods: voluntary enlistment upon the payment of a bounty (as in the case of the Regular Army); or, if sufficient recruits were not forthcoming, the balance was selected from among a wide range of able-bodied residents of the county; minus a wide range of exemptions, ranging from apprentices to dissenters. (Hence the element of conscription). It was not, however, a universal form of conscription, as those selected might opt to pay for a 'substitute' in their place (often at considerable expense). Once a Militia battalion had been formed in wartime, it conformed to a unit of the Regular Army in so far as it was engaged in permanent garrison duty throughout the United Kingdom. It was never based in the region in which had been recruited. This situation arose from the Militia's function as an anti-riot force (there then being no police force); a conflict of loyalties would have arisen should Militia forces been ordered to act against rioters who lived in the same district as Militia members. The Militia was supervised by the Home Office and its officers appointed by the lords lieutenant of the counties. In 1797 a supplementary Militia was created, in response to the exigencies of the Revolutionary Wars with France. The strength of this force was established at 63,878 and the commitment of men who served in it was for 21 consecutive days training in their own counties at one shilling per day, plus allowances for dependents.

The Local Militia Act of 1808 created two distinct forms of Militia. The 'local Militia' was embodied for the duration of the Napoleonic Wars and was, therefore, virtually a home army; whilst the 'new Militia' was an additional force to be embodied only in emergencies (eg in the case of a direct threat of invasion).

It is essential to bear in mind that the Militia forces were absolutely forbidden to serve overseas; and, indeed, the history of the Militia during the late 18th and early 19th Centuries was characterized by the tension between the county authorities (at the apex of which were the lords lieutenant) and the central government. The former were extremely jealous of the independence of the Militia forces, and fiercely resisted any endeavour to attenuate such an independent status by converting such forces into a reserve for the Regular Army. It should further be borne in mind that the intensely localized character of British administration (which enhanced the powers of the squirearchy and lords lieutenant), combined with the amateur, peace-time manning of the Militia, rendered the centralised organization of this force extremely difficult.

In 1795 the British Government was faced with an impasse regarding the Militia. On the one hand the exigencies of the war with Revolutionary France had created the dire need to increase the strength of the armed forces; whilst on the other hand the Militia was precluded from serving *en masse* overseas. (Conscription into the Regular Army was never an option and in this respect the British tradition decisively broke with the military practice of continental states. Only in 1916 was conscription introduced in Great Britain). In that year (1795) the British Government attempted to resolve the problem on the basis of individual recruitment. Up to 10% of the Militia were permitted to enlist in the Navy or Artillery. In 1805 the policy was extended into the Regular Army, which was permitted to call for volunteers from the Militia. Two major factors were instrumental in the ready access to Militia volunteers. The first was the bounty of 10 guineas that was offered (later increased to £14 for life enlistment and £11 for limited service). The second incentive was the very considerable pressure exerted on Militia men to enlist in the Regular Army; in the form of punishing drills and exercises reserved for those who did not wish to enlist.

Militia men could select the regular regiment in which they opted to serve; and thus naturally avoided those units that were based in disease ridden climates (the Caribbean was notorious in this regard). Conversely, such regiments enjoyed such high prestige that recruitment into their ranks had to be halted. The enormous popularity attained by the 95th Rifles (later the Rifle Brigade) was a case in point. In 1809, when the Regiment appealed for 350 recruits to replace their losses in the Corunna campaign, 1 282 volunteers immediately came forward from the English Militia alone. A second battalion had been raised in 1805 (only three years after the regiment had been included in the line infantry); and the Horse Guards (ie the senior military authority in England) forbade further volunteering for the regiment after the 95th Rifles had raised a third battalion. The number of Militia recruits increased from 1805 (the first year in which transfer to the Regular Army was sanctioned) until it accounted for half of all recruits. Between January and September 1809, of the 112 103 recruits within the British Isles, 54 299 (40%) derived from the Militia.

In 1814 Parliament sanctioned the wholesale transfer of complete companies or even regiments of Militia to the Regular Army. This gave access to foreign service for Militia units. Some fought with distinction against superior numbers of French in the Iberian Peninsula; acknowledged by the Duke of Wellington in a speech to the House of Lords, on 15 June 1852 occasioned by the impending Waterloo celebrations. A Militia officer would be granted a commission in the Regular Army if 40 of his men from the Militia unit had enlisted. In view of the extensive transfer of Militia men to the Regular Army, it is apparent that numerous Militia officers accompanied them. Indeed, one in five (19%) of new officers entered the Army via the Militia.

(5) Spiers, Edward M. *The Army and society 1815-1914*. London, New York: Longman, 1980, p 73.

(6) The authority is citing the following source: extract from the journals of Major Edward Macready. *United Service Magazine*, Part III, September 1852, p 68.

(7) Figures quoted by Skelly, A R. *The Victorian army at home*. Montreal: MaGill-Queen's University Press; London: Croom Helm, 1977, p 87.

(8) Douglas, John. *Douglas's tale of the Peninsula and Waterloo*; ed by S Monick. Barnsley (Yorkshire): Leo Cooper (Pen and Sword Press), 1997.

(9) Glover, Michael. Ibid item (3) above, p 75.

(10) Cannadine, David. *The decline and fall of the British aristocracy*. Rev ed. London, Basingstoke: Macmillan General Books, 1996, p 15.

(11) Cited by Glover, Michael. Ibid item (3) above, p 178.

(12) Glover, Michael. *Peninsular preparation: the reform of the British Army 1795-1809*. Cambridge: Cambridge University Press, 1963, p 178.

(13) Monagthan, David. *Jane Austen: structure and social vision*. London, Basingstoke: Macmillan Press, 1980, pp 2-3.

(14) Quoted by K H Powers in: The Sixty-Ninth Regiment of New York: its History, Traditions and Customs. *Quis Separabit: the Journal of the Royal Ulster Rifles*, Vol XXX, No 2, Winter 1969, p 106.

(15) Ibid item (14) above, p 107.

(16) Contained in an anthology of T S Eliot's selected prose: *Selected prose. T S Eliot*; ed J Hayward. Harmondsworth (Middlesex): Penguin, 1950, p 20.

(17) It is important to bear in mind that the efficacy of the line formation did not depend upon firepower alone. Its success was heavily dependent upon the selection of defensive positions that were concealed from the enemy by geographical location; further masked by light infantry units and riflemen. Wellington gained his

greatest renown as the master of defence (although at Vittoria and Salamanca he took the offensive). When selecting his positions for a defensive battle, wherever possible he selected a ridge; the troops being deployed below the crest and thus concealed from the enemy. French commanders encountering such a position rarely saw more than a few scattered guns and small groups of light infantry disposed along the forward slopes; and the accurate fire of these units, at remarkably close ranges, discouraged closer reconnaissance. When the French came to launch their attack their massed infantry, the true target concealed from them, would be largely ineffective. The folds of the terrain thus protected Wellington's troops from bombardment; whilst the French skirmishers would be unable to dislodge their British light infantry counterparts, who would continue to mask the main British force from the French heavy columns as they manoeuvred an uncertain path up the ridge. When the French force finally reached the crest of the ridge they would suddenly be confronted by the long lines of British infantry and the leading files of the French would be shot down before they had recovered from their surprise. The screen of British skirmishers was so effective that it was frequently mistaken for the main British force. Even as late as the closing stages of Waterloo Napoleon's Imperial Guard imagined that they had broken through the British line, only to be suddenly aware of the Foot Guards emerging from a cornfield. Similarly, Frenchmen who imagined that they had penetrated the main British line at Barossa (1811) had only repelled the skirmish screen; and when Reynier commented that he had been halted by Picton's 'second line' at Busaco (1810), he mistook the skirmish screen for the main British force.

The light infantryman was equipped with a lighter version of the Brown Bess musket, possessing a barrel of only 39 inches in length. They always acted in pairs; one a little in front of his comrade in order that they could cover one another when retiring. The intervals between pairs would vary from two to 12 paces; depending on the extent of the front that they had to cover. These skirmishers positioned themselves where the best cover could be obtained, and this enabled them to present an insignificant target whilst directing a galling fire upon the enemy's light troops. Being widely dispersed and presenting only the roughest of lines, they were signalled by the bugle call (as in the case of cavalry) and not the drums of the regiment. (Hence the device of the bugle horn born on the badges of light infantry and rifle regiments). In advancing the light infantry would close with the enemy's line and had to present an impenetrable front to the enemy's light troops. Once attacked in force, it was considered that their role had been fulfilled and they were permitted to withdraw to a flank; making sure that they did not mask the fire of their own troops by interposing themselves between the British and French forces.

The light infantry would be preceded by riflemen, who operated in advance of the light infantry units and were thus the foremost of the British skirmishers.

(18) Keegan, John. *The face of battle: a study of Agincourt, Waterloo and the Somme*. London: Barrie & Jenkins, 1976.

(19) Ibid item (19) above, pp 103-104.

Editorial Approach

Problems in editing

Pattisons's letters present not inconsiderable difficulties in the editing process. The problems - and their attempted resolution - are as follows:

(a) *Footnotes*: Pattison's text contains numerous footnotes, each numbered 1 on the page on which they appear. Such a numbering system obviously conflicts with a completely re-formatted text which includes the editor's numbered endnotes, contained in Part III. To overcome this problem, the writer's footnotes have been absorbed into the editor's numbered endnotes. The origin of the author's footnotes have been indicated by the appendage 'auth', which concludes the note; as opposed to the editor's note, which concludes with the appendage 'ed' (an eponym which also indicates editorial interpolation within the body of the text, contained within square brackets). This approach does not, however, entirely resolve the problems implicit in the author's original footnotes. Such notes require extensive editorial intervention, in so far as points within the footnotes require expansion or elucidation, as in the case of the numerous personalities contained therein.

The solution has been to reproduce the author's original footnote in the numbered sequence within the endnotes contained in Part III, but to elucidate the points contained therein in a succeeding editorial note. The points thus elucidated are 'signposted' by an alphabetic letter attached to the reference in question.

(b) *Mistakes*: Pattison's text contains numerous errors of historical fact, and these are invariably contained within the footnotes but also included in the main body of the text. For example, the name of his own Officer Commanding, Lt Col Elphinstone is consistently misspelt throughout the text, in common with the surname of Elphinstone's relative. One notes the same error in the spelling of the names of Sir Colin Halkett and that of Halkett's brother; as well as that of Gen Cooke. An outstanding example of a footnote requiring editorial emendation occurs in **Letter I**, in which the two brothers who served in the 33rd Regiment are cited as being the sons of Admiral Sir John Gore; whereas in actual fact Admiral Gore's only son was drowned whilst serving in the Royal Navy.

A further illustration of this problem occurs in another footnote appended to **Letter I**. Pattison mistakes a German light cavalry regiment which deserted the field of Waterloo (the Duke of Cumberland's Hussars, a unit within the Hanoverian cavalry brigade) for a Dutch cavalry regiment. One also notes the mistake regarding Queen Victoria's parentage, contained in a footnote appended to **Letter IV**, which features the Duke of Clarence (the future King William IV).

In such circumstances, the editor is faced with the problem of reconciling the integrity of the original text with demands of historical accuracy. The solution sought has been to reproduce the original text with complete exactitude, but to append the term [sic] indicating that this route has been followed. The attached editorial note then alerts the reader to the error in question. This note appears either in the sequentially numbered endnotes (where the error has appeared in the body of the text); or in an editorial emendation to the author's footnote (where the mistake has appeared in a footnote).

The editor has occasionally intervened in the main body of the text when:
- A mistake is particularly obvious (as in **Letter II**, when the author confuses the 1st Dragoon Guards with the Life Guards).
- The meaning of the author is obscure.
- A French phrase requiring translation has been used.

Such editorial intervention is indicated by being contained within square brackets, with the appendage ['ed'.]

Division of the text

It is self-evident that the text has been divided into three parts; Part I (the Introduction/Editorial approach), Part II (the letters and author's appendices) and Part III (the notes). This tripartite structure has been determined by the following considerations:

(a) It has been felt that the narrative fluency of the letters would be subject to serious and frustrating interruption if the relevant notes were appended separately to each letter; as opposed to being presented in a complete, composite block.

(b) In a curious manner, the division of the text between the original letters and appendices on the one hand, and the Introduction and notes on the other, embody that distinction between the private and public personas which has been referred to in the introductory essay. The letters exemplify the heart, so to speak, of the writer (his subjective, often emotionally highly charged impressions of the battle). The notes place those impressions within the context of the collective organization, to which the writer has to objectively respond (ie the 'head' of the writer). Thus, the notes contain the military-historical frame of reference within which the operations so vividly narrated by the author have occurred.

Detailed references

It is obvious that the editor's notes considerably exceed the need for mere identification and elucidation. They are clearly presented in more detail than is warranted if such were their sole purpose. These notes are invariably detailed in order to present that public frame of reference which has been discussed above. Such references prove to be highly illuminating once they are explored in detail. The backgrounds to the numerous personalities cited by Pattison lend colour and form to these individuals. (For example, we gain a vivid insight into Lt Col Hugh Halkett's colourful and adventurous character by the account of his capture of the French general at Waterloo). They also prove to be extremely informative with regard to such facets as the social complexion of Wellington's army; this point is underscored by a study of the careers of Maj Gen Sir Colin Halkett and his brother, and those of Sir Thomas Graham and Lord Uxbridge. The careers of the Halkett brothers exemplify the continuation of the mercenary tradition within the British Army and also alert us to the heavily cosmopolitan complexion of Wellington's army. This impression is powerfully reinforced by the references to the foreign corps in Pattison's work; viz the Brunswick Corps, Dutch-Belgian forces and the Hanoverian army. As will be elucidated in the relevant note, Graham's military career commenced when he was in his late 40s and his first rank was roughly the equivalent of a major. Conversely, Lord Uxbridge held the rank of lieutenant colonel at the age of only 25. The source of both situations (which appear so bizarre to a modern reader, schooled in the highly bureaucratic structure of the armed forces, in common with other institutions of the present time) is the peculiar structure of the 18th Century armed forces of Great Britain; in which a regiment could emerge as the private fief of a landed proprietor. The detailed exploration of the numerous senior officers to whom Pattison refers facilitates the wide angled focus which has been referred to above; ie it shifts the perspective from the individual, personalized vantage point to the universal. This transition in perspective from the specific and particular to the general is effected when one becomes aware of the contribution of the military personalities referred to in the text to the overall conduct of the battle. Invariably, such references are of a passing nature; although the accounts of Sir Colin Halkett and Sir John Colborne are obvious exceptions. To this extent, the detailed references exemplify the universalized landscape of the battle.

Such notes have thus sought to enhance the value of Pattison's work by facilitating access to the author's 'public world'; ie the socio-cultural and military frames of reference which underpin his observations. As stated in the Introduction, such access is especially difficult for the modern reader in the light of the vast distance which separates the military technology of our time from that of the Waterloo campaign. Admittedly, in some instances Pattison expands upon certain features of that science (as in the case of the discussion of the flintlock musket). In other instances, however, he refers to military concepts with which he assumes his readers to have been familiar. Not only are several of these terms totally alien to the modern reader, being symptomatic of a totally obsolescent military technology (as in the case of mounted artillery) but, indeed, were archaic at the time of the letters' publication (as in the case of the line and the square - tactical formations that were rendered obsolete during the second half of the 19th Century - or in the reference to grapeshot). (Where certain references frequently recur throughout the text (eg 'line', 'square', 'column', 'grenadier company') the terms have been elucidated within the Introduction, in order to furnish a generalized frame of reference).

The notes contained in Part II also embody the wide angled view of Pattison's society, in terms of its cultural landscape (to adopt the metaphor of the camera lens once again). Thus, the detailed references to Lavater and Canova, for example, cast an interesting light upon Pattison's tastes in art and reading, respectively. It may with justice be argued that the numerous biblical references which appear in the text (eg to Elijah, Saul and David) receive excessively detailed treatment. However, it is important to bear in mind that such references are significant pointers to the deeply religious cast of Pattison's mind, as has been intimated in the Introduction;

and a detailed acquaintance with such references (eg as when Pattison frames the heavy downpour which descended upon the field of Waterloo in terms of Elijah's inducing his God to break the drought which descended upon Israel) facilitates a full expression of the writer's terms of reference (especially in a society in which the Bible has largely lost the powerful cultural impact that it exerted upon Victorian society).

There is, admittedly, a grave danger in the provision of such detailed references. This is the threat of imbalance. When textual notes become too exhaustive (and exhausting) the reader may with justice form the impression that the editor is seeking to compete with the author; the reader being presented, in fact, with two rival texts. The editor has consistently sought to avoid this impression by restricting the notes to the purpose of elucidation. No attempt has been made to venture beyond the strict confines of Pattison's text. Thus, it has not been considered the editor's brief to expand upon the conduct of the battle beyond the elucidation of the biographical references contained in Pattison's work. Further, in the interests of securing the integrity of the author's work, the body of the text has been rigidly demarcated from both the Introduction and Notes; in order that the editor's intervention may be selectively disregarded by the reader.

Thus, whilst seeking to fully expose the reader to the military-historical and socio-cultural contexts of Pattison's work, the editor has striven to produce a balance between the need for interpolation and the vital preservation of the integrity of the author's original text. It is, of course, left to the final judgement of the reader as to whether the editor has succeeded in his objective.

PART II

Letter I

A night's march and the battle of Quatre Bras

It is an axiom, that events which occur in childhood or youth leave an imperishable impression on the memory; whereas those which take place in declining years "when the keepers of the house tremble" [1] may be likened to characters written on the sea-shore, perfectly legible when executed, but only remaining so until the receding tide returns to obliterate them for ever.

Realizing the truth of this mystery of our constitution, and trusting to the power of memory alone - for I took no note at the time, and have no memorandum beside me - I am willing to comply with your unceasing solicitations, to chronicle for you in some shape or other, some of those remarkable incidents which transpired under my own immediate observation, now more than fifty-four years ago, when I had the honour and good fortune (as a senior Lieutenant) to command a company of the 33rd, the Duke of Wellington's Own Regiment, during the three days campaign in Belgium. That campaign, as you are aware, spread an imperishable lustre over the British Army, dethroned Napoleon, and secured an uninterrupted peace to Europe for more than forty years. During all the interval we have been reaping the fruits of it. Men have had time to solve those problems in science, and to make those discoveries in art, which have been of unparalleled importance to the human race. Distance has been almost annihilated; materials are transported from one place to another with as great rapidity almost as the flight of the bird; and thought is conveyed from continent to continent across land and sea with the speed of lightning. And thus all peoples and nations are fast becoming united in those bonds of social communion which forbid war, and prepare the way for the speedy arrival of the happy time foretold in Scripture, when "the righteous shall flourish, and abundance of peace so long as the moon endureth." [2]

To begin with my narrative then at once. On the morning of the 15th of June, A.D. 1815, a report became current among the troops of Sir Colin Halket's [sic] brigade [3] (embracing the 30th, 69th and 73rd Regiments), quartered at Soignies and the adjacent hamlets, that important intelligence had been received at head-quarters of Napoleon's advancing with the army upon the frontiers of Belgium.

As the day advanced it was evident, from the very frequent arrival of couriers from Brussels, and in order to concentrate the brigade in Soignies, that what at first might have been a supposition was now a reality. Soignies being a small town, and the accommodation for the military being exhausted, the troops which were marched in from the adjacent villages in the evening, were sheltered for the night in a large church, which they completely filled.

The shelter was not long needed. Just as the bell of the large cathedral was striking the midnight hour, the drummers began to beat the "General" (4) preparatory to marching. Alas! how many of those brave fellows, who came out from that cathedral with buoyant spirit and earnest desire to meet the enemy, were numbered with the dead ere the sounding of the bell indicated the commencement of another day!

The march during the night was very exciting; and the jokes (compounding for a leg or an arm) (5) which were current, were such as none but soldiers under similar circumstances would have indulged in. Speculation of which might occur during the battle were rife. I recollect Lieutenant Hart of the Grenadier company [cf Introduction] addressing me in a jocular manner, 'Pat, you will be going to grass with your teeth uppermost [ie he would be lying dead] before night!' 'Take care of yourself, Jamie', was my rejoinder. Poor fellow! he fell at Waterloo.

As the sun began to appear above the horizon, and as we marched through a beautiful and highly-cultivated country, everything inspired the troops with life and animation; and the songs of the men, caught up by one company after another, expressed more the feelings of a party going to a banquet, than of soldiers marching to a field of blood.

The Brigade on getting to within a few miles of the battle-field, distinctly indicated by the roar of artillery, halted, intending to devote a couple of hours to rest and refreshment, but an express (6) arrived to hurry it on. Before starting, Lieutenant-Colonel Elphistone [sic] (7), who commanded the 33rd, called on the officers commanding companies to assemble together, and requested them to address their men, and encourage them by telling them what we and their country expected of them. The oration I made had an electric effect, awakening great enthusiasm amongst my men, evinced by an earnest desire to get into battle (8). Having performed this gratifying duty, I wheeled my company into line again, and left them standing at ease, to rejoin Colonel Elphistone [sic] and the other officers. On my way thither, I came into contact with my friend Lieutenant Boyce, whose countenance wore an unusual expression of anxiety. He addressed me in his ordinary friendly manner, saying, 'Pat, I feel certain I shall be killed.' I rebuked him for indulging such a feeling, saying, 'Banish such thoughts from your mind; no doubt some of us will be killed, but have the same chance as others.' This strange presentiment was soon fulfilled; he was one of the first officers killed. Boyce had always shown himself in action a brave soldier. After this incident, the command was given to the officers to join their companies immediately. The bugles sounded the advance, the band struck up The British Grenadiers, and the Brigade moved off with increased alacrity, high in spirit and in excellent moral condition to meet the enemy. It was not long ere the shrill rattle of musketry was distinctly heard, and arriving where two roads intersect each other (from which incident the hamlet, now historical, derives its name of 'Quatre Bras'), the battlefield appeared in sight. The Brigade having halted to load, a rather singular incident took place. James Gibbons, one of my men, came up to me, and, saluting me, said he was sick and wished to go to the rear. The request on such an occasion was altogether inadmissible; especially as this was not the first time he had shown the white feather (9); and, had I complied, the consequence might have been dangerous as an example to others. I at once called for the surgeon (Dr. Lever) to examine him, and have his opinion of him. The doctor felt his pulse, and told him there was nothing wrong with him, and that he must return to the ranks at once.

Gibbons before he enlisted was a journeyman (10) hairdresser, and became very useful in shaving, hair-cutting and setting (11) the razors of the officers. He might have made a capital valet-de-chambre to some effeminate 'Lord Dundreary' (12), who anoints his hands with cold cream, and sleeps with them in kid gloves, to soften and beautify them; but he was not made of stern enough stuff to qualify him for a good soldier in the hour of danger. Poor fellow! he never shaved a beard, cut hair, or set a razor again. He was killed at Quatre Bras.

Sir Colin Halket's [sic] Brigade unquestionably did not arrive a minute too soon on the field of battle. Reinforcements were greatly needed, 'The Duke' (13) being fiercely and incessantly assailed in every quarter by Ney (14), particularly by his cavalry, which rode over the whole field with impunity, not a single troop of British cavalry (15) being there to keep them in check. Beside this, the whole Dutch-Belgian troops (16), amounting to between seven and eight thousand, being disaffected to the cause, had left the field like traitors (17).

Orders were given that our Brigade should move to the right to support our Brunswick friends (18), who were vigorously attacked by the enemy's light troops (19), near the skirts of the wood of Bossu (the appuyer [support] of our right wing, which Marshal Ney was making strenuous efforts to turn). To accomplish this we had to move off the road and traverse an undulating field of grain, so luxuriant as to shut out from the view of all but mounted officers the direction in which we were marching. Advancing in open column of companies [cf **Introduction: Military/Historical Context**: *Tactics and drill*], a voice was heard calling aloud, 'Cavalry, cavalry, form square, form square!' [cf **Introduction: Military/Historical Context**: *Tactics and drill*]. The leading companies of the regiment halted immediately, and we were soon in a position to receive them. Having accomplished this important movement (we being in an elevated part of the field), a large body of French cuirassiers (20) were seen approaching at great speed. Perceiving, however, that we were ready to receive them, and that the 69th, which was to our left) was still in open column of companies, they brought their left shoulders forward, and passing by us at full gallop, dashed in amongst them, when a terrible sabring ensued. One of the officers

(Volunteer Clarke) (21), who carried the Regimental Colours (22) was cut and hacked in a fearful manner. Notwithstanding this he preserved the standard; but the other Colour was wrenched from the hands of the officer who bore it, and carried off as a trophy of success.

The 33rd were not left long to indulge the self-complacent feeling of defying cavalry. Infantry, if cool and collected in square, are invulnerable to cavalry. They might as well try to ride over St Paul's, as to break them. We laughed them to scorn. This dogma was fully illustrated at Waterloo, when the cavalry arm was pre-eminently in use; so much so that Waterloo might have been appropriately designated the battle of squares and cavalry. A far more formidable arm of war was now ready to be employed with fearful vengeance. Two French batteries which had stealthily advanced at point-blank distance, opened fire simultaneously on our helpless square, cutting down the men like before the scythe of the mower. At this juncture Lieutenant Arthur Gore (23) of the Grenadier company, who was standing close by me (an exceedingly handsome young man; like Saul (24), from his shoulders and upwards, he was higher than any of his compeers), was hit by a cannon-ball, and his brains bespattered the shakos (25) of the officers near him. In the twinkling of an eye he fell, like a stately oak from the last blow of the hewer, a lifeless corpse on mother earth. 'That's poor Pat', a voice immediately exclaimed. I, however, at once corrected this mistake by saying, 'It is not I, it is poor Arthur'. In a few minutes, if not a more awful, certainly a more touching catastrophe occurred. Captain Haigh (26), perceiving that the front of the square facing the artillery was bending inward, left his place much excited, and, flourishing his sword, called aloud vehemently with an oath, 'Keep up, keep up; I say keep up'. The words were vibrating on his lips, when a cannon-ball hit him in the abdomen, and cut him nearly in twain. He fell on his back; the separation between soul and body was most appalling. His eyes strained as if they would leap from their sockets, and the quiver of the lip with the strong convulsion of his whole frame, showed unquestionably how unwilling his spirit was to be driven in this ruthless way from her clay tenement. His poor brother (27) who was standing by was thrown into a terrible state of grief and anguish. Expressing his feelings by the wringing of his hands, and, shedding a flood of tears over the lifeless body, he cried aloud with bitter lamentation, 'Oh! my brother; Oh! my poor brother; my dear brother! Alas! alas! my poor old father!' Were I to live a thousand years this scene could never be effaced from my mind. The poor fellow was also shot at Waterloo, and, being carried to the village, died next day. (I saw him when he was sinking), thus leaving the old man bereft of his two gallant sons and childless.

Our position being untenable (a target for the enemy's artillery, which would soon have annihilated us), the enemy deployed into line [cf **Introduction: Military/Historical Context**: *Tactics and drill*] and moved to the point we assayed to reach when we entered the field. Encountering our assailants, we opened a vigorous fire, which we continued for a considerable time with decided effect. Many casualties occurred. Poor Boyce was killed here, and Lieutenant James Furlong [28] was wounded. I saw him hit; the ball entered his chest; he staggered and leaned on his sword for support, until a non-commissioned officer near laid hold of him, when he was carried to the rear.

Affairs being in this predicament, a loud cry was raised that cavalry were approaching to charge our rear. This announcement placed the 33rd in an anomalous position. To attempt to form square in front of a powerful assailing veteran infantry was altogether preposterous. Again, to resist a charge made on our rear was still more dangerous, and had the anticipated charge taken place, it would inevitably have subjected us to an ordeal similar to that which our friends of the 69th had undergone. On looking for a mode of escape, the only one presenting itself was the wood of Bossu, along the skirts of which we were contending with Ney's light troops. No time was left for deliberation, and the regiment, in rather a precipitous manner, sought and found shelter there.

When the regiment assembled in the wood, from the severe losses it had sustained, it was found not only desirable, but absolutely necessary to readjust companies. To accomplish this, as it was impossible to do so in the wood, a retrograde movement became imperative. Command was therefore given to traverse the wood, and, debouching on the Nivelle road, to our great joy and satisfaction we found that a division of the Guards [29] had just arrived under command of Major General Cook [sic] [30], amounting to above 4,000 men. They immediately dashed into the wood, and took our place, leaving us with the other regiments of our Brigade to reorganize companies and officers, preparatory to our again advancing to their support. On mustering our regiment it was found to be terribly crippled. In little more than an hour upwards of a hundred casualties, including ten officers, had taken place. However, notwithstanding all our losses, the morale of the men was as good, even better, than when they first entered the field. The adjustment of the Brigade being complete, it again advanced with a firm and undaunted step to the support of the Guards. The Guards nobly cleared the wood of the whole of Ney's light troops, and, after a determined and vigorous resistance, chased them into the plain. As a soldier I love the Guards [31] and have always done so, for the noble manner in which they invariably do their duty. When I think of their prowess at Inkermann, [32] my heart warms towards them with a brotherly affection; but surely Captain Siborne is unjustifiable in his laudatory language towards them on the present occasion, to the great disparagement of the troops of the line.

By the time the Guards succeeded in forcing the enemy from the wood, and chasing them to the plain, the shades of night were rapidly approaching. No doubt a gloom, darker than the gloom of night, was brooding over Ney's mind [33]. The sanguine hopes of forcing Wellington's position, which at the commencement of the conflict he was fully justified in cherishing, were now for ever dissipated. Frustrated in the whole of his daring attacks on every point of our position, and knowing that 'The Duke' had been largely reinforced with British troops, amongst which was a division of the Guards, he was forced to relinquish all further attempts, and to withdraw his army to the heights of Frasne, situated, I think, about two miles in his rear, where his army bivouacked, leaving 'The Duke' in possession of the field of battle. Strong pickets being thrown out, and every precaution taken to prevent surprise, the exhausted soldiery, after applying to their haversacks to relieve the cravings of nature, [ie had recourse to the rations in their haversacks, in order to relieve their hunger and thirst ed.] sought, amid the dead, dying, and wounded, 'Nature's sweet restorer - balmy sleep'. Thus terminated the battle of Quatre Bras, which gave Wellington a glorious victory, and relieved his mind of all doubts as to the concentration of his army, and the working out of his future contemplated plans.

The multitudinous thoughts which arose and passed through my mind in quick succession, after the termination of this bloody conflict were so complex and anomalous, that to attempt an analysis of them were altogether vain. The most prominent of these thoughts, however, was a deep sense of gratitude and thankfulness to the God of battles, who gives the victory to whom He pleases, for shielding me from those winged messengers of death that had cut down so many of my comrades on my right hand and on my left; summoning them with all their imperfections to his dread tribunal; and for vouchsafing to me the composure and presence of mind necessary to enable me, I trust, to fulfil my duty on that trying occasion. Had I entered the field with the same gloomy forebodings as those cherished by my friend Boyce, no doubt the result might have been very different; I therefore ascribed thanks and glory to God.

The battle of Quatre Bras does, in a peculiar manner, illustrate to a thinking mind the interposition of Divine power. There can be no doubt that 'The Duke' was taken somewhat by surprise. Whatever Captain Siborne may assert to the contrary, two facts alone will make this indisputable; viz. 1st. How was it that, during the whole battle, there was not a single regiment of British cavalry present, nor a battery of British artillery, except Lloyd's foot battery [34], which were late in entering the field? 2nd. How did it happen that, in bringing forward reinforcements from the rear, so much confusion prevailed among the Duke of Wellington's troops, a confusion so great as to make the luggage of General Halket's [sic] brigade a prey to the avarice of those traitors who had deserted the field in the early part of the conflict? Surely this can only be explained by 'The Duke's' not having sufficient time to bring forward those important arms of war, the absence of which necessarily gave Ney pre-eminent advantage in the contest, rendering, however, the victory all the more honourable to the Allied army.

It is unquestionable that had Napoleon not been blinded by some unaccountable infatuation in withdrawing D'Erlon's corps [35] from Marshal

Ney, the conflict might have terminated in a very disastrous manner to us, by enabling Napoleon to get to Brussels, where he had many emissaries longing for his arrival. The whole Belgian force had already shown that they would have joyfully placed themselves under his standard. Again, the scandalous conduct pursued by Castlereagh [36] and the Congress [37] towards Saxony [38], had inoculated the same feeling there as was known to exist in Belgium [39], and the conclusion therefore is warranted that Napoleon would in a few weeks have returned to Paris again - Emperor of the French - more firmly seated on his throne than ever.

My next letter will contain an account of our retreat on the 17th and an invitation to sup with me at our bivouac before Waterloo.

Mount Blow, 14th January, 1868

Editorial observations on Letter I

A distinctive feature of this letter is the manner in which Pattison introduces a fluent time scale through the agency of his footnotes (cf Part III). This is particularly exemplified in the footnote relating to Marshal Ney, in which the reference to the French marshal triggers a footnote which encompasses three generations of the Ney family's history. This fluid time dimension is similarly evident in the footnote relating to Capt Haigh; which looks backward to that officer's antecedents and also to the political scenario in Glasgow at the time of Pattison's father. The reference to Maj Gen Cooke also shifts the time scale (albeit a very brief interlude) to the attempted storming of Bergen-op-Zoom in 1814. The sources of these footnotes are of a domestic character; viz allusion to personalities known to the author. This process accords with the limited, highly personalized perspective of the narrative.

As intimated in the introduction, the device of the footnote prevents the disruption of the narrative flow, and permits such digressions to be easily absorbed into the main body of the text. It is feasible that Pattison's interlocutor, the Rev Hugh Macmillan, to whom he refers in a postscript to **Letter V**, was responsible for structuring Pattison's memoirs in this manner.

In this letter one also notes a recurrent theme that reappears in **Letter V**; viz the argument that the decisive defeat of the Imperial Guard in the closing phases of the battle was in the main directed, not by the Guards (as is popularly conceived) but by the 52nd Light Infantry, commanded by Sir John Colborne. It is a subject on which Pattison has clearly powerfully entrenched opinions; for the theme recurs, to reiterate, in **Letter V** and also features in an appendix.

Letter II

The retreat

My last letter to you left the exhausted soldiery victors on the field of Quatre Bras, seeking, amid the dead, the dying, and the wounded, renewed strength and energy from sleep.

The scene of blood and strife, which, a few hours before, had thrown even the birds of the forest and the beasts of the field into consternation, had now given place to a breathless silence, broken only by the occasional moaning of the wounded, the challenge of the sentries to the patrols on their visits to the pickets [1], or the discordant note of the night bird of prey in the adjacent wood of Bossu, led instinctively there in search of food.

As you may well imagine, the sun had made considerable progress towards the meridian, ere the troops were aroused from their dewy beds to the activities of another day. The sleep they had enjoyed was profound and refreshing, and they awoke (to use an agricultural phrase) in capital 'tid', either for hard fighting, hard marching, or any other hard duty that might come in their way.

Now that the fierce and cruel passions engendered by war had been softened down, the heart must have been hard indeed which could contemplate without deep emotion and poignant regret, those foul deeds of blood and devastation perpetrated the night before, and forced on our attention by the all-revealing light of another morning. Wives made widows, children fatherless, plighted vows broken, maidens' hearts desolated, these were the remoter associations of the scene. The immediate ghastly and revolting picture that lay before our eyes was made up of a beautiful country, bearing on its bosom the rich fruits of an approaching harvest, trodden under foot, polluted with the blood of our brethren and strewn with their corpses; cuirassiers dead, still cased in their armour; wounded sufferers fevered, calling for water; war-horses, artillery-carriages, muskets, pistols, swords, innumerable refuse of cartridges and other implements of war, promiscuously mingled together. O, War! War! offspring of hell and sin, disguise and mingle the cup as thou wilt, thou art yet indeed a bitter draught!

The attention of the reinvigorated soldiery was first given to breakfast, and although it is most certain that, in applying again to their haversacks, they found no luxuries there with which to regale their palates, there was enough to satisfy their appetites, and they were content. Breakfast over, the regiment was paraded on purpose to ascertain that the companies had been rightly adjusted after our severe losses. 'Powder dry, and arms in effective order for action', was the understood injunction when the men were dismissed, and we only waited orders from headquarters.

It would be about eleven o'clock when the Brigade got under arms and left their bivouac near the wood of Bossu. Moving to our left, apparently in a direct line towards Marshal Ney's right wing, the general impression among the officers was that Wellington contemplated an attack on that part of his position, and that shortly we should again be in action. This speculation was, however, soon found to be incorrect, the manoeuvre having been intended to mask our retreat, and it succeeded admirably. On reaching a woody covert, our right shoulders were brought forward, and diving into a by-road, we passed the defiles and bridge of Genappe without molestation from the enemy. This was, as usual with 'The Duke', an admirable piece of generalship - Marshal Ney's eyes not having been opened till too late to attempt to frustrate his design.

The protection of our rear was committed to our cavalry, light infantry [cf **Introduction: Military/Historical Context**: *Organization of the British infantry*], and flying field artillery (2), with whom the enemy kept up a ceaseless running fight, until we arrived and took up our position in front of Waterloo. I am told that during the retreat many chivalrous recontres [ie encounters during the course of reconnaissances] took place, when indominatable courage was exhibited by both parties; but a charge made by the 1st Dragoon Guards (3) at Genappe was so crushing and astounding to the enemy, that I cannot resist giving it, as admirably described by Captain Siborne:

'The Life Guards (4) now made their charge. It was truly splendid. Its rapid rush down into the enemy's mass was as terrific in appearance as it was destructive in effect; for although the French met the attack with firmness, they were utterly unable to hold their ground a single moment, were overthrown with great slaughter, and literally ridden down in such a manner, that the road was instantaneously covered with men and horses scattered in all directions. The Life Guards, pursuing their victorious course, dashed into Genappe, and drove all before them as far as the opposite outlet of the town.'

[There appears to be some confusion at this point between the 1st Dragoon Guards and the 1st Life Guards. Possibly the source of this error resides in the fact that both formed components of the Household Cavalry and both were, of course, heavy cavalry regiments. ed.]

After this, during the whole retreat the French cavalry showed a great deal more deference to the edge of the British sabre wielded by a Briton's arm. 'Burnt bairns dread the fire'.

From the dawn of day the heavens exhibited evident tokens of an approaching storm. 'The sky was red and lowering', the atmosphere oppressive and exhausting, and the sun in rising from his eastern bed looked morose and angry, and hid himself in a cloud of darkness. About ten o'clock, I was struck with the appearance of two very remarkable little clouds, rising from the horizon in juxtaposition, immediately to the rear of the French army. In contemplating them, a sudden thought traversed my mind, that, from their peculiar aspect, they might bear a notable resemblance to 'the cloud no larger than a man's hand' seen by Elijah's servant from the top of Carmel. (5) Be that as it many, one thing is certain, that their issue was identical. The atmosphere at this time was evidently impregnated with electricity, and there was not a breath of air to ruffle a feather; nevertheless, the clouds continued to enlarge very slowly but very perceptibly, until they united and formed a huge dark, impervious canopy to the rear of Ney's position - to weak and superstitious minds no favourable omen to us.

A very remarkable occurrence took place with regard to these celestial visitors. When the French army advanced in pursuit, this ill-omened stranger followed immediately behind, increasing in size and threatening gloom, until about one o'clock, when Heaven's artillery opened with a roar so terrible as to shake the very earth beneath us, and with the most vivid flashes of lightning illuminating the surrounding countryside with a light so powerful, that had it lasted many seconds longer it would have blinded the spectators.

'To whom, then, will ye liken God, or what likeness will ye compare to him?' The artillery of heaven on this occasion mocked into insignificance the puny attempts of man to rival it by the flash and the roar of his grandest cannonading. The rain descended as if the windows of heaven had been opened, or the bars of the mighty deep unloosed. I have witnessed the most violent thunder-storms when tossed to and fro on a tempestuous ocean; and also when resident in India, when the floods descend in overwhelming torrents, carrying everything away; but nothing that I have ever seen before or since can bear any comparison with this fearful visitation. The results of this storm in flooding and cutting up roads, impeded greatly the retreat of the army, and it was near the close of day before we reached and took up our position before Waterloo.

My next letter to you will contain an account of what transpired under my observation at the battle of Waterloo.

Mount Blow, 25th March, 1868

Editorial observations on Letter II

One notes that there is a marked absence of footnotes in this letter. This aspect is synonymous with a lack of digressions, which formed a prominent feature of **Letter I**. The narrative remains firmly rooted in the immediate context of the Waterloo campaign. The result is a variation in the pace vis-a-vis the preceding letter; symptomatic of an increasing sense of urgency in the latter.

Letter III

Waterloo

My last letter to you brought the Duke of Wellington's army, after its retreat from Quatre Bras, to its position in front of Waterloo. When our Brigade arrived on the ground, a General-officer (1) came up to Colonel Elphistone [*sic*] and asked him, 'Which Regiment is this?' On being told, he said, 'The 33rd will be out picket.' We therefore bivouacked that night on a grass field adjacent to the Brussels and Charlesrois road, somewhat in advance of the army. Our sentinels were so near those of the French, that it would not have required stentorian lungs for them to indulge in a social *tete a tete*, were it not that ignorance of each other's language interposed an insurmountable barrier to the possibility of such a fraternal enjoyment.

On hearing that the General-officer, who had given command for the disposition of our Regiment for the night was none other than Sir Thomas Picton (2), 'I was exceedingly glad, for I was desirous to see him for a long season'; my brother Alexander having served under him in many a hard-fought battle in the Peninsular War, and also having been attached to his personal staff as extra aide-de-camp at Salamanca, where he was thanked on the field by Sir Thomas for his conduct on that occasion. From the social intercourse which necessarily ensued when my brother was on Picton's staff, he became intimately acquainted with him both privately and officially, and always spoke with enthusiasm of his talent and bravery as a general, and of kind-heartedness as a man.

The unaccountable neglect Picton experienced from the British Government is a problem I believe no officer who served in the Peninsular could have been able to solve. Owing to his undaunted prowess and generalship, none save 'The Duke' himself had greater claims on his country. How came it to pass, then, that men, his inferiors both in active service and military genius, were elevated to a coronet, while he was entirely overlooked? It was not until long after he had fallen that the Government deigned to place even a piece of cold marble (cold as the heart of an ungrateful country) in Westminster Abbey, to tell posterity that Picton had faithfully saved her, and for her sake had watered with his blood the field of Waterloo!

From this digression I must return to our Regiment, which, as I have already informed you, had for its bed-chamber a grass field adjacent to the Brussels and Charlesroi road: a bed chamber certainly not encumbered with gorgeous drapery, the canopy of heaven being our curtain; and unceasing torrents of rain, accompanied by flashes of lightning and peals of thunder so terrible, that one might have thought they would have aroused the dead from their slumbers, our composing night-draught. Nevertheless, in defiance of wind and weather, the exhausted soldier slept soundly, and awoke refreshed by sleep, ready and longing to play out his role in the sanguinary drama that was to decide the destiny of Europe for half a century. My berth between Colonel Elphistone [sic] and Captain Knight, was under a gnarled hedge, which entirely afforded us no protection from the elements. Just as we had bid one another good night, a message was brought to the Colonel, that his brother Captain James Drummond Elphistone [sic], (3) of the 7th Hussars (4) had, while leading a charge at the head of his troops against a body of French Lancers, (5) at Genappe, been wounded, unhorsed, and taken prisoner. Our Colonel, who was a very amiable man, and much attached to his family, was deeply affected by this intelligence.

As the day began to break, the fury of the elements gradually subsided, and the voice of God in His thunders, uttering as it were a solemn protest against the violation of His law of love, which His omniscient eye saw would be perpetrated on His holy Sabbath, retired into silence with an ominous muttering.

At an epoch when such momentous events were going on, Britain having just terminated a continental war with the French in Spain of more than seven years duration, gunnery was still in a very primitive and inefficient state, particularly with regard to musketry. The weapon then used by the troops of the line, nicknamed by the soldiery 'Brown Bess' (6), was a heavy, unwieldy, awkward arm, weighing more than fourteen pounds, discharged by a lock and flint (detonating the caps being unknown) (7); thus exposing the connecting powder in the pan of the lock to the inclemency of the weather, so that after rain such as we had encountered in our retreat and bivouac, its discharge became a mere peradventure. To prevent the possibility of such a terrible disaster as no discharge in action, a searching supervision into the working conditions of the musketry became imperative. This led immediately after daylight to their discharge, preparatory to their being thoroughly cleaned out and put in reliable condition for the approaching contest. The unceasing rattling noise, which, on this account, for several hours ensued on both sides of the belligerents, might be likened to skirmishers driving in out-pickets (8) before the commencement of a battle.

Although on rising from his grassy couch, the outer man of the soldier, owing to the severe weather which he had encountered, seemed altogether transformed into the appearance of a half-drowned rat, yet his British pluck was burning with unquenched ardour, so that when our commissary (9) arrived with bread and Geneva (10), and we partook of a good breakfast (alas the last meal to many a brave fellow), we entered the bloody arena determined either to conquer or to die.

Time moved on as it does in sorrow or joy, but the troops of both armies remained in *status quo*, until about nine o'clock, when the two great Captains having devised and determined their schemes, the one for attack, the other for defence, a general and simultaneous movement began.

Although half-a-century has now transpired since this magnificent and heart-stirring spectacle occurred, yet I never can forget the overwhelming impression it sealed on my mind. Picture to yourself for a moment such a vast sea of living men, from one hundred and seventy five thousand to one hundred and eighty thousand armed *cap-a-pie* (11) - curassiers in their bright shining armour - lancers with their gay flitting flags - heavy dragoons and light dragoons (12) - with huge masses of infantry and artillery passing to and fro to their appointed positions, preparatory to that terrible onslaught which so immediately ensued!

The position of Sir Colin Halket's [*sic*] Brigade being on the right centre flank of the army, having Maitland's Guards (13) to the right, and Keilmansegg's Hanoverian Brigade (14) to the left, we moved from our bivouac, crossed the Brussels and Charlesrois road, and marched to the position assigned to us. On reaching our ground the Brigade was divided. The 73rd and 30th Regiments formed contiguous columns of companies at quarter distance, the former right and the latter left in front. The 33rd and 60th were also formed in contiguous columns of companies at quarter distance [cf **Introduction - Military/Historical Context**: *Tactics and drill*] in second line to the right of the 73rd and 30th Regiments, they being at an intermediate distance to the rear of from eighty to a hundred paces, intersected by the Wavre road, each Brigade preserving its relative distance so as to deploy in line in case of a simultaneous advance, which actually took place at the crisis.

Wellington's arrangements being complete, his army now only waited with stoical patience Napoleon's attack. It must now have been past eleven o'clock before the first cannon was fired. Tradition in the French army attributes its discharge to the Emperor himself. This is not improbable, for a love of stage effect was a prominent feature of his somewhat superstitious character. Be that however as it may, it is most certain that the vibration of its thunder had not ceased, ere the signal was acknowledged by more than 400 pieces of artillery, belching forth death and destruction from their adamantine throats. And thus the battle began; a terrible fight fought for a terrible stake: freedom or slavery to Europe.

It would manifestly be impossible for one who held so narrow and circumscribed a position as I did in the battle, being merely an officer commanding a company of infantry, to attempt a detailed account of the stupendous incidents which transpired during this momentous day. To do so adequately would have required ubiquity of body or omniscience of mind. To avoid, therefore, all risk of misrepresentation, I shall confine myself entirely to the incidents which occurred in my immediate neighbourhood, and fell directly under my own observations.

Our position, as I have already stated, being on the right centre flank of the army, on rather elevated ground, it afforded us a fine perspective view of what was in front, as also the chateau and out-buildings of Hugomont, as far as they could be distinguished among the surrounding foliage, and forming the appuyer of our right wing. The battle had hardly commenced, when it was evident that Napoleon's first great manoeuvre was to take possession of the chateau and thus to turn our right wing. To accomplish this important purpose, he left not a stone unturned. Fierce, persevering and unceasing attacks were made during the whole day, by the Emperor's choice troops. The fighting which took place here was of so sanguinary and murderous a character that it has secured imperishable renown to the brave fellows who defended this important and now world-famous position. It is recorded that Bonaparte, on finding all his attacks in this quarter frustrated, expressed, like a petted spoiled child, his chagrin and disappointment in words which have since passed into a proverb, 'Ces chiens Anglais ne savent quand se sont battus'. ['The accursed English do not know when they are beaten.' ed.]

The scene at the chateau and its environs on the following morning was even to the oldest Peninsular veteran altogether revolting. It was a perfect charnel-house of the enemy: dead heaped on dead: the trees in the surrounding orchard perforated with musketry, and the habitation, from fire and artillery, a complete desolation. But I must stop here, and reserve the remaining incidents of the battle for another letter.

Mount Blow, 10th April, 1868

Editorial observations on Letter III

A marked feature of this letter is the lengthy digression - encapsulated in a footnote (cf Part III) - relating to the French character; especially its emphasis upon good manners and polite behaviour. Pattison's observations, however, are far from being pedestrian or tedious; for their import is communicated through an actual lived experience; viz his being the host of a French family whilst he was en route to Paris following the battle of Waterloo. Pattison's Proustian recall of this domestic incident in minute detail - evincing a verbatim recollection of an incident which occurred over half a century earlier - embodies a certain novelettish piquancy. The detailed reconstruction of this charming scenario was probably generated by the deep impression which his daughter, Marie, exerted upon Pattison's sensibilities; remaining securely anchored in his psychological landscape thenceforth.

Letter IV

Additional incidents of the battle

The next grand move in this sanguinary game on which Bonaparte had staked his crown and empire, was a concentrated attack on the centre and left wing of Wellington's position. For the execution of this important design he selected his favourite Marshal Ney - 'Le brave des braves', one greatly beloved whose name alone was a tower of strength and confidence to the French army. No doubt from the complete preparations made by this renowned soldier for the assault, the Emperor was not only assured, but confident, that our centre would be forced and a way opened for his army to reach Brussels that evening. We are told by Captain Siborne, that the troops selected for this service amounted to no less than seventy-four pieces of artillery, and 18 000 veteran infantry, flanked by legions of cavalry. The fighting which ensued was fierce, persistent and tremendous. The attack, however, was too much to our left to admit of our Brigade being brought into action, but near enough to give us a pretty correct view of the contest, which was exciting beyond description, but, like all other attempts, frustrated and set at nought.

It was soon after the commencement of this attack that the British Army sustained an irreparable loss. The brave, the gallant, the renowned Picton, of whom Napoleon himself was jealous (his first inquiry on the morning of the battle being, 'Where is Picton's division situated?'), in leading a charge at the head of Kempt's Brigade, one of the Brigades of his own division, embracing the 28th, 32nd, 79th and 95th Regiments, against three times their number, which they dispersed like chaff before the wind, fell shot through the head, the words, 'Charge, charge, hurrah!' still vibrating on his lips. It was a source of deep regret to the whole British Army that the noble career of the distinguished soldier should have been thus suddenly cut short, but he could not have perished in a more appropriate way than in the most renowned battle of modern history, to which his military genius and brave deeds lent such imperishable glory.

At this juncture the Earl of Uxbridge [1] introduced a new feature into modern warfare, by simultaneously charging with his heavy Brigade [2] both the infantry and cavalry of our assailants, to their complete consternation and overthrow. I believe I am right when I aver, that never before this period was the arm of cavalry so pre-eminently brought forth in a general engagement. Prior to Waterloo, the sole use of cavalry was to protect the rear and flank of infantry, when they deployed into line preparatory to their assault against the enemy.

For many hours after the commencement of the battle, Sir Colin Halket's [sic] Brigade was placed in the most trying position in which a soldier can find himself. Held in reserve in complete inaction, except in resisting repeated charges from the French cavalry, which we invariably repulsed, he was yet exposed to the fire of destructive artillery, which ever and anon sent showers of fractured shells and canon-balls [3] into our ranks, occasioning many casualties. In order to shelter the men as much as possible in this hazardous situation, orders were given for them to lie down and thus to let the shots pass over them. This manoeuvre saved the life of many a brave fellow. When in this prostrate position, it so happened that Lieutenant Pagan, Captain Trevor and Lieutenant Hart were lying on the ground close to one another in the centre of the square. I was standing up much interested in what was going on to our left, when a missile, supposed to be the fracture of a shell, hit Hart so severely on the shoulder as to cause sudden death, and passing over Trevor, scooped out one of Pagan's ears. [4] He got up staggering and bleeding profusely, when I with other assistance placed him on a bearer [stretcher] to carry him to the rear. The men thus employed had hardly left the centre of the square, when a cannon-ball hit one of them and carried off his leg. Another man took his place, when he was then carried in safety to the village of Waterloo, where medical attention was paid to his wound.

I have often been asked if there is much difference in men when in action. Taking troops collectively, *en masse*, actively engaged, this becomes a difficult question to answer; but there are occasions - and certainly the position in which Sir Colin Halket's [sic] Brigade was placed for many hours after the commencement of the battle, as already described, was one - which give the cool observer ample opportunity of finding his way to a pretty clear solution of the inquiry. It is a dogma I have long entertained, and which I have often seen exemplified, that there is a great difference between bravery and courage; the former being an instinctive virtue which may be traced from the cradle to the grave, whereas the latter is merely an acquirement to which all men may attain more or less by precept, encouragement, and example: the poor hairdresser's case being altogether unique and exceptional. Thus all men will fight courageously when properly commanded and led, but it is the brave man alone who sets danger at defiance, and by a calm self-possession despises it when it comes into conflict with his honour and duty. The character assumed by the merely courageous man in time of trial, is either too excited or too desponding; the unseemly laugh in some, the restless eye and inexplicable nervous expression of mouth in others, betray an internal warfare which the natural force of character in the brave man has completely extinguished. I am therefore forced to the conclusion, that although all men may become courageous, it is the brave man alone that can depend upon a leader in an extremity. [5]

During the battle, my attention was directed with much interest to what

was termed 'spent cannon balls', leaping about the field, and giving it much the appearance of a giant cricket match, so as almost to induce an earnest prayer to step forward and bat them. But woe betide the man who would be so presumptious as to interfere with their course, for although they seemed harmless, they would instantly have cut him in two.
Mount Blow, 6th May, 1868

Editorial observations on Letter IV

The footnote generated in this letter (cf Part III) by a discussion concerning the character of courage illustrates the danger which besets the narrative when the author's digression is not triggered by an actual personality or experience. The footnote generated in this instance by an abstract concept assumes a somewhat vague and incoherent complexion. The implicit comparison of William IV with Charles XII of Sweden smacks of eccentricity. Nevertheless, the footnote is valuable in so far as it furnishes valuable biographical information concerning the author's past military service. Historical value also resides in the charming anecdote relating to the future William IV. The detail concerning Carnot's feat of military engineering in frustrating the British efforts to destroy the French fleet anchored at Antwerp is also worthy of historical note.

Letter V

The approaching crisis

The shadows of evening were now rapidly approaching. The battle had raged with terrible and unabated fury for more than nine hours; the slaughter had been frightful, when 'The Duke', quite alone, mounted on his celebrated charger with telescope in right hand, and reins relaxed in his left, at walking pace, unexpectedly passed near our square. A veteran who had served with him in India, on observing him, called aloud, 'Let us have three cheers for our old Colonel!'. (1) The men at once began to give effect to this suggestion, when 'The Duke', holding up his telescope, and looking at them with a gratified but commanding aspect, said 'Hush, hush, hush'. In an instant the command was obeyed and perfect silence prevailed. I state this incident as being highly honourable to the discipline of the 33rd.

Immediately afterwards, 'The Duke' reined up close to our square, which afforded us an admirable opportunity of seeing this remarkable man. His outward apparel was noticeable for its great simplicity, a simplicity, however, which, in contrast to his brilliantly-attired staff, marked him out as a target for the French rifles (2), and might have cost him his life, and England the defeat and ruin of her army. Nelson fell at Trafalgar on the quarter-deck of the *Victory* owing to a similar imprudence; and in our own day, when rifle practice has been brought to such proficiency (3), the sooner the dress of officers in action is assimilated to that of the private soldier the better. (4) It is likewise to be hoped, that by the *multitudinous wisdom concentrated in the Horse Guards* [author's italics], something should be devised for the dress of standard bearers of the regiments. (5) Should the old practice be persisted in, there can be no doubt that all the officers in battle will soon be shot down. And what then? Certain ruin and defeat!

But to return to the description of 'The Duke', a splendid subject for the chisel of a Canova. (6) The noble development of forehead, the marble-like repose of every muscle in the countenance, and the calm, searching, inflexible expression of eye, showed that although the issue of the battle seemed at this moment to tremble in the balance, yet he was enabled to maintain the composure of his spirit; and I believe, even now, saw his way to lead his army to victory, through what most other men would have considered an inexorable labyrinth. An occurrence took place here which fully illustrated the intrepidity of his character, and is worth relating. It was evident from the use he made of his telescope when he reined up, that he was reconnoitering what was going on to the east, the left of our position, it being from that quarter he looked for aid, the period for Blucher's appearance having arrived. While thus intensely occupied, a bomb-shell from the enemy's artillery fell so near him, that the fizzing noise of the fuse attracted his attention from his telescope. Regardless, however, of what might have been the probable result of its explosion, he paid not the slightest attention to it, and at once resumed his examination. The shell did explode, but, blessed be to God, proved innocuous either to him or his horse. In a short time after this occurrence, he put up his telescope, spurred his horse, and moved rapidly out of sight to our right. It might be a quarter of an hour after his departure, that the long-looked for command arrived for Sir Colin Halket [sic] to concentrate his Brigade, preparatory to a simultaneous advance of the whole army, to receive Napoleon's last great attack by the Imperial Guard, led on by Marshal Ney.

When our different regiments met to be united again in brigade, no one could feel indifferent to the sad havoc which had taken place since they entered the field. Alas! Alas! how many familiar faces were now absent, many of them numbered with the dead, and others, writhing with pain, lacerated and disabled. The 73rd, which had taken its position with a full staff of officers, was now commanded by a junior lieutenant (Lieutenant Stewart). The 69th, which had suffered so terribly from French sabres at Quatre Bras, as already described, had greatly increased its casualties. The 30th had likewise come in for its full share, in loss of officers and men; and the 33rd had by this time been reduced more than one-third; yet, notwithstanding all these depressing circumstances, the Brigade was longing for a more active application of its physical power, and therefore was glad to find itself now to be the assailer instead of the assailed, by being brought into immediate contact with the enemy. Each regiment having been formed four deep, right wing in front, took its relative position, when our brave and gallant General, Sir Colin (with what feelings of love and admiration did I behold him!) placed himself in front of the centre of his Brigade, and taking one of the Colours (I think of the 73rd), supported it on his right stirrup and gave the word of command for the Brigade to advance.

The contest soon became fierce and exterminating, men dropping in quick succession all round. My right-hand man, a brave fellow, was at this instant shot through the head. He leaned on me in falling; the ball entered his left temple, and I can never forget the expression of his countenance in the momentary transition from life to death. Directly after this my shako shook on my head. I took it off to ascertain the cause, when I found that a ball had gone right through it grazing my skull. When a lieutenant in the Grenadier company, I often wished in stature that I had been two inches higher. 'Vain man would be wise, though man be born like a wild ass's colt'. This miraculous escape ought to have taught me the truth of this scriptural declaration, and kept my soul humble and trustful on Him who alone holds in his hands the issues of life and death.

Although the contest could not have lasted more than ten or fifteen minutes, the losses on both sides must have been prodigious. Our brave

General was shot right through both cheeks and removed from the field. Lieutenants Buck and Cameron, the latter of whom carried the Regimental Colours, were killed. Lieutenant Haigh, shot through the back, died at the village of Waterloo next day. Adjutant Thain, Lieutenants Bain, Meikland, Westmore, and Ogle, were also at this juncture shot down, Captains M'Intyre and Harty were wounded, besides between thirty and forty of our rank and file. On the removal of Sir Colin, the command devolved on Colonel Elphistone [sic], and well do I recollect that matters became so serious as to create much apprehension as to the final issue of the contest. On assuming the command, Elphistone [sic] at once put forth all his energies to encourage the troops, and flourishing his sword in mid-air, called aloud, 'Come on, my brave fellows! let us die like Britons, sword in hand, or conquer.' While matters were in this critical state, an event took place so astounding and inexplicable as to fill everyone with amazement. The fire of the enemy, which had been decimating our ranks in the manner I have described, suddenly relaxed and almost in an instant ceased entirely, so that when the smoke had disappeared, not a man was to be seen except those who were retreating in great disorder and consternation. Captain Siborne attempts to account for this sudden denouement, averring that it was caused by a charge of Maitland's Guards, in which they routed Napoleon's Imperial Guard. This is now ascertained from *unquestionable authority* [author's italics] to be altogether a myth. No doubt the panic and dispersion was caused by a charge, but it is equally true that Maitland's Guards had nothing whatever to do with it. It is now an undoubted historical fact that Napoleon's last grand attack on Wellington's line was entrusted to Foy [7], Ney and Donzelot. [8] Foy was again to manoeuvre and attack Hugomont; Ney with the Imperial Guard to attack our right centre wing; and Donzelot to push with increased vigour and perseverance his attack on 'The Duke's' centre and left wing. This last service Donzelot was much encouraged to do, having already driven the Germans from 'La Haye Sainte', and established himself in great force in that important position on our centre.

The simultaneous advance of the whole of 'The Duke's' army which now took place was intended to resist and overthrow this last grand attack and expiring struggle of the Emperor. Preparatory to this important movement, command was given to Generals of Brigades to concentrate their Brigades, each regiment to be formed four deep, right wing in front on a collateral line, preserving their relative distances. When this disposition of the forces had been completed, Maitland's Guards were immediately to our right; indeed, this had been their position during the whole day. The intermediate ground between them and Byng's Guards [9] being now occupied by the Light Brigade of Lord Hill's Division [10], enumerating six companies of the 95th Rifles, and the 52nd and 71st Regiments.

It is recorded, and I believe truly, that while the Imperial Guard were advancing to the attack, under their renowned leader, Napoleon placed himself in reviewing position, so that they might pass close to him and thus afford him an opportunity of awakening, as if by a magic wand, those feelings of enthusiasm which he well knew to be so characteristic of the nation. The influence which this remarkable man had acquired over his troops was something more than romantic, and this spell of inspiration the Guards advanced to the contest, each one carrying in his bosom an assurance of victory, as undoubted as did the shepherd boy of Bethlehem (11) when he went forth, sling in hand, to encounter the champion of the Philistines (12). An interesting incident which occurred in one of the hospitals in Brussels, after the battle, will fully illustrate the force of what I have asserted. A bullet having lodged in the breast of an Imperial Guardsman, the surgeon found it necessary to remove it. While this painful operation was going on, not a word of complaint passed the sufferer's lips; but ever and anon he ejaculated with an earnest and emphatic voice, 'Coupez, mon ami, coupez un peu plus profondement, et vous verrez l'Empereur'. ['Cut, my friend, cut more deeply, and then you shall see the Emperor'; ie the image of the Emperor was engraved upon his heart, and would be revealed by the incisions of the surgeon's knife. ed.] Surely, with such men, what but victory was to be expected.

Certainly, it was not by fighting, but by a stratagem, a unique flash of military genius, devised by Sir John Colborne (13) afterwards Lord Seaton, and executed entirely on his own responsibility, with his regiment, the 52nd Light Infantry, that gave the 'coup de grace' to the Imperial Guard, and spread panic and consternation through the whole French army. It was an axiom of war, on no account to change front in face of an attacking enemy; but it was by a direct violation of this axiom that Sir John succeeded in charging the left flank of the first division of the Imperial Guard, numbering about 5,000, while advancing in close column of companies [cf **Introduction - Military/Historical Context**: *Tactics and drill*], thus taking them in as helpless a condition for self-defence as were the unfortunate victims that perished in the 'Black Hole of Calcutta' (14). As the 52nd advanced to charge, the Imperial Guard had but the choice of two fates left them, either to submit to being massacred by the fire and bayonet of their assailants or to fly. They naturally chose the latter course, and it is hardly necessary to observe that the panic which ensued being infectious, the disaster was complete and irreparable - opening for 'The Duke's' army an undisputed road from the plains of Waterloo to the gates of Paris.

There is not a shadow of doubt in my mind, that had the sudden defeat of the Imperial Guard not taken place, matters would have fared far otherwise with us. From the arrival of the Prussians in great force, I do not doubt that we should have succeeded in forcing the enemy from their position, and compelled them to retreat; but with a general such as Napoleon supported by men of renown in war, having his Imperial Guard, numbering from ten to twelve thousand, fresh and unexhausted (held in reserve during the whole day) to form a rear guard, it might have been expected that the retreat would have been accomplished with some sort of order, and with the preservation of at least a great part of the artillery. It is also needless to disguise the fact, that before this crushing event to the Emperor had taken place, the aspect of our affairs was by no means encouraging. Donzelot's attacks was shaking our centre *au coeur* [at its heart]. Byng's Guards, whose ammunition was nearly expended, along with our Hanoverian friends (15) - who were commanded by Colonel Halket [*sic*] (16), a distinguished Peninsular officer and brother to our Sir Colin Halket [*sic*] - had enough to do to meet and resist Foy's renewed attack on Hugomont; and our assailants, who no doubt were part of the left wing of Donzelot's attacking party, were now committing fearful devastation on our nearly exhausted Brigade - our casualties amounting at this time to no less than 76 officers, 983 rank and file and 40 non-commissioned officers and drummers - nearly the half of the whole of our effective force on entering the field on the 16th at Quatre Bras. The sudden and unaccountable cessation of their fire - at the time a mystery - is now explained. Foy and Donzelot, after the defeat of the Imperial Guard, saw clearly that a way had been opened by which Wellington would outflank them; and to avoid such a disaster they immediately ordered a retreat, and their troops coming into contact with the fugitive Imperial Guard, the flight became universal.

A very old friend of my father's (the late Robert Graham of Whitehill) used to propound a dogma, that there was not a sane man or woman in the universe, and that the point in which the infirmity had the mastery was invariably that which was repudiated by the subject of it. [ie the greatest error is reflected by the intensity of the defence by those who perpetrate it. ed] Substantially I believe Mr. Graham was right in this doctrine; and from the manner in which Captain Siborne talks of the Guards, both at Quatre Bras and Waterloo, to the great disparagement of the troops of the line, his infirmity appears to have been an unbounded servile devotion to aristocracy. In this remark let it not for an instant be imagined that I would insinuate anything derogatory to the honour of the *British Guards* [author's italics]. I have already expressed my love and admiration of them; and I repeat it, I love them as I love all brave and honourable men. But in recording the history of so momentous an epoch as the campaign in Belgium in 1815, Captain Siborne should have made himself better acquainted with facts before he extolled the Guards for a deed with which they had nothing whatever to do. If he merely means to say that the 3rd Battalion of Maitland's Guards drove in the skirmishers of the Imperial Guard, who had been sent forth thick as the Egyptian locusts (17), and were decimating their ranks, his assertion will not be disputed. The 33rd did the same with Ney's skirmishers at Quatre Bras. But if he avers that they charged either of the two columns of the Imperial Guard, when advancing to the attack under Marshal Ney, I must decidedly contradict him. They never had the opportunity of performing such service, although I have no doubt, had opportunity offered, they would have acted *as gallantly* [author's italics] as did the 52nd Light Infantry.

The sudden dispersion and flight of the Imperial Guard, forced on by the hot and persistent pursuit of the gallant 52nd, created a panic (18) – that mysterious and ungovernable impulse which makes fools of wise men and cowards of heroes – which quickly spread through the whole of Napoleon's forces, everywhere creating and multiplying confusion beyond description. The once formidable soldiers, who had planted the imperial eagle (19) on the ramparts of Vienna and the walls of Moscow, and who had never before known defeat, became a spectacle of amazement and consternation to the whole French army. Denuding themselves of their arms and encumbrances to facilitate flight, their exulting shouts of 'Vive l'Empereur!' with which shortly before they were rending the air, were changed into the doleful and paralysing cries of 'Save qui peut' ['Every man for himself' ed.] now engraven on the page of history – an appropriate motto for a defeated army and a lost empire.

'Darkness visible', extinguishing every ray of hope, had now overshadowed Napoleon's star. His army, physically and morally the finest every collected in France, was completely routed and dispersed; and he himself a fugitive hurrying to Paris, the forerunner of news which would make the ears of both his court and les bourgeois tingle with fear and astonishment. What a wonderful change of circumstances! Napoleon the great – Napoleon the conqueror of Europe – the dethroner and enthroner of kings at pleasure – the man who had even on one occasion, in defiance of the superstition which throws a sacred halo around the head of the Roman Catholic Church, dared to seize the holy father himself, and imprison him, until he was compelled to acquiesce in all his political schemes (20) – was now himself reduced to the last extremity.

The last political act in the drama of this remarkable man's life proved a complete failure. Reaching his capital in the hope of raising the Parisians *en masse* to defend his throne and crown, he found that *disappointed* [author's italics] France had now begun to feel that the ocean of blood she had already shed to gratify his insatiable ambition was more than sufficient. Notwithstanding his earnest solicitations, therefore, and overwhelming appeals to the glory the empire had achieved under his sway, both his court and les bourgeois remained inflexible in refusing to entertain such a gigantic project.

Deserted now by his friends, surrounded by his enemies, many of whom he knew would willingly have 'betrayed him with a kiss' (21), and isolated from all regal power, he sought protection for his person under the British flag. On the 15th of July, on board the *Bellerophon*, he resigned himself into the hands of Captain Maitland as a prisoner of state.

By the joint determination of the allies, he was sent to the island of St. Helena. There, under the vigilant eye of a stern and unrelenting jailer (22), whom he no doubt regarded as being unworthy to unloose his shoe-latchet, he lingered out a few years in degradation and neglect, save for the unwearied devotion and heartfelt sympathy bestowed on him by a few old friends and faithful attendants. For the love they bore him, and the admiration they entertained for his gigantic intellect, these men had forsaken their country to accompany him in his exile. *Let imperishable honour be accorded them* [author's italics] for this godlike manifestation of self-sacrificing love!

On the 5th May, 1821, nearly six years after the battle of Waterloo, he died of cancer in the stomach, the disease being no doubt aggravated and hurried to a fatal termination by that war of emotion which must have agonized his soul during the many solitary hours of his imprisonment.

The sudden rise and the still more sudden fall of this extraordinary man, are events altogether unique in history. On account of the clouds of prejudice which still envelop his memory, it must be reserved to a later posterity to write an appropriate epitaph for him. That epitaph, although it may be justly emblazoned with many deeds of imperishable renown, nevertheless, if faithful, must likewise be tarnished with many others of a mean and humiliating character. It is to be regretted for the glory of his name as a soldier, that he did not place himself instead of his Lieutenant [Ney] at the head of his Imperial Guard, in his last grand attack on Wellington's line, carrying with him an unalterable determination, like our gallant Colonel Elphistone [sic] either 'to die sword in hand or conquer'.

The fate of the eagle struck down by lightning from his lofty elevation, while with expanded wing and inflexible eye set on the sun - majestically soaring heavenwards - will undoubtedly awake emotions of a very different nature from those excited by the demise of 'the caged bird', whose pinions have been paralysed, and whose heart has been broken, by a debasing imprisonment. The case of the first commands a noble commiseration, that of the latter a feeling somewhat akin to contempt.

It had therefore been well, assuredly well, for the glory of Napoleon's setting sun, had he, instead of deserting his army, led on his Imperial Guard to the attack, and like our noble and gallant Picton, found a hero's grave on the field of Waterloo, instead of a prison-house on the island of St Helena, where with his honour trodden under foot, and his heart broken like the poor captive bird's "his lamp was put out in obscure darkness", his whole career being only a remarkable illustration of the truth of Scripture, "that kings reign and princes decree justice" solely by the will of God.

As I would not wish, like Bonaparte, to be a deserter from the field of battle, I must after this long digression beg you to return with me to the scene of conflict. The advance of 'The Duke's' army was now unimpeded and triumphant. Feelings were glowing in the breasts of our troops altogether inconceivable, save by those who participated in the victory. Our army have taken possession of the French position, which was now entirely deserted, halted, and a most interesting inquiry took place as to the extent of our losses. It would be difficult to express the feelings awakened and to describe the congratulations evoked, as we clasped the hands of those of our brother officers who had escaped unhurt.

As for myself, I felt as the Brigade advanced, my step so elastic and my heart so joyous, that I seemed as if treading on air. On halting, a number of little coteries were formed to discuss the proceedings of the day, when a dark and unexpected cloud suddenly overshadowed the joy and gratitude which reigned, I am sure, in every breast. The officers composing my circle were Colonel Elphistone [*sic*], Captain Gore, and Major Chalmers. Major Chalmers having commanded the 30th Regiment for some time previous to the termination of the battle, was in high spirits, and had just remarked 'that having been in command, he would no doubt be gazetted a Lieutenant-Colonel at once'. We all acquiesced in this, and congratulated him on his anticipated promotion. While engaged in this social conversation, our attention was directed to some desultory firing going on in front. A few shots having passed close by us (in passing they make a sharp whistling noise) I quitted my friends saying, 'I will go and see what those fellows are about'. On getting to a rising ground close to the circle I had just quitted, I saw a few straggling skirmishers firing towards the Brigade. On a shot passing close to my left, I involuntarily turned round, when I saw poor Chalmers leave his friends, advance towards me, put his hand to his breast, lay himself down close to me, and immediately expire. This sad event was the cause of great regret, as Chalmers was much liked and respected in his regiment and by all who knew him. He was, I think, the last man - certainly the last officer - killed in our Brigade at Waterloo. His unexpected death was indeed a remarkable verification of the old adage, 'that each ball has its own billet'.

The destroying angel had now stayed his arm and assailed his sword. The voice of the cannon which had shaken the earth was stilled, and a silence reigned around as peaceful as that of a sleeping infant or the surrounding dead. A great battle had been fought, and a stupendous victory achieved. The exhausted soldiery sought and found again, as at Quatre Bras, rest among the wounded, the dead, and dying. And their repose, notwithstanding the horrors which surrounded them, was more refreshing that that of the voluptuary on his bed of down.

The shooting rays from the east, which heralded the birth of another day, spread light over a scene of blood and desolation unparalleled in modern warfare. Lavater [23] held the opinion that the passions which govern man in life are fixed, so that even the cold hand of death cannot remove them from his countenance. Here indeed was a large field for contemplation; and among the many dead around me, one instance was so illustrative of the truth of this statement that I cannot resist giving it. A French gunner, whose back had been placed in an erect position against the wheel of a broken gun-carriage, wore an expression so life-like it required almost minute examination to realize that the vital spark had fled. His shako, which lay at his right side, had fallen from his head, and completely exposed his face. His large blue eyes seemed fixed on *me* [author's italics], and wore even in death a living expression. His right hand was raised as if under great excitement, and for a second I imagined him to be yet alive, and in the act of enthusiastically exclaiming 'Vive L'Empereur.'

In further pursuing my examination of the dead, who were scattered over the field like sheaves cut down by the hand of the reaper, I was struck with the diversity of expression still lingering on the countenances of those around me. From the distortion of their faces (like poor Captain Haigh's), many of them must have had a terrible struggle 'with the king of terrors'; others, from the placidity of their expression, seemed as if they had sunk into refreshing slumber. The separation between soul and body in their case must have been instantaneous.

Another dark phase in this revolting spectacle was the prodigious destruction of war-horses. The official return given in by the allied armies of Wellington and Blucher amounted to no less than 2 610; and from the unceasing use Napoleon made of his cavalry during the battle in charging our squares, and the severe chastisement they met with from our heavy dragoons, his loss must have been nearly double that of ours. It was indeed painful to witness the lingering sufferings which those noble animals, who had rendered such distinguished service during the battle, must have endured before relieved by death - indeed no one who had witnessed their prowess could withhold from them a meed of admiration. As I leisurely walked over the field, my attention was attracted to one of them standing at a considerable distance from me. I went towards him to ascertain how he remained in this isolated position; judge then of my surprise when I found the poor animal on three legs - one of his fore-legs having been taken off near the shoulder by a cannon ball. His suffering seemed terrible, and his beautiful face wore an aspect of great pain, which so touched me that I only regretted I had not a pistol by which I might have put an end to his anguish! As the day advanced hosts of visitors and marauders from Waterloo and Brussels spread over the field of battle - the former to alleviate the sufferings of the wounded - the latter to destroy and rob them. Preparations were soon set on foot to bury the dead by digging large trenches, into which they were thrown promiscuously - friend and foe together - there to rest in PEACE until the resurrection trumpet shall, by a long blast, awake them from their long sleep! Solemn thought! - let us no longer linger on this field of blood - let us rather try to forget it - for me, alas! impossible!

It is not my purpose, neither is it my inclination, to animadvert [pass judgement] on the general conduct of the two great captains who commanded during this momentous struggle; that has been left to the tribunal of history. However correct or incorrect its declared judgement may be, that is all that remains to posterity. I shall only remark that, from the complex and exciting character of a great battle like Waterloo, together with the strong party and individual jealousies that such a stirring event must needs awake, it is not surprising that much must has been written and said about it entirely derogatory to truth.

Mount Blow, 18th June, 1870

P.S. - When I undertook this narrative, I had not the most remote idea of ever printing it. My sole motive was to please and gratify my grandchildren; but having received much encouragement from several friends on whose judgement I could rely, I have been emboldened to put it in this form, so that they and my family may have copies as a memento of my respect and affection. To my esteemed friend, the Rev. Hugh Macmillan, who kindly agreed to edit and see my little bantling swaddled and cared for before the tiny creature showed [its] face to my friends, I return unfeigned thanks; and only hope that those who may read these letters will be indulgent, and bear in mind that the writer of them is now over fourscore, and that his profession was not the art of writing but the art of fighting.

Editorial observations on Letter V

This letter is distinguished by several important features. The first is the profusion of powerful visual imagery. The atmosphere of the battle is communicated to the reader through a series of dramatic, emotionally charged images: the brigade commander, Sir Colin Halkett, seizing the Colours and ordering the advance; Lt Col Elphinstone assuming the command of the brigade upon Sir Colin being wounded and urging forward the brigade, sword in hand; the French Imperial Guardsman who urged the surgeon to cut more deeply with his knife, in order that the image of the Emperor engraved upon his heart could be revealed; the frozen posture of the French gunner who still projected the image of the life that had been severed; and - probably the most unnerving and pathetic - the terrible image of the mutilated horse, whom we can readily, and all too painfully, imagine pleading for death to end his silently borne suffering. The last named image possesses distinct images of the terrible indictment of war embodied in Picasso's painting, *Guernica* (inspired by the Fascist atrocity of bombing the village of that name during the Spanish Civil War of 1936-1939), which features a dead mare and its still-born foal. To this series of images one must add the portrait of the 'eagle caged' - the forlorn Napoleon confined on St Helena. The reader can readily imagine these vivid images being evoked in the course of Pattison's recollections; possibly being created in his mind's eye at the base of the oil lamp on his desk as he recounted his memories to his friend, the Rev Hugh Macmillan, late into the night.

The second noteworthy aspect of this letter is Pattison's instinctive awareness of recent dramatic advances in military technology; an insight which, regrettably, was not shared by many arch-conservative senior officers either of his or a succeeding generation. His comments regarding the extreme vulnerability of the Colour escorts to modern small arms fire is symptomatic of his awareness of the need for camouflage in the context of a radically altered battlefield scenario compared with that of Waterloo. His remarks proved to be prophetic in a dual respect. First, the abandonment of

Memories of the Waterloo campaign

conveying the Colours in battle occurred 11 years after the publication of his letters. Second, the universal introduction of camouflage followed some two decades later. It is apparent from Pattison's remarks in these contexts that he had a close and informed interest in contemporary military affairs.

Third, as stated in the editorial observations on **Letter I**, Pattison strongly reiterates his argument to the effect that the unwarranted credit devolved upon Maitland's Guards Division has detracted from the true role played by the 52nd Regiment in this respect.

APPENDIX I

The effective strength of Sir Colin Halket's [sic] Brigade on entering the field of Quatre Bras on the 16th June, 1815.

<u>5th British Brigade, commanded by Major-General Sir Colin Halket [sic]</u>.

2nd Batt. 30th Regiment - Lieut.-Col. Hamilton commanding . . .615
33rd Regiment - Lieut.-Col. W. Elphistone [sic] commanding . . .561
2nd Batt. 69th Regiment - Col. C. Morrice commanding 516
2nd Batt. 73rd Regiment - Col. G. Harris commanding 562

Casualties at Quatre Bras and Waterloo including non-commissioned officers, drummers and those missing
Quatre Bras 304
Waterloo . . . .<u>679</u>
                                                                                                                 983

Add officers killed and wounded as stated above 77

Total amount 1060

Not far from half of the whole Brigade.

The following is a List of the Officers of the 33rd Regiment who were engaged at Quatre Bras and Waterloo. (1):

	killed	wounded	unhurt
Lieut.-Col. W. Elphistone [sic] commanding,	0	0	1
Major G. Coclough,	0	0	1
Major E. Parkinson,	0	1	0
Captain W M'Intyre,	0	1	0
Captain C. Knight,	0	1	0
Captain J. Haigh,	1	0	0
Captain J. Harty,	0	1	0
Captain R. Gore,	0	0	1
Captain J. Longden,	0	0	1
Captain A. H. Trevor,	0	0	1
Captain J. Reid, ★	0	0	0
Captain G. Barr, ★	0	0	1
Captain Fred. Hope Pattison, ★	0	0	1
[★ Lieutenants in command of companies]			
Captain G. D. Haigh,	1	0	0
Captain J. Boyce,	1	0	0

Captain A. Gore,	1	0	0
Captain J. Hart,	1	0	0
Captain J. Mirkland,	0	1	0
Captain R. Westmore,	0	1	0
Captain J. G. Ogle,	0	1	0
Captain S. A. Pagan,	0	1	0
Captain E. Clabon,	0	0	1
Captain J. Archibald,	0	0	1
Captain J. Lynam,	0	0	1
Captain J. Furlong,	0	1	0
Captain J. Cameron,	1	0	0
Ensign H. Bain,	0	1	0
Ensign J. Alderson,	0	1	0
Ensign J. A. Howard,	0	1	0
Ensign A. Watson,	0	0	1
Ensign C. Smith,	0	0	1
Ensign W. Hodson,	0	0	1
Ensign G. Blackall,	0	0	1
Ensign G. Duery,	0	1	0
Adjutant Thain	0	1	0

36 officers of the 33rd Regiment entered the field;
of them [*sic*] 7 were killed, 15 wounded, 14 escaped unhurt.

MEMORANDUM

I am very desirous that Field Marshal Lord Seaton's letter to his friend, the late Lieut. Colonel Bentham, who served in the 33rd for many years, should be given in this Appendix, as it is conclusive of the fact that the Guards never did charge the Imperial Guard at the crisis of the battle, and it ought for ever to set at rest that disputed question. It is most certain that the glory of this astounding achievement belongs to Sir John Colborne and his gallant corps alone, although the reward was given to others. An extract from page 102 of *Lord Seaton's Regiment at Waterloo* is also given, together with what is contained in pages 103 and 104; these facts will support what I have averred in my narrative.

Deer Park, Honiton, October 15, 1853

My Dear Bentham,

With reference to your letter of the 7th, it may be more satisfactory to you, instead of replying to your queries, to draw your attention to the principal movements which accelerated the termination of the battle of Waterloo, and to the facts which would have been admitted as evidence in support of the claims of the 52nd, to the merit of having first checked the advance of the Imperial Guard at the crisis of the battle, and of having completed their *deroute* [rout], by marching directly on their dense columns, and by a flank movement charging them so vigorously, that the whole gave way, and retired in confusion. The statement of officers, engaged at Waterloo, I found were generally so different and conflicting, that it was impossible to draw up any correct account of them. Captain Siborne, I believe, consulted every officer in command with whom he was acquainted, or to whom he was introduced, and endeavoured to make *their* version correspond with the facts generally known relative to the movements of regiments, brigades, and divisions. I have never read his account. If you bring the 52nd into a contest with the Guards by attempting to prove from rumours that the latter were retiring at the time they are said to have charged and defeated the French troops, you will raise up a host of opponents to your account, which would rather injure the cause of the 52nd. I suppose the Guards must have made some forward movement, and that many officers must have seen it, but I contend that the French column had been checked and thrown into disorder before the Guards moved. I saw the column of the Imperial Guard steadily advancing to a certain point, and I observed them halt, which was *precisely* [writer's italics] as the skirmishers of the 52nd opened fire on their flanks. My attention was so completely drawn to our position and dangerous advance – a large mass of cavalry having been seen on our right, exposed as it was, that I could see no movement on the part of the Guards, and, indeed, as we advanced, I believe we were too much under the position to have been able to have them in sight. Sir John Byng's Brigade remained in line without firing or making any movement while we passed along in front, our line forming a right angle with that Brigade, and being about two hundred yards nearer to the French. Sir John Byng told me afterwards at Paris that he had his whole attention drawn to our movements, and that his Brigade had no ammunition left. He gave *us* [writer's italics], at that time, full credit for our advance. Till the Duke of Wellington's despatch was made known at Paris *we* [writer's italics] had never heard of the charge of the Guards; and I am inclined to believe that the attack on the French had been checked by the advance of the 52nd, and the movements afterwards of the whole of Sir H. Clinton's division (2) before any forward movements had been made by the Brigade commanded by Sir P Maitland. This account corresponds with that given to me by Lord Hill, who was close to the Guards, and 'saw us moving across the plain'. When we followed the French towards La Belle Alliance (3), no troops from the part of the position occupied by the Guards was near us, and we passed eighty guns and carriages a short time after the French had retired, which they had left on the road between La Haye Sainte and La Belle Alliance.

I have written this, as circumstances have occurred to me to remind me of the part we performed, without method - but with those remarks and the facts measured in the inclosure [sic], you may be able to judge correctly of the claims of the 52nd.

Yours very faithfully,

Seaton.

The following passages, bearing upon the defeat of the French Imperial Guard by the single-handed attack of the 52nd, are extracted from some remarks on Waterloo by Lord Seaton:-

'The crisis may be called the period when the French columns, advancing with the intention of penetrating our centre, were checked and compelled to halt by the flank movement and fire of the 52nd. The attackers were attacked and checked in their assault, and driven from the ground they had gained before they could deploy ... The whole of the Imperial Guard advanced at the same time, and their flank was first attacked by the 52nd, before any forward movement was made to check them in front ... The Prussians could not have attracted the attention of the French so as to cause the throwing back of their right wing, until after the Imperial Guard had commenced their attack on our centre ... No regiment except the 52nd fired on the flank of the Imperial Guard.'

The late Mr. Wm. Crawley Yonge, of the 52nd, in a letter to Colonel Bentham, written in November 1853, says:-

'He [Lord Seaton] was saying here last week that after his conversation with the French cuirassier officer, he kept watching the heavy column advancing, saw it directed against a very weak part of the line, saw no attempt at preparation to meet it, and therefore (making light of his own exercise of judgement and decision), he said there was nothing else to do, having such a strong battalion in hand, but to endeavour to stop them by a flank attack, for it seemed quite evident that, if something of that sort was not done, our line would unquestionably be penetrated. With a man looking on in this intelligent way, and acting on what he saw, how is it possible that all this fanfaronade [fuss] of Guards charging the head of this column, can have the smallest foundation of truth?'

The same officer writes:-

'It is the dearest wish of my heart to see that affair put to rights in the eyes of the world. As to Lord Seaton, I think there never was a man so ill-used as he was - only fancy how many men were there at any time who would have done what he did, being only the commanding officer of his own regiment, without orders or sanction from any superior officer, his own general of brigade yet on the field, to take upon himself such responsibility; first, in acting without orders, and secondly, daring to expose his flank to the enemy as he did? How few would have seen and caught the right moment; and was there another man in the army who would have ventured on it, if he had seen it? As for the regiment, if they had their rights, they ought to have more credit for their exemplary steadiness under heavy fire for a good while previous to the charge, than for the charge and pursuit itself. It was capitally done, and few regiments could have borne to be handled without getting into confusion, but it was easy work compared with the other.'

On another occasion he speaks of Lord Seaton's characteristic humility and modesty in the following terms:-

'Meeting him in London a little while ago at the house of a lady, a mutual friend, she, hearing us talk over some of the occurrences of the war, remarked, "How proud you gentlemen may feel at the recollection that you had a share in those great events;" on which he replied very gently, "Proud! No, rather humbled, I think."How characteristic this is, is it not? It puts me in mind of two lines in "The Christian Year" [4] on St. Philip and St. James's Day. The stanza ends -

   Thankful for all God takes away,
   Humbled by all he gives."

In "The United Service Journal" for 1833, Colonel Gawler publishes a letter from Colonel Brotherton, from which the following is an extract:-

'Some years ago, not long after the battle of Waterloo, in conversation with a French officer of the staff, who had accompanied the column led by Marshal Ney at the close of the day, we were describing the relative merits of our different modes of attack. I observed to him that it seemed surprising and unaccountable that our gallant opponents should obstinately persist in a practice, which experience must have taught them to be so unavailing and destructive to themselves, viz. their constant attacks in column against our Infantry in line. I cited as a last and conclusive instance, the failure of the attack at the close of the day at Waterloo, where a column composed of such distinguished veterans, and led by such a man as Ney, was repulsed and upset by some comparatively young soldiers as our Guards (for such I understood the brigade in question to be composed), adverting [referring] also to the singular coincidence of the Imperial Guard encountering our British Guards at such a crisis. Upon which he observed, without seeming in the least to detract from the merit of the troops which the column had to encounter in its front, who, he said, showed 'tres bonne contenance' [ie a good spirit. ed.] that I was wrong in adducing this [author's italics] in support of my argument, or in supposing the attack was solely repulsed by the troops opposed to it in front; 'for', he added, 'nous fumes principalement repousse *par un attaque de flanc, tres vive*, QUI NOUS ECRASA' [We were principally repulsed by a very powerful flank attack, which crushed us. ed] [author's italics and capitals].

As far as I can recollect, these were his very words. I retain all the feelings of a Guardsman, in which corps I served several years, and should feel as jealous of its honours as if still in its ranks, etc.

Horror recollected in tranquillity

PART III

NOTES

LETTER I

(1) *keepers of the house tremble*: Pattison is referring to the mental and physical faculties which ensure the body's consciousness of its physical environment. *ed*.

(2) *the righteous shall flourish*: Possibly a reference to Psalm 92 (Verse 12): 'The righteous shall flourish like the palm tree, he shall grow like a cedar in Lebanon.' *ed*.

(3) *Sir Colin Halket's Brigade*: Sir Colin's name is in fact misspelt in Pattison's text. He is referring to Sir Colin Halkett (1774-1856). He was the eldest son of Maj Gen Frederick Godar Halkett and was born on 7 September 1774 at Venlo (his father then being a major in the Regiment of Gordon of the Scots Brigade of the Dutch army). His grandfather was Lt Gen Charles Halkett of the Dutch army and colonel of a regiment of the Scots Brigade. On 2 March 1792, having previously served seven months as a regimental cadet, he was nominated ensign, with the rank of lieutenant, in the 2nd Battalion of the Dutch Foot Guards; and subsequently lieutenant with the rank of captain in the 1st Battalion of the Dutch Foot Guards.

Halkett was instrumental in the formation of a unit that was to prove the genesis of the renowned King's German Legion. In June 1803 the French occupied Hanover, the 15 000 strong Hanoverian army being unable to resist. The Convention of the Elbe (5 July 1803) had disbanded the Hanoverian army, but permitted its members to journey wherever they wished; with the proviso that they should not again bear arms against France until they had first been formally 'exchanged' as prisoners-of-war. (This latter provision never came into effect, as the King of England, George III - in his capacity as Elector of Hanover - refused to ratify the convention; the union of England and Hanover, consequent upon George I's accession to the English throne in 1714, meant that the Hanoverian army owed its allegiance to the English monarch). Somewhat surprisingly, the French permitted the recruitment of Hanoverian troops in the English service within Hanover itself, notwithstanding the fact that England and France were at war; although the French obviously tried their utmost to discourage such recruitment. (This latitude probably derived from the fact that Hanover was an English possession). Halkett, described as a major in the Dutch service (which at that point in time he appears to have left) was authorized by the British government to raise a battalion of light infantry in Hanover, to consist of 489 men. He was given the rank of major commandant, with the promise of a lieutenant colonelcy when the number reached 800 men. Simultaneously, a German officer, Col Frederick von der Decken, was authorized to raise a second corps in Hanover. The separate forces raised by von der Decken and Halkett were integrated into a unit known as the King's German Regiment, in which the forces created by Halkett and von der Decken were designated the 1st and 2nd Light Battalions. They were uniformed in riflemen's camouflage green and stationed initially in the New Forest, and latterly at Bexhill, Sussex. The influx of German recruits into England proved to be so great that the King's German Regiment was expanded into a force that was virtually a miniature army, designated the King's German Legion; comprising five regiments of cavalry (three of hussars and two of dragoons); the two original battalions of light infantry; eight battalions of line infantry; two troops of horse and four batteries of foot artillery; and a small engineer corps. At Waterloo the Legion (which, by virtue of the Hanoverian Army's special relationship with the English Sovereign, was never regarded as an allied contingent, but as an integral formation of the British Regular Army) fielded six infantry brigades and one cavalry brigade. They were regarded as the finest of the foreign troops; acknowledged by Wellington (never prolific in his praise) when he stated: 'It is impossible to have better soldiers than the real Hanoverians'.

On 17 November 1803 Halkett was appointed lieutenant colonel. At the head of the 2nd Battalion, King's German Legion, he served under Lord Cathcart in the north of Germany (1805-1806) and in Ireland (1806). In 1808 he served in Sweden and Portugal; in the latter theatre the King's German Legion formed part of Lt Gen Sir John Moore's force as it retreated towards Corunna. The German light battalion formed part of the force that retired on Vigo. The King's German Legion repeatedly distinguished itself in the ill-starred Walcheren expedition of 1809. Commanding his battalion, Halkett joined Beresford's army before Badajoz, in April 1811, and commanded the brigade at the battle of Albuera (1811). He was appointed brevet colonel on 1 January 1812 and served with his battalion at Salamanca (1812) and in the operations against Burgos. He subsequently commanded the German Light Brigade serving with the 7th Division during the retreat from Burgos; his services in this operation being especially commended by the Duke of Wellington. Halkett commanded the German Light Brigade during the succeeding operations in the Peninsular War; including the battle of Vittoria (1813), the passage of the Bidassoa, and the battles on the Nive and at Toulouse. On 4 June 1814 he was promoted to major general, and commanded a brigade at Quatre Bras and Waterloo; being hotly engaged on both occasions and receiving four severe wounds at Waterloo. Wellington referred to him in his despatch as 'a very gallant and deserving officer.'

Halkett remained in the British service following Waterloo. He was for some years lieutenant governor of Jersey. In 1830 he was promoted to lieutenant general and appointed a full general in 1841. Halkett served as commander-in-chief in Bombay between July 1831 and January 1832. He was appointed colonel successively of the 71st Highland Light Infantry, the 31st and 35th Regiments. Appointed a Knight Grand Cross of the Order of the Bath (GCB) and Knight Grand Cross of the Order of Hanover (GCH), Halkett was made a knight of numerous foreign orders and an honorary general in the Hanoverian service. He was appointed lieutenant governor of Chelsea Hospital in 1848, succeeding as governor on the death of George Anson in 1849. He died at Chelsea on 24 September 1856.

As Pattison informs us (**Letter V**), Sir Colin's brother, Gen Hugh von Halkett, also played a memorable role at Waterloo, serving in the desperate defence of Hougoumont. Halkett is perhaps the most interesting of the many figures introduced by Pattison; in view of the marked cosmopolitan character of his career, being grounded in the Dutch service and the King's German Legion. In a very real sense Halkett's career exemplifies the continuance of the mercenary tradition within the British Army. ed.

(4) *the 'General'*: ie a specific rhythm of drum beat which denoted that the troops gathered should 'fall in', or assemble. This drum call was also known as the 'Assembly' or 'Gathering.'*ed.*

(5) *compounding for a leg or an arm*: The meaning of this phrase is obscure, but the sense would appear to be that the jokes were based upon grim puns relating to the loss of limbs. *ed.*

(6) *express*: ie a message delivered by a courier. *ed.*

(7) Lieutenant Colonel William George Keith Elphistone [sic] (a), aide-de-camp to the king, was son of the Honourable William Elphistone [sic], and East Indian Director (b), and previously commander of an East Indiaman. (c) He was also cousin to the late Lord Elphistone [sic], and uncle of the present peer, who is son of the late Colonel James Drummond Elphistone [sic], who was wounded at Genappe. (d) In 1813, Lieutenant colonel Elphistone [sic] was appointed to the command of the 33rd Foot, and fought with his regiment at Antwerp, Bergen-op-Zoom (e), Quatre Bras and Waterloo. During the assault on Bergen-op-Zoom he was wounded; and at the crisis of Waterloo, when Sir Colin Halket [sic] was removed from the field severely wounded (shot through both cheeks) he assumed command of the Brigade, which he led on most gallantly, ejaculating, when the issues of victory or defeat were trembling in the balance, 'Come on, my brave fellows, let us die like Britons, sword in hand, or conquer.' For this service he was rewarded with the distinction of C.B. (f) In 1837 he became a Major general and was appointed to take command of the Bengal army, when his health gave way, and he died at Cabul in 1842. *auth.*

Editorial observations on above footnote
(a) The name is in fact misspelt. It should read 'Elphinstone'. The following biographical details are intended to supplement Pattison's concise outline.

Maj Gen William George Keith Elphinstone (1782-1842) entered the army as an ensign in the 41st Regiment of Foot on 24 March 1804; was promoted lieutenant on 4 August 1804; and captain in the 93rd Regiment on 18 June 1806. He exchanged into the 1st Regiment of Foot Guards on 6 August 1807, and into the 15th Light Dragoons on 18 January 1810. On 2 May 1811 he was appointed major in the 8th West India Regiment and on 13 September 1813 purchased the lieutenant colonelcy of the 33rd Regiment (in succession to Arthur Wellesley, later Duke of Wellington).

On 27 May 1825 Elphinstone was promoted colonel and appointed aide-de-camp to King George IV. In 1839 he was appointed to the command of the Benares Division of the Bengal army. From this peace-time role he was, regrettably, selected, at the end of 1841, to take command of the British army at Cabul, succeeding Sir Willoughby Cotton. The Afghan War of 1839-1840 had ended. Dost Mohammed had been removed from the Afghan throne and the English nominee, Shah Suja, was believed to be firmly established. The greater part of the army that had served in the 1839-1840 campaign was withdrawn from Afghanistan, where there remained only a single division to support Shah Suja and the English resident, Sir William Macnaghten. When Elphinstone took command of the division at Cabul the situation appeared totally stable and quiescent. The troops stationed there amused themselves with pony racing and theatricals, as if they were based in a friendly country. Elphinstone made no effort to place the garrison in a battle-worthy condition; and, misled by the political officers (Burnes and Macnaghten) appeared to be ignorant of the perils of his position and his isolation from any assistance from India. When, therefore, Macnaghten was assassinated on Christmas Day 1841 by Akbar Khan (Dost Mohammed's son), Elphinstone proved to be totally unsuited to deal with the grave crisis that ensued. His age and poor health also militated against sound judgement in the emergency. He refused to heed the advice of some of his officers that he should seize the citadel. Crippled by gout, Elphinstone delegated all authority to Brig Gen Shelton. The Afghans promptly closed all communications between India and Cabul, and even between the capital and Jellalabad, where a British brigade had gallantly established itself. The British garrison was virtually besieged in Cabul. On 6 January 1842 Elphinstone began a disorderly and dangerous retreat to Jellalabad, minus the greater part of his stores and guns. The army was hampered by a mass of Afghan camp followers and also had to protect the women and children of the garrison. Akbar Khan had provided spurious guarantees of safe conduct but, in the event, could not, or would not, help the retreating British force against the depredations of the tribesmen, who attacked it at every point. Finally, the women and children, and some of the officers - including Elphinstone himself - were surrendered as hostages, on 28 January. The attacks continued, and the British troops made their final defence in the pass of Jagdallak. There was only one survivor, a Dr Brydon, who reached Jellalabad. Whilst still a captive, Elphinstone died in Cabul of dysentery, on 28 April 1842. The Jellalabad garrison survived and was eventually relieved.

It is, perhaps, significant that Pattison, who is usually voluble in biographical details, passes over this final, disastrous, phase of Elphinstone's career in silence.

(b) *East India director*: ie a director of the East India Company. The East India Company was formed for the expansion of British trade with east and south-east Asia, and India. It was incorporated by royal charter on 31 December 1600. The company, having wresting trading concessions from the rulers of the Moghul empire in India, traded in cotton and silk goods, indigo, saltpetre and spices. Commencing as a monopolistic trading body, the East India Company acted as the agent for the expansion of British interests for a century; from the mid-18th Century until its role in India was superseded by the British Crown in 1858. In 1708 the fusion with a rival company led to the creation of the United Company of Merchants of England trading to the East Indies. The United Company was controlled by a board ('court') of 24 directors. Popularly known as 'John Company', the East India Company maintained its own armies and navy. The major areas of the company's control were Bombay, Madras, and Bengal (acquired in 1757). In 1809 the Treaty of Amritsa fixed the river Sutlej as the north-west boundary of the Company's sphere of influence. It extended its interests to the Persian Gulf, south east Asia and east Asia. After the mid-18th Century the cotton goods market declined, whilst tea became an important Chinese import. Beginning in the early 18th Century, the company financed the tea trade with illegal opium exports to China. Chinese opposition to this trade triggered the first Opium War (1839-1842), which resulted in the acquisition of Hong Kong and the expansion of British trading privileges following upon the predictable Chinese defeat. A second Opium War, often called the 'Arrow War' (1857-1860) brought increased trading rights to Europeans. Following the Regulating Act (1773) and Pitt's India Act (1784) the company gradually lost both its political and commercial independence in India. Its commercial monopoly was broken in 1813, and from 1834 its trading activities ceased entirely, thenceforth serving as the managing agency of the British Government in India until it was deprived of this role following the end of the Indian Mutiny in 1858. The company ceased to exist as a legal entity in 1874.

(c) *East Indiaman*: A large sailing vessel, of the type constructed between the 16th and 18th Centuries for the trade between Europe and southern Asia. The first were Portuguese and Dutch. English Indiamen appeared late in the 16th Century and eventually came to dominate the trade. The ships varied in size from approximately 400 to 1 500 tons and more; and often were larger than contemporary men-of-war. They were three-masted and invariably well armed to defend themselves against piracy.

(d) *Genappe*: The action referred to occurred on 17 June 1815, on the day following Quatre Bras. On that day Lord Uxbridge (the commander of the cavalry and horse artillery in Wellington's army) had been ordered to remain at Quatre Bras for as long as he conveniently could, in order to allow time for the allied forces to retire to Waterloo. He remained there until 13h00, and then retired in a leisurely fashion before the French advance. After passing through Genappe he placed his old regiment, the 7th Hussars, on the high road, some 200 yards behind that town, with the 23rd Light Dragoons in support. As soon as the lancers, who headed the French advanced guard, issued from Genappe, they were charged by the hussars; but the latter were not able to penetrate the French cavalry. At length Uxbridge sent forth two squadrons of the 1st Life Guards, which overcame the lancers and pursued them into Genappe.

(e) *C.B*: Companion of the Most Honourable Order of the Bath.

(8) *The oration I made get into battle*: It is possible that a strong element of irony is present in this statement; Pattison is feasibly engaging in a humorous exercise in self-mockery. *ed*.

(9) *white feather*: the traditional symbol of cowardice. The symbol derives from the barbaric practice of cock-fighting, an extremely popular 'sport' during the 18th and 19th Centuries. Those cocks which appeared the least aggressive were found to have a white feather in their tails (a symptom of anaemia). *ed*.

(10) *journeyman*: A journeyman was one who had completed his apprenticeship, but continued to work for his employer, as he had not yet established his business. *ed*.

(11) *setting*: ie preparing the razors by sharpening their blades. *ed*.

(12) *Lord Dundreary*: A character in the play, *Our American cousin* (1858), by Tom Taylor. Lord Dundreary was an indolent brainless peer, whose long drooping whiskers became proverbial. *ed*.

(13) *'The Duke'*: Arthur Wellesley, 1st Duke of Wellington (1769 - 1852). He was the son of the 1st Earl of Mornington and a younger brother of the 1st Marquess Wellesley. He gained an army commission in 1789 but saw no regimental service until 1793, when he purchased a majority in the 33rd Regiment of Foot; becoming Officer Commanding of the regiment (with the rank of lieutenant colonel) in the same year. Wellesley served in the futile Dutch campaign of 1794, but his first opportunity for distinction presented itself in India, where his brother was Governor General of Mysore (cf note re Seringapatam) and held an independent command in the Mahratta wars. His greatest triumph in India occurred at the battle of Assaye (1803).

In 1808 he commanded an expedition despatched to Portugal to extirpate the French from that country. He secured a victory at Vimeiro (1808) but a cloud was cast over his career by the Convention of Cintra; the agreement which permitted the French to withdraw from Portugal. In 1809, following the death of Lt Gen Sir John Moore at Corunna, Wellesley was re-appointed to the command of British troops in the Iberian Peninsula, which was once again subject to French invasion. He gained a victory at Talavera (1809), which earned for him the title of Viscount Wellington and enabled him to assume a secure position in the prepared fortified lines of Torres Vedras. Here, after checking the French at Busaco (1810) he was sufficiently strong to advance in turn, but had to await the fall of Cuidad Rodrigo (January 1812) and Madrid (May 1812). Although he subsequently captured Madrid, he was forced to retire and winter in Portugal once more. In 1813, possessing the advantage bestowed upon him by the severe depletion of the French forces in the disastrous Russian campaign launched by Napoleon in 1812, he advanced across Spain; and, following the victory at Vittoria (July 1813), forced the enemy to retire to its homeland of France. Wellington's forces, in pursuit, secured the final victory of the Peninsular War at Toulouse (April 1814). The title of Duke was bestowed upon him in recognition of his achievements of that year.

Whilst attending the Congress of Vienna (1815) as one of the British delegates, he heard that Napoleon had escaped from Elba. Wellington was placed in command of the allied army of the Netherlands. Although Napoleon succeeded in dividing his opponents, defeating the Prussians at Ligny and checking the British at Quatre Bras, this did not prevent Wellington - with the help of Blucher in the latter phases of the battle - from gaining the final victory at Waterloo (18 June 1815).

Wellington retained his position as commander-in-chief in France until 1818, when he returned to England to take part in political life. For this he was temperamentally ill-suited; and there was constant friction with his colleagues in the Tory ministry, Castlereagh and Canning, until he resigned in 1827. He served as prime minister during the period 1828-1830. Although (predictably) a staunch Tory (implacably opposed to the reform of the electoral system), he was very far from being a bigoted reactionary; and his ministry is renowned for the Act of Catholic Emancipation (1829), which removed discrimination against Roman Catholics. Wellington's opposition to the Reform Bill of 1832 made him increasingly unpopular, and induced the fall of his government. He was again briefly prime minister in 1834 and served in Peel's ministry of 1841-1846. Although he then retired from public life, he retained his position as commander-in-chief. His burial at St Paul's Cathedral marked the English public's farewell to one of its greatest military commanders; of whom only Marlborough has attained equal status. The epithet of 'the Iron Duke' was symptomatic of his austere nature, but his character also possessed a gentler and more humane aspect. He was a man of complete integrity who, although little loved, commanded total and unequivocal respect.

The Duke of Wellington has an especially close association with the regiment that bears his name. To reiterate, he had entered the 33rd Regiment as a major in 1793, rising to be officer commanding in the same year. Wellington subsequently commanded the regiment for 13 years, until, in 1806, he was elevated to be colonel of the regiment; a role which he fulfilled until 1813. There is a charming anecdote in this connection, which Pattison relates in **Letter V**; when the Duke, reigning in beside the 33rd Regiment, received the message of a veteran who shouted 'Let us have a huzzah for our old Colonel'. The soldiers responded by cheering lustily; in response to which the Duke (characteristically) held up his hand and declaimed 'Hush! Hush!' Indeed, his family continued to exert an impress upon the regiment in the 20th Century. The 6th Duke of Wellington was killed at Salerno in September 1943. He was Lt the Earl of Mornington, eldest son of the 5th Duke and a direct descendant of the 'Iron Duke' (having succeeded as the 6th Duke of Wellington in 1941). *ed.*

(14) *Ney*: Marshal Michael Ney, duc d'Elchingen, Prince de la Moscowa, Marshal of France (1769-1815). He was popularly known as the 'bravest of the brave'. Ney was the most renowned and popular of Napoleon's marshals. The son of a barrel cooper, he was an Alsatian who had enlisted as a trooper in the hussars in 1787. Clearly demonstrating his ability and courage, he was commissioned soon after the

outbreak of the French Revolution of 1789, but his advancement was slow compared to that of his contemporaries (eg Brune and Soult, who were both generals by 1794). He was not promoted to general until the August of 1796, after seeing much service as a cavalry commander on the Sambre, Meuse and Rhine; and in 1799 was still serving as a general of a division. However, his role in the victory at Hohenlinde decisively highlighted him as an officer whose abilities clearly transcended those of the merely competent. Having briefly and provisionally commanded the Army of the Rhine in 1799, in 1802 he was appointed commander of the Army of Switzerland, and in this role negotiated peace between France and Switzerland. In 1804 he was created Marshal. In 1805 he commanded the 6th Corps and blocked the escape of Mack from Ulm to Elchingen (hence his title). In 1807, in the fighting that occurred in the regions of Eylau and Friedland, in each instance his corps contributed greatly to the victory over the Russians.

He was then despatched to Spain. The Peninsular War proved invariably a graveyard for military careers and Ney's experience proved to be a confirmation of this adage. Quarrels with Massena created an irretrievable breach between the two marshals and Ney was recalled to France early in 1811. However, the disastrous Russian campaign of 1812 re-established his reputation. In 1812 he commanded the 3rd Corps in the invasion of Russia and the rearguard in the retreat. In that role he was exposed to numerous attacks by Cossacks and Russian artillery fire. It was his conduct in this operation that won for him Napoleon's sobriquet, 'le brave des braves'. (However, his soldiers described him as 'le rougeaud' ('ginger'); his livid temper conformed to the stereotyped image of the redhead). He was among the very last Frenchmen to leave Russian soil. In 1813 and 1814 he served Napoleon most creditably in the campaigns of Leipzig and France (being wounded for the sixth time at Lutzen). However, he affirmed his loyalty to the Bourbons upon the establishment of Louis XVIII on the French throne.

Sent to recapture Napoleon following the latter's flight from Elba, and promising to return the former emperor in a cage, he found that the population of his military district was intensely anti-Bourbon. Therefore, after receiving messages from Napoleon, he changed his allegiance for the second time and announced his decision to join Napoleon; whereupon he was deliriously cheered by both his soldiers and the populace. He was given command of the left wing in the invasion of Belgium. Ney led this force at Quatre Bras; and at Waterloo he commanded the entire army which, predictably, he led in person (disastrously, as it proved). He had four horses shot from under him and retired from the field only after he had failed in every effort to secure his death. Arrested by the Bourbons for treason, he was tried by a body which included five fellow marshals, and shot in the Luxembourg gardens on 7 December 1815. He himself delivered the orders to the execution squad. Three of his sons became generals in the Second Empire of Napoleon III, and a grandson a general in the service of the Third Republic. Ney was a 'soldier's soldier', totally lacking in political judgement or ambition. He attained his heights in the campaigns for France's natural frontiers at the beginning and end of his career. The dignity of his death rendered him the most heroic figure of his time; a status which clearly emerges in Pattison's memoirs. *ed.*

(15) *troop of British cavalry*: The majority of cavalry regiments were organized on the basis of squadrons and troops; there being two troops to a squadron. Each troop was usually commanded by a captain, and included one or more lieutenants and a cornet (the equivalent of a 2nd lieutenant). A typical establishment of other ranks within a troop, in 1793, was: three sergeants, three corporals, one trumpeter and 47 'private men' (the term 'trooper' not being then in use). The number of troops in a cavalry regiment was subject to great variation, but the majority maintained eight troops within four squadrons. *ed*.

(16) *Dutch-Belgian troops*: For the major part of the Napoleonic Wars the territory which is today defined by Belgium and Holland was under the control of France. The region which constitutes modern Belgium was, prior to the outbreak of the Revolutionary Wars in 1792, known as the Austrian Netherlands. It had been transferred from Spanish to Austrian suzerainity in terms of the Treaty of Utrecht (1713). The territory was overrun by France during the early stages of the Revolutionary Wars and was annexed as an integral part of France in 1797. Holland (then known as the United Provinces) was also conquered by France, but maintained its separate national status as a French satellite state. It was initially styled the Batavian Republic but, from 1806, was designated the kingdom of Holland, ruled by Louis Napoleon, Bonaparte's brother. Louis, however, proved to be an unwilling ally of the French emperor and abdicated in 1810; whereupon Holland (and its army) was integrated into the French Empire. It continued in this state until 1813, when the French collapse in northern Europe precipitated the Dutch rebellion and liberation. William Frederick (Prince of Orange) became 'Sovereign Prince of the Netherlands' (the House of Orange being Holland's hereditary ruling family). (In 1806 he had been deprived of the principality of Nassau when he had refused to join Napoleon's satellite organization, titled the Confederation of the Rhine). In 1814, in terms of the Congress of Vienna, the former Austrian Netherlands (now separated from France) was united with Holland in a new state designated the Kingdom of the Netherlands (William Frederick becoming the state's first king (as William Frederick I).

It was the troops of this newly created political entity which joined the allied troops on the field of Waterloo. There was thus no distinctly Belgian army, as the state of Belgium only emerged as an independent nation in 1830 (following the revolution and rebellion against Dutch rule in that year). One can readily understand the lack of enthusiasm on the part of the Dutch-Belgian force in supporting the allied cause, due to two principal factors. The first related to the frustration of Belgian aspirations to independence at the Congress of Vienna (to which Pattison refers in the penultimate closing paragraph of **Letter I**). The unification of Holland and Belgium had been decreed in the Act of the Congress of Vienna, dated 8 June 1815 (ie only 10 days prior to the battle of Waterloo). Second, one had the long tradition of Dutch service under Napoleon. This is reflected in the army's command structure. The head of the Ministry of War was General Janssens who, having fought against the British at the Cape of Good Hope and Java, could not be expected to be greatly sympathetic with the British command under whom the Dutch troops served. General David Chassé had commenced his military career with the Dutch army but had gained greatest distinction with the French army, serving with them in the Peninsular War until 1813. In 1810 he had been appointed a general and, in the following year, a baron of the empire. Nevertheless, his loyalty to the allied cause, after he had returned to the Dutch service in 1813, was unquestioned. He became a lieutenant general in 1815 and served with distinction at Quatre Bras and Waterloo. Chassé was, arguably, the most competent of the Dutch commanders in 1815. The quartermaster general of the Netherlands army was Constant de Rebecque, who was similarly pro-British.

The nominal head of the army was King William Frederick I. He was the son of the *Stadtholder* (the traditional title of the Dutch ruler). William's father had died in England in 1806, having taken refuge there in 1795. The effective head was William's eldest son, the Prince of Orange (1792-1849). He had known British service, and had served as Wellington's aide during the Peninsular War. In 1813, at the age of only 21, he had been appointed a major general in the British Army. At Waterloo he was overall field commander of the Netherlands army and in nominal command of the allied 1st Corps of Wellington's army. The appointment was of course clearly political in motivation, for the Prince of Orange was obviously totally inexperienced to hold such commands; a factor which led to the incompetent wasteage of a number of units to no purpose. However, Wellington was supreme commander of the Netherlands forces (a concession which had been wrung from the Dutch king on 4 May 1815).

Although there was no separate Belgian army, the Netherlands force was divided between Dutch and Belgian units. These names were not in common use at that time and the national groups were described as 'North Netherlands' and 'South Netherlands'. The Netherlands infantry comprised 36 numbered regiments (in the main single battalions). Of these, the 1st, 2nd, 4th, 7th, 34th and 36th regiments were Belgian; the last named two being jager (ie light infantry) battalions. The remaining infantry battalions (with the exception of the 29th - 33rd and the two Nassau regiments) were Dutch: the 5th, 10th and 11th and 19th - 26th Dutch colonial regiments (the 5th, 10th and 11th being formed in the Dutch East Indies); the 16th - 18th and 27th were Dutch *jagers*; The 29th - 33rd were Swiss mercenary units and the 34th a garrison battalion. The 28th regiment derived from Nassau and in addition there was a 2nd Nassau regiment, not numbered in the line. The militia comprised 45 battalions, a number of which served at Waterloo. The regiments numbered 1 - 20 were Dutch, the remainder Belgian. The eight cavalry regiments were numbered consecutively, despite being of different types. The 1st and 3rd Carabiniers, 4th Light Dragoons and 6th and 7th Hussars were Dutch (the last named deriving from the Dutch East Indies); whilst the 2nd Carabiniers, 5th Light Dragoons and 8th Hussars were Belgian. Seven of these cavalry regiments served at Waterloo (the 7th Hussars then being stationed in the East Indies). The heavy dragoons (carabiniers) were designated cuirassiers (presumably because they wore a breastplate, conforming to the French pattern). There was in addition a small elite unit formed as an escort for the commander-in-chief in February 1815 (the *Guides te Paard*).

Memories of the Waterloo campaign

The Netherlands infantry were uniformed in blue tunics cut in the British style; all units having white facings (save for the militia, who wore orange facings). The *jager* regiments wore similar uniforms, but coloured green with yellow facings. The uniforms of the Dutch and Belgian units were distinguished by their shakos; the former having bell-topped caps with front and rear peaks, whilst the Belgian shakos conformed exactly to the British 1812 pattern, save for the 'W' cypher on the plate.

The Netherlands troops engaged in the 1815 campaign numbered some 22 440, with 48 guns; of whom approximately 466 were killed, 2 054 wounded and 1 627 'missing (a number that included many deserters). Pattison's extremely poor opinion of the Netherlands army was shared by virtually all his comrades, and the Dutch were generally considered to be the most inferior components of the allied forces. To correct the balance, however, one should add that some units behaved with great credit. The defence of Prince Bernhard of Sax-Weimar, commanding a force of outnumbered Netherlanders during the early stages of Quatre Bras probably saved the allies from defeat. *ed*.

(17) Much has been said, and I believe truly said, about the disaffection and infidelity of the Belgian troops both at Quatre Bras and Waterloo. Captain Siborne (a) calculated that no less than 7 500 of them deserted their standard during the former engagement; and I myself can bear witness to the shameful misconduct of a regiment of their light cavalry at Waterloo. It might be between the hours of six and seven o' clock - for in fight 'we take no note of time' - when the battle was raging with terrible fury, that a regiment of their light cavalry traversed our position. Even at this distance of time I can still picture them as they passed close to our Brigade, clothed in French-gray uniform (b) with silver facings, and wearing the 'sabre tache' (c), admirably mounted on strong horses with switch tails (the cruel custom of docking being at this period unknown on the Continent). As they passed near the 73rd Regiment, then in square, Sir Colin Halket [*sic*] (who spoke and understood German perfectly (d) commanded them to halt. Then he earnestly addressed them, and proposed they should charge a menacing body of French cavalry to his right. He drew his sword to lead the charge, but they hesitated, and in spite of his noble example and earnest exhortations, nothing could induce them to follow him. Soon after this leading troop went threes about, and, followed by the whole regiment, galloped off the field, pursued by the indignant execrations, hissings, and hootings of our Brigade. It is said so great was their panic, they did not halt until they reached Brussels, spreading a report all along the road that Wellington was defeated, and that Napoleon would be in the city that night (e) *auth*.

Editorial observations on above footnote

(a) *Siborne or Siborn, William (1797 - 1849)*: Historian of the Waterloo campaign. He was the son of Capt Benjamin Siborn of the 9th (Norfolk) Regiment of Foot, who was wounded at the battle of Nivelle in the Peninsular War and died whilst serving with his regiment at St Vincent (in the West Indies) on 14 July 1819. William Siborne was born on 15 October 1797 and was partly educated at the Royal Military College, Sandhurst. In March 1826 Siborne was appointed assistant military secretary to Lt Gen Sir George Murray (1772-1846), commanding British forces in Ireland; and held the same appointment with Murray's successors - Sir John Byng, Sir R Hussey and Sir Edward Blakeney - until 1843, He was promoted to captain (unattached) on 31 January 1840 and on the same date was placed on half-pay; although he continued to hold the staff appointment of military secretary in Ireland. In 1822 he published *Instructions for civil and military surveyors in topographical plan-drawing, founded upon the system of John George Lehman*; and in 1827 *A practical treatise on topographical surveying and drawing, containing a simple and easy mode of surveying the detail of any portion of the country, to which are added instructions in topographical modelling*. The book was dedicated to his chief, Sir George Murray.

In 1830 Siborne was commissioned by the commander-in-chief to undertake the construction of a model of the field of Waterloo. He accordingly lived for eight months at the farm at La Haye Sainte, on the former field of battle, and made an accurate survey of the entire ground; upon which he based the construction of his model. The execution of the task occupied some years, as Siborne could only devote his leisure time to the project. Siborne consulted surviving officers who had taken part in the campaign. The progress of the work was interrupted in 1833 when the new government refused to allocate any further funds to the project. The work thus had to be financed after 1833 by Siborne's own private resources. He completed the work in 1838, at which point the cost to him had reached £3 000. The model was exhibited in London and other cities; but the receipts barely covered the cost of exhibition and Siborne never recuperated his outlay. He also constructed a similar model, on a larger scale, of a portion of the field of battle. *A guide to Captain Siborne's new Waterloo model* was published (nd). The huge amount of information that Siborne had amassed in the course of the model's construction furnished the source of his publication, *History of the war in France and Belgium, containing minute details of the battles of Quatre Bras, Ligny, Wavre and Waterloo* (published in 1844). It appeared in two octavo volumes, together with a folio atlas. The work reached a fourth edition in 1894, and remains a standard textbook on the subject. To judge by its frequent appearances in Pattison's work, it served as the author's principal source of printed reference.

On 6 November 1844 Siborne was appointed secretary and adjutant of the Royal Military Asylum in Chelsea; and died there whilst holding the appointment on 9 January 1849. Siborne had two sons and two daughters. The second son, Maj Gen Herbert Taylor Siborne (born 18 October 1826), edited, in 1891, with explanatory notes *Waterloo letters: a selection from original and hitherto unpublished letters bearing on the operations of the 16th, 17th and 18th June 1815, by officers who served in the campaign*. It is a selection of the letters his father received concerning the Waterloo campaign.

(b) *French-gray uniform*: The reference is somewhat misleading, for the colour grey denoted, not the uniforms, but the overalls in which all Dutch cavalry units were clothed. The uniforms of the individual cavalry regiments were as follows:

1st Carabiniers: blue coat; red cuffs; blue collar; white trousers.
2nd Carabiniers: blue coat; red cuffs; blue collar; white trousers.
3rd Carabiniers: blue coat; yellow cuffs and collar; white trousers.

4th Light Dragoons: blue coat, yellow cuffs and collar; white trousers.
5th Light Dragoons: green coat; yellow cuffs and collar; grey trousers.
6th Hussars: light blue coat; red cuffs and collar; light blue trousers.
8th Hussars: light blue coat; light blue collar and cuffs; light blue trousers.

(c) *Sabre tache*: The term is derived from the German; a pocket or pouch (*tasche*) attached to a sabre. The early Hungarian hussars wore tight breeches which did not permit pockets, and so their purse or pouch was worn on a waist belt. Although worn extensively on the continent, sabretaches were not introduced into the British cavalry until the end of the 18th Century. Light dragoons and hussars adopted them, and so also heavy cavalry by 1812. Troopers of the heavy cavalry discontinued the wearing of sabretaches in 1831, but they were not completely abolished until 1902.

(d) *spoke German fluently*: It will be recalled that Sir Colin Halkett's early military career had been performed in the Dutch service; whilst, prior to Waterloo, his service under the British had been undertaken as a senior officer in the King's German Legion. (cf Note (3) above).

(e) *As they passed … Napoleon would be in the city that night*: Pattison is confused in this footnote. The unit involved was not Dutch but German; specifically, the Duke of Cumberland's Hussars, one of the three hussar regiments continued within the Hanoverian army that had been reformed after 1813 (and which should be clearly distinguished from the King's German Legion). The regiment was contained within the 1st Hanoverian Brigade. It quit the field during the battle, conveying tales of Wellington's defeat. As a punishment the unit was disbanded and attached to various corps as escorts for the commissaries.

(18) *Brunswick friends*: Pattison is here referring to the reformed Brunswick army. The origins ot this army lay in the Brunswick Oels Corps. The unit was formed in 1809 by the Duke of Brunswick-Oels (whose father had been killed in 1806 and who was himself killed at Quatre Bras). The unit had originally fought in the Austrian service, but, following the Habsburg defeat at Wagram (1809) the force boldly retreated through Westphalia and was evacuated by the Royal Navy (an audacious, gallant and resourceful exploit). The force then enlisted in the British service. The Legion then separated into the Brunswick Hussars (serving in eastern Spain) and the Brunswick Oels Jagers (serving in the Peninsula from 1810 onwards). Their record was very far from being unblemished; due largely to the dilution of their original ethnic component through the influx of former prisoners-of-war (including Dutch, Italians, Danish, Croats and Poles), which created terrible problems of desertion. One commentator (Leach of the 95th Rifles) remarked that the British only 'leased' the unit (implying their implicit disloyalty). Brig Gen Robert Craufurd, commanding the Light Division, caustically stated that any member of the Brunswick Oels who wished to desert would be granted an official pass 'for we are better without such'. The Brunswick army was reconstituted in 1813, following the expulsion of the French from Germany in the War of Liberation, and served at Quatre Bras and Waterloo with credit. In that campaign the Brunswick troops constituted in effect the army of Brunswick; including

cavalry, infantry, light infantry and artillery. A nucleus of Peninsular veterans was represented, but in the main the force consisted of newly recruited young soldiers inexperienced in combat who, under such circumstances, performed creditably.

The Brunswick Oels and the reformed Brunswick army chose black uniforms and the death's head badge on their shakos, symbolizing their mission of revenge against the 'rape' of their country by French troops. Their uniform earned for the corps the sobriquet of the 'Black Legion'; whilst the death's head device on the shako bestowed upon them the nickname of the 'Death or Glory men' by the British. Lady De Lancey described the unit as resembling 'an immense moving hearse.' ed.

(19) *Ney's light troops*: ie the skirmishers who harrassed the British line preparatory to the columnar attack. These troops were termed *voltigeurs* (literally 'leapers') and *tirailleurs* (ie members of light infantry regiments). The *voltigeurs* were highly mobile skirmishers who formed a company within each *tirailleur* and line formation. They were supposedly capable of keeping pace with trotting cavalry. With regard to the *tirailleurs*, these were distinguished by tall plumes on their shakos which were detachable. Both *voltigeurs* and *tirailleurs* were armed with smoothbore muskets. ed.

(20) *Cuirassiers*: Members of the French heavy cavalry regiments. The term 'cuirassier' derives from the word 'cuirass'. The cuirass was originally a jerkin or leather garment worn by soldiers. In the Middle Ages the name was applied to metal plate armour protecting the body, front and back, from the neck to the waist. The name 'cuirassiers' was applied to heavily armed cavalry of the first half of the 17th Century, whose armour extended from the head to the knee; and, later, to mounted troops wearing a helmet and breast and back-plate only (the French *casque*). The cuirassier was thus a survivor of the men-at-arms and mailed knights of the feudal armies, and of the troopers of the 16th and 17th Centuries. The first Austrian corps (*kryissers*) was formed in 1484 by the Emperor Maximilian and by 1705 there were 20 such regiments in the army of the Habsburgs. The cuirassiers played a major role in the Prussian army of Frederick William I and in the wars of Frederick the Great (1740 - 1786); the latter formed 14 regiments of cuirassiers. In France the first cuirassier regiment was formed in 1666. Napoleon's cavalry contained 14 regiments of cuirassiers, the first of which was created in 1803. In Britain the heavy cavalry abandoned the cuirass at the beginning of the 18th Century. The British equivalents of the cuirassiers were the regiments of Household Cavalry, Dragoon Guards and Dragoons. However, the cuirass was re-introduced into the Household Cavalry (the two regiments of Life Guards and Royal Horse Guards), who were issued with the steel cuirass in 1821 (largely due to the promptings of George IV, at whose coronation, in that year, it was first worn). The cuirass, however, was only worn for ceremonial and guard duties and never in a practical battlefield scenario. The Prussians retained their breastplates until after the close of the Seven Years War (1757-1763). The principal motive in discarding the breastplate was to reduce the weight the horse had to bear (combined with the total vulnerability to musket balls). France alone retained the cuirass on

active service; and, indeed, regiments of cuirassiers were serving in their traditional dress at the outbreak of World War I.

As heavy cavalry, the cuirassiers' principal role was to defeat and drive the enemy's horsemen from the battlefield and to hammer their way through any weakness in the opposing enemy line; a role clearly exemplified by the massive strokes delivered by the French cuirassiers at Eylau (1807), Borodino (1812) and, of course, Waterloo. The cuirassier regiments formed the core of Napoleon's heavy cavalry and were the direct descendants of Cromwell's 'Ironsides'. Armed with a heavy sword and two pistols the French cuirassiers charged in dense column, and their pace rarely proceeded beyond a trot. An eye-witness (Count von Bismarck) wrote: 'The cuirassiers laid special stress upon riding boot to boot'. One should bear in mind that the original strength of the cuirassier force had been gravely and irreparably attenuated by the Russian campaign initiated in 1812, in which all the regiments perished in the snows of Russia. Virtually all the horses died and towards the close of the catastrophic campaign Napoleon was obliged to unite the 500 remaining horsemen into the 'Sacred Squadron', in which full generals were to be found serving as troop commanders. It was never possible to surmount the dearth of mounts and trained men thereafter. *ed.*

(21) *Volunteer Clarke*: *Volunteer* - A volunteer was a member of the regiment who occupied a socially ambivalent role in so far as, whilst serving in the ranks, he had access to the officer's mess; cf **Introduction - Military/Historical Context**). Upon the death of an ensign he would be appointed to the vacancy. Pattison is, strictly speaking, inaccurate in referring to Clarke as an 'officer'.

Clarke: Christopher Clarke was aged only 16, having volunteered for the campaign as a Sandhurst cadet. Isolated, when the regiment was caught whilst its square was still only half-formed, he clung to the Colour despite having received 22 sabre wounds and killed the French cavalryman with his own sword. The second Colour lost, as recorded by Pattison, was the King's Colour. Had it not been for Clarke's incredibly tenacious courage, therefore, the regiment would have been deprived of both Colours (a profound source of shame to the regiment); the humiliation resulting thereby would have been compounded by the fact that the 69th had lost its previous Regimental Colour at Bergen-op-Zoom the year previously. Clarke was awarded an ensigncy in the 42nd Highlanders, and died whilst serving as a subaltern in the 33rd Foot in 1831.

(22) *Regimental Colours*: The Colours were the focal point of the battalion and the rallying-point in battle. Each battalion possessed two Colours: the King's Colour (basically a Union flag with battalion identification); and a Regimental Colour (normally of the regimental facing colour - blue, yellow, green, white as the case might be - with a Union in the upper canton nearest the staff. The Colours symbolized the battalion's honour and devotion to its Sovereign and, as intimated in the introduction, evoked a deeply ritualistic significance, with religious overtones embodied in the consecration of each new pair.

The role of the Colours at Waterloo, as a rallying point and source of inspiration, are frequently mentioned in accounts of the battle; and their contribution to the stability of the square explicitly emphasized. It has become fashionable to attenuate this significance; a process illustrated by a contributor to the *New Statesman* who, writing in October 1973, stated that 'all the stories of deeds of heroism in defence of military colours can only have been so much myth-making'. Such an argument is not borne out by the memoirs of Waterloo, which cite numerous acts of incredible heroism either in their defence, in or in the endeavour to capture them. The steadfastness of the square may, in some instances, have depended upon certain geographical features such as its alignment with some territorial landmark or boundary. Whilst such factors were certainly present (especially in the centre of the battlefield, where the position was traversed by hedgerows and embanked roadways), little significance is attached to such topographical features in the records of Waterloo.

The loss of a Colour was deemed the greatest disgrace that could befall a battalion and as a result the Colours were the focus of the most desperate struggles, generating deeds of heroism unequalled in the military history of any nation. Of the innumerable examples, one may cite the defence of the Colours of the 3rd Regiment (The Buffs) at Albuera (1811); in which Lt Matthew Latham suffered appalling disfiguring wounds and had his arm severed rather than relinquish his grip upon the Colour. He finally fell dead beneath the hooves of the French cavalry rather than allow the precious standard to be captured by the French. Volunteer Clarke's incredible heroism (cf note (21) above) was certainly not an exceptional case in the Waterloo campaign. Ensign Christie of the 44th was charged by a Frenchman whose lance 'entering the left eye, penetrated to the lower jaw. Christie, notwithstanding the agony of his wound, flung himself [upon the Colour], wrested it from the Frenchman, and fell to the ground on top of it.' (He survived this terrible wound, to die of fever in Jamaica in 1833). Equally incredible acts of valour and self-sacrifice were displayed in the attempt to capture the Colours. Several Frenchmen virtually committed suicide in hopeless (and quite unnecessary) efforts to carry British infantry Colours back to their lines. Thus, Belcher, conveying the Regimental Colour of the 32nd Regiment, found himself close to a French officer who had become dismounted during D'Erlon's attack. He did not accompany his men, who were retreating but, as Belcher records,

> 'suddenly fronted me and seized the staff, I still retaining a grasp of the silk. At the same moment he attempted to draw his sabre, but had not accomplished it when the covering Colour-Sergeant, named Switzer, thrust his pike into his breast, and the right rank and file of the division, named Lacy, fired into him. He fell dead at my feet.'

The modern Colours have been diminished to modest proportions. Those borne at Waterloo were of gargantuan dimensions; 6 feet square, obviously demanding great strength to be carried in a wind. They were borne by two of the most junior subalterns, each escorted by two senior sergeants. (The rank of colour sergeant, introduced in 1813 to recognize the most meritorious sergeants, does not indicate a member of the Colour escort, but was equivalent to the modern company sergeant major). The Colour escort party represented the most dangerous post that could be held in action. Sgt Laurence, of the 40th Regiment, when ordered to the Colours at 16h00 on the day of Waterloo, recalled his reluctance:

'This ... was a job I did not at all like; but still I went as boldly to work as I could. There had been before me that day fourteen sergeants already killed and wounded while in charge of these Colours, with officers in proportion, and the staff and Colours were almost cut to pieces.'

Colours were last carried into battle in the course of the First South African War of Independence of 1880-1881; specifically, at the battle of Laing's Nek in 1881. *ed.*

(23) Lieutenant Arthur Gore was brother of Captain [Ralph] Gore of the 33rd, who was also in action at Quatre Bras. They were sons of Admiral Sir John Gore (a) of the Royal Navy, a distinguished officer in that service. Sir John's brother, Colonel Gore (b), commanded the regiment for many years in India, and came home with his regiment in 1812. He was killed as a volunteer in the storming of Bergen-op-Zoom, on the 8th of March, 1814. A monument bearing the following inscription:

'ERECTED AT THE PUBLIC EXPENSE TO THE MEMORY OF MAJOR-GENERAL'S ARTHUR GORE AND JOHN BYNE SKERRET, WHO FELL GLORIOUSLY WHILE LEADING THE TROOPS TO THE ASSAULT OF THE FORTRESS OF BERGEN-OP-ZOOM ON THE NIGHTS OF THE 8TH AND 9TH MARCH, 1814.'

is erected in St. Paul's, in commemoration of his gallant services. *auth.*

Editorial observations on above footnote

(a) *sons of Admiral Sir John Gore*: There appears to be some confusion at this point. *The Dictionary of National Biography* (DNB) states that Admiral Sir John Gore had only one son, who drowned while serving as his flag lieutenant, in the attempt to save a seaman who had fallen overboard. *The Waterloo Roll Call* states that the Gore brothers who served at Waterloo were in fact the sons of Lt Col Ralph Gore, of the 33rd Regiment.

Admiral Sir John Gore: Vice Admiral Sir John Gore (1772-1836) was the second son of Col John Gore of the 33rd Regiment, subsequently lieutenant of the Tower of London, and was born at Kilkenny on 9 February 1772. He joined the *Canada*, under the command of the Hon William Cornwallis, in 1781, and served in her during the eventful West Indian campaign of 1782. In 1789 he was promoted to lieutenant and served with distinction in the operations in Toulon and Corsica, and in those leading to the surrender of Bastia on 22 May 1794. In November of that year he was appointed to the command of the *Windsor Castle*, of 98 guns, being the flagship of Rear Admiral Linzee; serving in the actions off Toulon in March and July 1795. He was then appointed to the command of the *Censeur*, in which ship he was captured by the French in the action off Cape St Vincent on 7 October 1795. Whilst commanding the *Triton*, a 25-ton frigate in which he served in the Channel for five years (and to which he was appointed in 1796) he captured a considerable number of small cruisers and privateers. On 18 October 1799 he assisted in the capture of *Santa Brigida* and *Thetis*, two Spanish frigates, each of 36 guns, homeward bound with treasure from Vera Cruz, and of enormous value. Gore's share alone, as a captain, amounted to upwards of £40 000. As the result of an injury he received from a bursting gun, he was compelled to leave the *Triton* in the spring of 1801.

In July 1803 Gore was sent to Gibraltar as senior officer in command of a small squadron to cruise in the Straits, with special orders to search and intercept French ships of war sent to strengthen the Toulon fleet. In this service he continued for upwards of a year; and on 5 October 1804 his squadron captured the Spanish frigates, carrying cargoes to a value of considerably more than £1 million. Gore's share of the prize money must have amounted to at least a further £40 000. On 21 February 1806 he was knighted and sailed for Calcutta on 15 April. He returned to England in the following year and was shortly afterwards appointed to the *Revenge* of 74 guns; in which he was actively employed in the Bay of Biscay. On 4 December 1813 he was promoted to the rank of Rear Admiral, his flagship being the *Revenge*, and commanded the detached squadron in the Adriatic until the close of the Napoleonic Wars. In January 1818 Gore was appointed a Knight Commander of the Bath (KCB) and on 27 May 1825 was advanced to the rank of Vice Admiral. Between December 1831 and 1835 he served as commander-in-chief of the East Indies station. He died on 21 August 1836.

(c) *Sir John's brother, Colonel Gore*: Pattison is referring to Arthur Gore, who commanded the 33rd regiment during the period 1802-1813.

(24) *Saul*: Saul, King of Israel. Saul, Son of Kish from the tribe of Benjamin, was the first king of Israel. He probably reigned circa 1020 - 1000 BC, although the precise dates and exact duration of his reign are disputed. The Old Testament *Book of Samuel* (I, versus 9 - 12) contains several independent and conflicting accounts of Saul's elevation to the kingship, but three points appear consistent. First, the desire for a king arose because the poorly organized tribal confederation of the Israelites could not meet the military threat posed by the Philistines. Second, Saul's military prowess and personal bravery rendered him a prime candidate for the kingship. The remainder of *Samuel I* records Saul's reign, but with a pro-Davidic bias. Saul enjoyed a considerable degree of initial success and greatly enhanced the cohesion and strength of the Hebrew nation. He extirpated the Philistines from the central hill country and extended his authority into Judah and southern Jordan. Samuel soon broke off relations with him, however, and the subsequent lack of religious support, combined with Saul's escalating envy and suspicion of David, his brilliant young commander - which assumed paranoiac proportions - began to destroy Saul's judgement. He reacted tardily to the Philistine threat, resulting in his eventual defeat at Mount Gilboa, where he committed suicide rather than be captured. *ed*.

(25) *shakos*: The shako was a peaked cap. The word derives from *czak* (Magyar for 'peak'). This headdress was issued under *General Order* of 23 February 1800, and issued to the British infantry; this pattern being commonly referred to as the 'stovepipe'. A high, flat topped cap had been worn by the Austrian infantry in the 18th Century; in the course of which there was a marked tendency for the crown

to be decreased in height. The stovepipe shako was superseded in 1812 by a new pattern, eventually styled the 'Waterloo shako.' It was a black felt cap with a black leather peak; and was distinguished by the raised front, which extended above the top of the body. The front plate is a cartouche with a raised edge and crown in the centre (gilt for officers and brass for other ranks). In the centre of the plate are the letters GR ('Georgius Rex'). Decorative cord is draped across the front in the form of a V shape. This cord is of gold and crimson for infantry officers, white for other ranks and green for light infantry units. (The light infantry does not appear, however, to have adopted the 1812 pattern on a very large scale, preferring to retain the former pattern). At the top left side was positioned the red and white plume. *ed.*

(26) *Captain Haigh: The Waterloo Roll Call* records the Haigh brothers serving in the 33rd Regiment as being named Lt Thomas D Haigh and Capt John Haigh. Both are cited as being killed at Waterloo and it is therefore impossible to ascertain as to which brother was killed at Quatre Bras and which at Waterloo two days later; especially as Pattison does not distinguish between lieutenants and captains in his appendices. *ed.*

There is something interesting and politically instructive in the rise of Captain Haigh's family. His father, who was either a private or non-commissioned officer, went to India with the 33rd, under the command of the Duke of Wellington, then Sir Arthur Wellesley. He was present at the storming of Seringapatam (a) in 1799, where his regiment greatly distinguished itself. Haigh became a great favourite of 'The Duke's', who made him quarter-master (b) of the regiment. It was in the balmy days of Toryism, when a man was hanged in Glasgow for stealing half-a-crown, and your great-grandfather was exhibited in effigy on the lamp-posts in the Trongate (c) of Glasgow during the day, and burned in the evening as a democrat; when the noble patriot Muir (d) was expatriated for entertaining and promulgating those rational and Christian principles which are now universally held by all parties, even by the most rabid Tories - the old Quartermaster Haigh applied to 'The Duke' and obtained a commission for his son, Captain Haigh, who fell at Quatre Bras, the emoluments accruing there from being more than sufficient to defray his education in England; (e) so that when he joined his regiment at Seringapatam in 1810, he stood at the head of the lieutenants, thus allowing a beardless stripling to take precedence of those veterans who had been doing their duty under a vertical sun for many years.

The late Mr. Houldsworth, of Coltness, grandfather of the present proprietor, has often told me, that on one occasion, while conversing with my father on the Anderston Walk, he observed a stranger on the opposite side looking earnestly at them. On Mr Houldsworth leaving my father, the stranger accosted him, saying, 'Is not that Mr. Pattison of Kelvingrove?' On Mr. Houldsworth replying in the affirmative, and inquiring how he came to know him, he drew from his waistcoat pocket a miniature likeness, saying, 'I have been sent by the government to watch the gentleman'. *auth.*

Editorial observations on above footnote

(a) *Seringapatam*: Seringapatam was the capital of Mysore, a state in India. Its ruler, Haidar Ali, had attacked the British on the Carnatic, with French aid, but was defeated at Porto Novo in 1781, and died the following year. His son, Tipu Sultan, continued the war against the British in the Second Anglo-Mysore War, which was terminated when French aid was withdrawn. In 1790 Tipu attacked Travancore, initiating the Third Anglo-Mysore War. Lord Cornwallis (governor general during the period 1786-1793) allied himself with other Indian princes, and Tipu was defeated in 1792; paying a huge indemnity and ceding half his territory. Tipu continued to solicit French aid and in 1799, having proved successful in these approaches, initiated a further war against the British. The new governor general of Mysore, Richard Wellesley (the brother of Arthur Wellesley, the future Duke of Wellington) despatched two armies into Mysore to crush Tipu. The forces included the armies of the Bombay and Madras Presidencies, the army of the Nizam of Hyderabad (commanded by Col Arthur Wellesley) and various British regiments. [A Presidency was a division of the East India Company's territory]. These latter included the 33rd Regiment of Foot (of which Arthur Wellesley was then the Officer Commanding, having been appointed in 1793, although on this occasion command was vested in a Maj Shee). Command of the expeditionary force was vested in Gen George Harris. The force arrived before Seringapatam on 5 April 1799 and an attack was made on the enemy's outposts that night; of which one, under Wellesley, was repulsed. Wellesley determined 'never to suffer an attack to be made at night upon an enemy who is prepared and strongly posted, and whose posts have not been reconnoitred by daylight'. On 4 May 1799 Seringapatam was stormed and Tipu slain. The 33rd Regiment stormed through the breaches of one of the strongest fortresses in India, and hunted the defenders through a labyrinth of buildings, pleasure gardens and bazaars.

(b) *quarter-master of the regiment*: The quartermaster was the officer responsible for the supply of essential materials (eg uniforms, accoutrements, weapons and ammunition) for the regiment. It was a distinct post. The quartermaster's commission reflected a peculiar social characteristic of British regiments, whereby an officer could be in the regiment, but not of it, so to speak; ie was a member officially but was not fully integrated into the social fabric of the mess. Popular social prejudices of the period categorized the quartermaster as a 'tradesman', as opposed to a 'gentleman'. The quartermaster's commission was thus a popular method of rewarding meritorious service in the ranks. (An equivalent social complexion was attached to the riding master in cavalry regiments).

(c) *Trongate*: A famous thoroughfare in Glasgow. It formed one of the four original main medieval streets. It was originally named St Thenew's Gate (later corrupted into St Enoch's Gate, from a chapel at its western end. The term 'tron' means 'wayby'. The first reference to the Trongate occurs in the middle of the 16th Century, 60 years after the the city obtained the right to a free tron. It eventually ceded its earlier importance to Ducanon Street and Sauchiehall Street, with the relocation of the city centre. [The editor is indebted to Glasgow Central Library for this information].

(d) *Muir*: Pattison is referring to Thomas Muir (1765-1798), a Parliamentary reformer. He was born in Glasgow on 24 August 1765, being the only son of James

Muir, a prosperous tradesman. He was educated at Glasgow Grammar School and at the University of Glasgow, whence he graduated with an MA degree in 1782. He intended to enter the Church, but ultimately read for the Bar, and was admitted to the Faculty of Advocates in 1784. He was of a radical political persuasion and an enthusiastic advocate of Parliamentary reform. Muir became a member of the Scottish branch of the Society of the Friends of the People; created in Glasgow in 1792 on the model of the London Society, and dedicated to Parliamentary reform. At one of the meetings held in Edinburgh he read an address from the United Irishmen (the rebel movement that had spearheaded the Irish insurrection of 1797-1798), intimating the hope that Scotland would adopt the same attitude towards the English government as had the rebellious Irish. On 2 January 1793 Muir was arrested on a charge of high treason, but was freed on bail. Shunned or insulted by fellow advocates, he immediately started for France and was entertained *en route* by the London Society, who commissioned him to intervene on behalf on Louis XVI; but Muir did not reach Paris until the day following the execution of the French king. Whilst enjoying the hospitality of the French revolutionary regime he was outlawed by the Edinburgh Society and struck off the Roll of Advocates of Scotland.

After several months absence he returned to Scotland, was arrested and on 30 August and tried for treason in Edinburgh. He was accused of exciting a spirit of disloyalty and disaffection, of endorsing Paine's *Rights of Man*, of distributing seditious publications and reading aloud from one of these. Muir was convicted and sentenced to 14 years exile in Australia. In 1794 he was despatched to Botany Bay. Muir purchased a small farm (which he called Hunter's Hill). His situation attracted much sympathetic attention in the United States; to the extent that a ship, commanded by a Captain Dawes, was despatched from New York to rescue him. The rescue was effected on 11 February 1796. A variety of adventures followed, including: shipwreck on the Nootka Sound; captivity by American Indians; hospitable treatment in Mexico; and imprisonment in Havana, Cuba. Muir was sent in a Spanish frigate to Cadiz, but the vessel was attacked by English ships. Muir had one eye and part of his cheek shot off. He was numbered among the dead but an old school friend is said to have recognized him by the inscription written in the Bible clasped in his hand. Muir was sent ashore with the remainder of the wounded; to be detained in Cadiz as a British subject and prisoner-of-war. The French Directory (the revolutionary government) procured his release and offered him both citizenship and hospitality. After a public reception at Bordeaux, Muir reached Paris on 4 February 1798. However, his wound proved fatal and he died in Paris on 27 September 1798.

(e) *emoluments accruing there from education in England*: The sense of this appears to be that Haigh procured the Duke of Wellington's patronage for his son, and that his patronage included sufficient financial provision for the youth's education in England.

(27) Arthur Gore's brother was Capt Ralph Gore, who also served at Waterloo. The *Waterloo Roll Call* faintly implies a blemish on Capt Ralph Gore's career, as it

curtly states in a note that he 'quitted the regiment as a captain'. *ed.*

(28) Lieutenant James Furlong was a Glasgow man; and son of William Furlong, Esq., of Welshot. He was a capital officer and a great enthusiast in his profession. He afterwards attained the rank of Lieutenant colonel, and went out in command of the 43rd Light Infantry - a crack regiment - to Canada, where he married, and died, carrying with him to his grave the French lead which had wounded him at Quatre Bras. *auth.*

(29) *division of the Guards*: Pattison is referring to the 1st Division, which comprised two Guards brigades. The 1st Brigade was formed from the 2nd and 3rd Battalions of the 1st Regiment of Foot Guards); the brigade commander being Gen Sir Peregrine Maitland; cf **Letter III**/note (13). The 2nd Brigade consisted of the 2nd Battalion of the 2nd Regiment of Foot Guards (Coldstream Guards) and the 2nd Battalion of the 3rd Regiment (Foot Guards); the Brigade being commanded by Sir John Byng; cf **Letter V**/note (9). As stated above (cf **Introduction - Military/Historical Context**: *Organization of the British Army*) a Guards battalion was normally considerably greater in strength than its line infantry counterpart. (The two battalions of the 1st Guards Brigade comprised some 1 000 men each) and accordingly the Guards Brigade encompassed two (as opposed to the normal three) battalions. *ed.*

(30) The first time I had the honour of meeting General Cook (a) was at Bergen-op-Zoom (b) on the morning of 9th of March, 1814, when Sir Thomas Graham (c) attempted to take that celebrated fortress by a *coup-de-main* - General Cook as a volunteer had accompanied Lord Proby (d) and his Guards (e). The attempt virtually succeeded, putting us in possession of the ramparts for more than seven hours; and it would be impossible to express our chagrin and disappointment when, owing to the shameful mismanagement of those in command, we were forced to relinquish this noble prize. The troops, instead of being concentrated and claiming the fortress as conquerors, had been dispersed, and were caught as birds in a trap; being isolated and without a leader, they became a helpless prey to our adversaries. So confident had I been of success, I well recollect saying to my friend Lieutenant Hart (who afterwards fell at Waterloo), 'Well, Jamie, this is a glorious achievement, we shall all have medals; and after we have had a sleep in our billets, I will go and search for my scabbard'; which had been wrenched from my side by a discharge of grape-shot (f). *auth.*

Editorial observations on above footnote
(a) *General Cook*: This name has been misspelt. Pattison is referring to Maj Gen George Cooke, who commanded the 1st (Guards) Division at Waterloo. He was commissioned as an ensign into the 1st Regiment of Foot Guards in 1794, and subsequently served in Flanders. As a lieutenant colonel in the Guards he was severely wounded whilst serving in Holland in 1799. During the Peninsular War he held a command under Sir Thomas Graham. He was appointed brevet major

general on 4 June 1811. He lost his arm at Waterloo, and was made a Knight Commander of the Bath (KCB) on 22 June 1815. His other honours included Knight of St George of Russia. He died on 3 February 1837.

(b) *Bergen-op-Zoom*: cf **Introduction**; note (c) below. Although this reference has been elucidated at the two points noted above, it is recapitulated at this point in order to facilitate ease of reference.

Bergen-op-Zoom was a French fortress situated in Holland. On the night of 8-9 March 1814 it was assaulted by a British force, as part of the offensive against Antwerp, undertaken in conjunction with Bulow's Prussian army. All four of the assaulting columns stormed the outer walls; only to be repulsed by the superior numbers of veteran French troops manning the inner defences.

(c) *Sir Thomas Graham*: Thomas Graham, Baron Lynedoch (1748-1843), of Balgowan, Perthshire, general. He was the third and only surviving child of Thomas Graeme, laird of Balgowan, who died in 1766. He was educated privately and at Christ Church College, Oxford (which he left without taking a degree). In 1774 he married Catherine, second daughter of the 9th Earl of Cathcart. Lady Graham's consistent ill-health necessitated the couple's migration to a warmer climate but after a lingering illness she died on board ship at Hyeres, on 26 July 1791. En route through France, whilst the French Revolution was raging, his wife's coffin was desecrated. The act exercised a significant influence upon British military history; for it induced a profound francophobia on Graham's part, which motivated his pursuit of a military career and, specifically, the creation of the British Army's first light infantry regiment.

He raised a battalion titled the 'Perthshire Volunteers', which was officially established as the 90th Regiment of Foot. Through the good offices of Lord Moira, the new battalion was drilled and equipped as light infantry; being in fact the senior light infantry corps of the British Army (although it did not receive the designation 'light infantry' until 1815). Graham's (temporary) commission as lieutenant-commandant was dated 10 February 1774; Rowland Hill (afterwards Lord Hill) was the regiment's lieutenant colonel. Graham served with his regiment in various camps in the south of England, in the operations at Quiberon and Isle Dieu, and afterwards accompanied it to Gibraltar. On 22 July 1795 he became lieutenant colonel. In 1796 he was appointed British military commissioner with the Austrian army in Italy and confined in Mantua with General Wurmser's force during the investment of that city by the French. As the siege continued the garrison's provisions became seriously depleted; and it was resolved at a council of war to acquaint the imperial forces' commander-in-chief, Alvinza, with their dire straits. Graham offered himself as a volunteer for this purpose, left the fortress (disguised as a peasant) on the night on 29 December 1796 in the midst of a heavy snowstorm. Concealed during the day, and travelling through swamps and marshes by night, he succeeded in eluding the French patrols and reached the Austrian headquarters on 4 January 1797.

He subsequently distinguished himself, whilst serving with the 90th Regiment, in the siege of Minorca, in 1798; and in May 1799 was despatched with two British regiments to organize the defences of Messina. The strategic importance of this place had been strongly emphasized by Lord Nelson, then in the bay of Naples. Graham remained in command of a mixed force of British and Neopolitan troops until November 1799, when he was sent as brigadier general in command of the troops despatched to Malta; then in enemy hands and blockaded by sea by Captain Alexander Ball of the Royal Navy. Graham resolved upon a siege, in order to starve the defenders into surrender. With the regiments that had accompanied him, together with some corps organized on the island, Graham established a close land blockade of the French garrison at Valetta. This was maintained for two years, until September 1800, when the French capitulated. Immediately prior to their surrender, Graham had been superseded in the command of the British forces by Maj Gen Pigot.

Lt Gen Sir John Moore was instrumental in securing for Graham a permanent commission. Graham accompanied him to Sweden in 1808, and afterwards to Spain. He took part in the Corunna retreat and was one of the few personages actually present at Moore's death and burial. In 1809 Graham received the permanent rank of major general and commanded a brigade in the ill-starred Walcheren expedition; in the course of which his brigade participated in the siege of Flushing. He was invalided home.

Graham was appointed to succeed Gen Sherbrooke in Portugal in 1810 and was sent to Cadiz, with the rank of lieutenant general, to assume command of the British troops aiding in the defence of that place against the French. In the February of 1811 he embarked with an expeditionary force to attack the rear of the French blockading army; and on 5 March 1811 obtained a memorable victory over the French at Barossa. The results, however, were neutralised by the gross misconduct of the Spaniards. Graham, who refused a Spanish dukedom, was ordered to join Wellington in June 1811. He was given command of the 1st Division and assisted in the siege and capture of Cuidad Rodrigo in January 1812. Graham was invested as a Knight of the Order of the Bath (KB) at Elvas, near Badajoz, on 12 March 1812. He commanded an army corps comprising the 1st, 6th and 7th Divisions, with two brigades of cavalry, in the course of the final operations against Badajoz and Wellington's advance against Salamanca. A painful affliction of the eyes, aggravated by the constant use of a telescope under a vertical sun, compelled Graham to return to England at the beginning of July 1812.

Rejoining Wellington early in 1813, he was placed at the head of the left wing of the army, comprising some 40 000 men, which he commanded at the great battle of Vittoria on 21 June 1813. He subsequently captured Tolosa, at which he was wounded, and was despatched by Wellington to invest the fortress of St Sebastian, 20 miles south west of Bayonne. The position was defended by Emmanuel Rey. Graham besieged and bombarded the fortress from the beginning of July 1813 and on 24 July endeavoured to carry it by assault, but was repulsed with heavy losses, and three days later was compelled to raise the siege. He resumed it after Wellington's defeat of Marshal Soult at the foot of the Pyrenees and was master of the most important outworks on 31 August; the citadel finally surrendering on 9 September. With the left of the army, Graham was ordered to cross the Bidassoa, the natural boundary dividing Spain from France, an operation which he successfully accomplished; establishing the British Army on French soil on 7 October 1813. Graham's health then obliged him to return home again, Sir John Hope succeeding him in the command.

Feeling his health improved, in November 1813 Graham accepted the offer of command of the troops to be despatched to Holland, to co-operate with Bulow's Prussian army in the offensive against Antwerp. He defeated the enemy at Merxem, but failed in a desperate attempt to storm the fortress of Bergen-op-Zoom in a night assault of 9 March 1814. This operation is recurrently referred to by Pattison who, to reiterate, took part in this action.

Graham returned to England following the peace, and on 3 May 1814 received the thanks of Parliament. He was created Baron Lynedoch of Balgowan in the peerage of the United Kingdom. Graham became a full general in 1821; and appointed colonel successively of the 58th Foot, 14th Foot and 1st Royals (the Royal Scots). He was created a Knight Grand Cross of the Order of the Bath (GCB) and Knight Grand Cross of the Order of St Michael and St George (GCMG); as well as receiving the Order of the Tower and Sword (Porgugal), San Fernando (Spain) and William the Lion (Netherlands). In his later years Graham continued to evince a deep interest in husbandry, which he had developed prior to his military career; and his love of farming and stock breeding persisted to the end of his life. (His name repeatedly appears as a breeder of prize stock in the catalogues of the Highland and Agricultural Society of Scotland. Queen Victoria congratulated him for winning a prize at the Epsom meeting of 1839, for a two year old colt of his own breeding, named Jeffy, with which he won a further prize at the Newmarket Craven meeting of 1842). In 1815 he commenced a long cherished project, that of founding a military club on the principle of the civil clubs then existing in London. A site was eventually secured in Pall Mall, and in 1817 the foundation stone of the present senior United Services Club was laid. He died on 18 December 1843, at the age of 95.

Graham's military career exemplifies three especially noteworthy themes. The first is the manner in which it is 'fixed in time', so to speak. That career was a peculiar manifestation of the social fabric of the 18th Century military establishment, in two important respects. First, it exemplifies the manner in which the regiment remained in many instances the creation of a wealthy individual; exampled by his foundation of the 90th Regiment of Foot, upon which Graham's subsequent career was anchored. To this extent, the military forces powerfully reflected the impress of the patronage exercised by the aristocracy and landed gentry. Second, one notes a situation that would be clearly impossible in the structured bureacracies characteristic of the modern state; viz the manner in which Graham commenced his military career at the level of a senior officer (broadly the equivalent of a major). The third noteworthy feature of Graham's military career is the late point in his life at which it commenced (when he was in his mid-40s). Fourth, it is a remarkable aspect of that career that he attained the heights of his profession, and exhibited great expertise and talent in the process, despite the fact that he appears to have had no formal training in the military arts whatsoever (a further common characteristic of the 18th Century military officer).

(d) *Lord Proby*: Lord John Proby had been appointed a lieutenant colonel in the 1st Regiment of Foot Guards on 27 April 1803. At Bergen-op-Zoom he commanded the fourth attacking column.

(e) *Guards*: Six companies of the 2nd Battalion of the 2nd Regiment of Foot Guards (the Coldstream Guards) served in the assault on Bergen-op-Zoom. On 4 August these six companies were moved to Brussels and shortly afterwards the battalion was completed by the arrival of the headquarters component and four other companies from England. Most fortuitously, therefore, the battalion was at full strength when news arrived of Napoleon's escape from Elba and his arrival in Paris.

(f) *grape-shot*: The term, when applied to ammunition employed by guns engaged in land warfare, is in actual fact a misnomer. Grape shot proper consisted of some nine cannon balls sewn together in a canvas bag that dissolved after the rounds left the gun. Its name derives from the ammunition's resemblance to a bunch of grapes, and was employed only at sea. When used in land warfare, the term 'grape shot' refers to 'case' or 'cannister' shot. This consisted of metal cases filled with small balls which, in effect, transformed the cannon into gigantic shotguns. The container disintegrated as the rounds left the muzzle. Two types of case shot were employed: 'light case' (which, for 6 pr, contained 85 cans, each holding 18 bullets); and 'heavy case' (43 cans, each containing 42 bullets). Case shot was not normally fired at ranges above 350 yards, being employed as a last resort for repelling a charge. Heavy case, however, would strike its target at a range of up to 600 yards. Grape shot, when employed within the context of land warfare, refers to heavy case shot and the term 'grape shot' in this particular instance thus refers to heavy case.

(31) *Guards*: The Guards have been referred to in various parts of the text. However, some of the information contained therein is recapitulated within the context of this note, in order to concentrate the data and facilitate ease of access.

The term 'Guards' properly refers to the (then) six regiments which comprised the personal escort of the Sovereign; these being the three mounted regiments (the 1st and 2nd Regiments of Life Guards and the Royal Horse Guards) and the three infantry formations (the three regiments of Foot Guards). Pattison is specifically referring within this context to the Foot Guards. Their role as the Sovereign's escort conferred upon the Foot Guards a uniquely elite status and they undertook most of the ceremonial duties in the capital (as, indeed, they continue to do); always being stationed in and around London.

The 1st Foot Guards is the senior infantry regiment in the British Army. Its date of formation is generally accepted as being 23 November 1660, following the restoration of Charles II; although its antecedents reside in the regiment of Guards maintained by the exiled son of Charles I from at least 1656. At Waterloo the regiment was represented by the 2nd and 3rd Battalions, which formed the 1st (Guards) Brigade, within the 1st (Guards) Division. The Brigade was commanded by Gen Sir Peregrine Maitland. Their light companies assisted in the defence of Hougoumont; and, at the culmination of the French attacks, claiming the credit for repelling the assault of the Imperial Guard (a point on which Pattison expresses strong feelings). In recognition of this latter service the 1st Regiment of Foot Guards was awarded the distinction of forming an entire regiment of grenadiers. (Hence the subsequent title of 'Grenadier Guards'. At the time of Waterloo, therefore, it was not yet designated the Grenadier Guards). The regimental motto is: '*Honi Soit Qui Mal y Pense*' ('Evil be to him who evil thinks').

The 2nd Regiment of Foot Guards (the Coldstream Guards) can trace its lineage to an even earlier point in time than the 1st Regiment. The formation was originally designated 'Monck's Regiment of Foot', raised in 1650. The 2nd Regiment was unique in so far as it embodied an unbroken tradition extending from the Commonwealth (1649-1660) to the Restoration. Although junior in precedence to the 1st Regiment of Foot Guards, it has never regarded itself as such, exemplified in the regimental motto, *Nulli Secondus* ('Second to None'). (This subordination to the 1st Regiment of Foot Guards may possibly be based upon the Coldstream Guards' association with Cromwell's hated Parliamentarian army). The 2nd Battalion served at Waterloo (contained, together with the 3rd Regiment (Scots Guards) within the 2nd Brigade, commanded by Gen Sir John Byng). It especially distinguished itself in the French assault on Hougoumont; when Capt and Lt Col James Macdonell of Glengarry (styled the 'bravest man in the army') closed the gates of Hougoumont at the point where the French almost succeeded in breaking in. (However, Macdonell generously insisted in sharing this sobriquet with Sgt Graham of the Coldstream light company, another hero of Hougoumont).

The 3rd (or Scots) Regiment had its origins, as its name suggests, in several companies formed in Scotland. The regiment was officially raised in 1662 at the express instructions of Charles II. However, the antecedents of the regiment extend back to 1642. In that year Charles I raised in Scotland a Royal Regiment commanded by the Marquess of Argyll for service in quelling the Irish rebellion of that period. The remanants of this prototype regiment returned to Scotland in 1649. In 1650 it became styled the 'Foote Regiment of His Majestie's Lyffe Guardes', under the command of Lord Lorne (the son of the Marquess of Argyll). The regiment became fragmented following the battle of Worcester (1651). On his restoration in 1660 Charles II ordained that English garrisons in Scottish cities should be replaced by Scottish units. Two companies were raised for this role. In May 1662 Charles ordered that these two companies be supplemented by four new companies to form a new regiment of Foot Guards. This new formation had a powerful lineage with the erstwhile 'Foote Regiment of His Majestie's Lyffe Guardes'. Until the formation of the Irish and Welsh Guards (in 1900 and 1915 respectively) it was the only Guards regiment which bore a distinct ethnic complexion; as, throughout its history, the majority of its recruits appear to have derived from Scotland. To reiterate, the regiment was brigaded with the 2nd Battalion of the Coldstream Guards at Waterloo, within the 2nd Guards Brigade. The regimental motto is: 'Nemo Me Impune Lacessit' ('No one provokes me with impunity').

The elite status of the Guards was not reflected in any distinctive uniform, which resembled the style currently adopted by the line infantry (with the blue facings which distinguished 'royal' regiments; ie those with a royal title or named after a royal personage). Rather, such status was embodied in the peculiar seniority enjoyed by Guards officers within the British Army; the vastly enhanced price of commissions; and the predominance of the aristocracy within the officer establishment.

With regard to the first factor - seniority - in the Foot Guards all officers possessed a double rank; being higher in the army than in the regiment. It was customary for officers in line regiments to be awarded a 'brevet' rank. Brevet rank was bestowed upon an officer as a reward for meritorious service, despite there being no immmediate vacancy for promotion within the regiment. It was thus possible for a company officer to hold, for example, the regimental rank of captain whilst simultaneously possessing the army (brevet) rank of major. However, in the Foot Guards all officers were thus entitled to a higher brevet rank. For example, a Guards lieutenant would be the equivalent of a line regiment captain; and would therefore have the confusing title of 'lieutenant and captain'.

Second, the cost of purchasing a commission in the Guards was enormous. Although not all commissions in these regiments were procured through purchase, when such was the case (in the majority of instances), the prices were staggering compared with those prevailing in line regiments. For example, a lieutenant colonelcy in the Guards cost £6 700 in 1815; a majority £6 300; a captaincy 33 500 and a lieutenancy £1 500. These may be compared with their respective counterparts in infantry regiments; £3 500, £2 600, £1 500 and £550 respectively. Moreover, a Guards officer could not possibly hope to survive without a substantial private income. (This was despite the fact that the rates of pay for Guards officers were higher than those prevailing in the remainder of the army. A major in the Foot Guards, for example, received £1.4s.6d per day, a captain 16s.6d and a lieutenant 7s.10d; compared with the equivalent line pay of 16s, 10s.6d and 6s.6d per day respectively)

The high costs of commissions and necessity for a substantial private income was symptomatic of the Foot Guards' social exclusiveness. In general, only the members of the most senior echelons of British society - the aristocracy and landed gentry - and the most affluent (the two aspects often being synonymous) could hope to gain access to a commission in the Foot Guards.

This introduces the third important facet of the Foot Guards, their social exclusiveness. This may be gauged from an assessment of the backgrounds of officers who served at Waterloo; in both their regimental capacity and as staff officers. They included at least seven peers (or the heirs to high ranking peerages, with the right to be called 'lord'); 25 sons or heirs of peers (including one 'natural' - ie illegitimate - son); five knights (in the main honoured for their previous services); nine sons or heirs of baronets; and even the son of a Count of the Holy Roman Empire (Capt CAF Bentinck of the 2nd Foot Guards). The Guards battalions (including the mounted regiments) formed a marked exception to the generally socially variegated backgrounds of officers within line infantry regiments. Of the 140 officers drawn from the peerage in 1809, 43 were serving in the Foot Guards and 36 in the cavalry. Conversely, only 50 aristocratic officers were serving in line infantry regiments; distributed over 35 regiments. Of the 283 officers who had been educated at the major public schools, 80 served in the Foot Guards (and 96 in the cavalry).

It is important to bear in mind that this elite status - of which the Guards social exclusivity was symptomatic - was not based upon their purely ritual impress upon the public imagination as the personal escort of the Sovereign. They undoubtedly represented the finest combat troops in the army; especially renowned for the maintenance of the highest standards of discipline in the face of the most desperate pressures. To cite but one example, Lt Gen Sir John Moore is said to have commented upon the appearance of the Guards in the retreat to Corunna (1808-1809). They were distinguished from the remainder of the army by marching in immaculate barrack-style formation, their drum major at their head. *ed.*

(32) *Inkerman*: In order to break the British/French siege of Sebastapol during the Crimean War of 1854-1856, the Russian commander, Prince Aleksander Menshikov, prepared a large scale sortie towards the east of the port. At dawn on 5 November 1854 the Russians thrust out of the city against the thin allied line near the mouth of the Chernaya rivers. The British commander, Lord Raglan (Fitzroy Somerset) and the French general (Aimable Pelissier) rallied their troops to make a stand at Inkerman. In savage hand-to-hand fighting the Russians were finally repulsed by the smaller allied army. Menshikov retired behind Sebastapol's defences again, having lost some 12 000 men. *ed.*

(33) It was on the 7th of December, 1815, while I was in Paris with the army, that Marshal Ney was taken from his prison, and, in *violation* of the *true* [author's italics] construction of the articles of amnesty made at the capitulation of Paris, (a) shot like a dog. I well remember the feelings of indignation which this foul deed engendered in my mind, and which were keenly reciprocated by every honourable soldier. What surprised me then, and has surprised me ever since, is the fact that the Duke of Wellington, whose power was omnipotent, and who declared the sentence of death awarded by the Peers of France to be in contravention of the capitulation to which *his name* [author's italics] was adhibited [ie appended], allowed such a procedure to take place. It is most certain that had he exercised the same authority he put forth to prevent that old barbarian Blucher (b) from blowing up the bridge of Jena (c) at Paris, he would have saved the life of a renowned brother warrior, and shed additional lustre on his own great name. (d) It, however, being otherwise, I have always looked on this cruel affair as a blot on The Duke's 'escutcheon.' (e)

Ney, at his execution fully verified his title to that enviable distinction for a soldier, accorded him by the whole French army, and which he had won in a hundred fights, *Le brave des braves* [Bravest of the brave. ed.]

In executions such as his, the eyes of the culprit are invariably covered, but this proposition the marshal scornfully rejected; and, standing erect with calm, dignified and unshaken *mien* before the platoon which was to perform the sad duty, looking them steadfastly in the face with a benign and unreproaching expression, and pointing with his right hand towards his heart, he ejaculated, 'A mon coeur, mes camarades' ['At my heart, my comrades' ed.] The discharge was instantaneous, and

Ney ceased to live. But let us cast a curtain over this heart-rending spectacle, and forget, if possible, the noble opportunity Wellington lost to himself and his country of magnifying the God-like attribute of mercy, which every human being needs. 'Blessed are the merciful, for they shall obtain mercy'. (f) Marshal Ney had five horses killed under him at Waterloo, and his cloak was actually riddled by musket-balls. He was the idol of the French army, and many a veteran cheek was bedewed with tears of indignation and sorrow when his cruel death was made known.

Since the above was written, the following extract from *The Daily Telegraph* appeared in *The Glasgow Herald* of 26th January, 1869:-

'INTERESTING MARRIAGE IN PARIS

In the chapel of the Tuileries (g) there was solemnized on Sunday week a marriage - one of the prettiest marriages, so far as the names of the contracting parties go, which it has ever been our lot to record. The Prince de la Moskwa was married to Madame le Comtesse de Labedoyere. "Eh bien!" ["Oh good"] the cynic may say, with a shrug and a yawn; "what then?" It is a "marriage in high life" - no more. Princes marry countesses every day. Ere now, they have been known to marry chambermaids. Nevertheless, the marriage of Sunday week has a significance when the names of the bride and bridegroom are remembered, that is at once historic and pathetic. Fifty-three years ago, on a dark December morning, armed men bearing lanterns brought forth from his cell in the palace-prison of the Luxembourg a stout, simple, bourgeois-looking man in a civilian's garb, who had been doomed to death by the Bourbon's Court of Peers. They conducted him to a remote corner of the Luxembourg Gardens, close to the Boulevard de l'Observatoire. They set him up - he refused to have his eyes bandaged - and a file of grenadiers shot him to death. The victim's name was Michael Ney, a peasant's son of Sarre-Louis, but famous throughout the world as Duke of Elchingen, as Prince of Moscow, as "Bravest of the Brave". He fought at Waterloo. Could the great British captain who won that fight have saved the life of the heroic Frenchman in December? It matters little now. Ney had got to die; and he died as he had lived. Very shortly after his execution another sacrifice was made to the offended majesty of Bourbonism. The brave Colonel Labedoyere, one of the most devoted among Napoleon's adherents, was tried by military commission, found guilty of "treason", condemned to death and shot. Need we say anything more to show the interest, both historic and pathetic, which must cling to that marriage in the Tuilleries chapel, where, under the auspices of the Third Napoleon, the heir of Marshal Ney was wedded to the widow of Labedoyere's son?' *auth*.

Editorial observations on above footnote

(a) When Ney was brought to trial in November 1815, he claimed Wellington's intervention; under the 12th Article of the Convention of 3 July, by which the allied powers (Great Britain and Prussia) occupied Paris. The Article provided that no action should be taken against any individuals on account of their past position and opinions.

(b) *Blucher*: Gebherd Leberecht von Blucher, Prince of Wahlstadt, Prussian general. He was born at Rostock in Meklenburg, Schwerin, and joined the Swedish army as a cavalry officer in 1757, in the course of the Seven Years War (1756-1763). Having immediately been taken prisoner by the Prussians, he joined the army of his captors. He resigned in 1772, but in 1793 he rejoined to oppose the French revolutionary armies. In the ensuing campaigns he gained renown as a cavalry commander. In 1806, by then a lieutenant general, he was captured following the battle of Jena, but was exchanged a fortnight later for the French general, Victor. When Prussia re-entered the war in 1813 he regained Silesia from the French and played an important role in Napoleon's defeat at Leipzig. Having fought his way through France in 1814, his forces entered Paris on 31 March. When Napoleon escaped from Elba, he and Wellington concentrated their forces south of Brussels. They were, of course, aware of Napoleon's favoured strategy when faced with two opponents; viz interposing his forces between the two, confining one with the minority of his army, destroying the second with the bulk of his forces and then returning to defeat the first. It was essential, therefore, that the Prussian and British forces be mutually supportive. Blucher was defeated at Ligny (16 June 1815), but was able to rally his troops to arrive at the decisive moment at Waterloo. This occurred at 16h30. The Prussians conducted the pursuit following Waterloo, the British forces being too exhausted to do so. Blucher personified the stern and aggressive martial qualities traditionally associated with Prussia. He was nicknamed 'Marshal Vorwarts ('forward').

(c) *bridge at Jena*: The bridge was named Jena in order to commemorate the crushing defeat inflicted upon the Prussians by Napoleon in the battle of Jena (14 October 1806). The Prussians were routed and for the ensuing six years Prussia was humiliated. She lost half her territory under the terms of the Treaty of Tilsit and was reduced to virtually the level of a French satellite. Blucher was no doubt animated by the same spirit which moved Hitler when, in June 1940, he orchestrated the French surrender in the same railway carriage in which the Armistice of 11 November 1918 had been ratified; thereupon ordering the demolition of the carriage. Wellington had to frequently intervene to deter the Prussians from committing excesses motivated by their zeal for revenge.

(d) *saved the life of a renowned brother officeron his own great name*: Wellington replied to Ney's plea for the former's intervention in the latter's trial that the Article in question (Article 13; cf note (a) above) was not, and could not be, interpreted to imply that a French government could be prevented from acting as it thought fit. Accordingly, he did not take, and the British ambassador was forbidden to take, any official steps to rescue Ney; but Wellington did all that he could in his private capacity on Ney's behalf.

(e) *escutcheon*: Pattison is referring to the coat of arms in a general sense. The strict heraldic definition of an escutcheon is the heraldic shield emblem bearing the coat of arms.

(f) *Blessed are the merciful for they shall obtain mercy*: This is one of the eight

Beatitudes, which Christ preached at the Sermon on the Mount (Matthew, Chapter V, verses 3-10).

(g) *Tuilleries*: Pattison is referring to the Palais des Tuilleries, a French royal residence adjacent to the Louvre in Paris. The palace was destroyed by arson in 1871. Construction of the original palace, commissioned by Catherine de Medici, commenced in 1564; and during the succeeding 200 years there were many additions and modifications.

(34) *Lloyd's foot battery*: The officer referred to is Maj William Lloyd (1778-1815), who died in Brussels on 29 July 1815, as the result of wounds received at Waterloo.

foot battery: As stated in the introduction [cf **Introduction - Military/Historical Context**: *Organization of the British Army*] the artillery - together with the engineers - fell outside the control of the commander-in-chief; being the province of the Board of Ordnance, headed by the Master General of the Ordnance.

At this time the Royal Regiment of Artillery was divided into three main arms: viz, field, siege and garrison artillery. The field artillery was further sub-divided into foot and horse artillery. This sub-division was a most important distinction, for the latter followed the basic cavalry pattern of organizatiion (being structured on the basis of troops, as opposed to the foot artillery, which was modelled upon infantry companies). Pattison draws the distinction between 'foot artillery' and 'flying artillery' (ie horse artillery). He refers to the latter in **Letter II** (cf **Letter II**/note (2)). The Royal Horse Artillery were distinct not only in terms of organization but also uniforms (although the personnel were then interchangeable between foot and horse artillery).

To reiterate, the foot artillery followed the infantry organisational pattern of companies. These companies were structured in battalions. After 1808 there were eight battalions, each of 10 companies. However, these battalions did not function as integrated units, but operated independently on a company basis. These companies were known as 'brigades' or 'batteries' (although the term 'battery' more properly referred to a gun emplacement). The authorized establishment of a company was: two captains, three subalterns, four sergeants, four corporals, nine bombardiers (lance corporals), 120 gunners and three drummers; furnishing a total of 145 of all ranks. In the field, however, its strength probably fluctuated between 110 and 130. In addition the company might have allocated to it some 100 drivers, with horses and mules, resulting in an overall strength of almost 200. The company was equipped with five field guns (9 prs or heavy 6 prs) and one 5½ inch howitzer (a short barrelled weapon which fired a high angled trajectory with the object of delivering a bomb onto fortifications). Teams of eight horses harnessed in pairs were normally used to move the guns, but mules were frequently employed to haul the ammunition and baggage. (A standard field battery might possess eight ammunition and three baggage waggons, in addition to a mobile forge). The drivers would theoretically have a commissary officer attached to them and, being mounted - and therefore incapable of responding to drum calls - would have their own trumpeter. *ed.*

(35) *D'Erlon*: Drouet, Jean-Baptiste, Comte D'Erlon (1765-1844). Born on 29 July, 1765, the long career of this French soldier encompassed service in the armies of both Louis XVI and Napoleon; and was climaxed by his appointment as the first governor general of Algeria and marshal of France under Louis Philippe. A volunteer in the regiment of Beaujolais from 1782, Drouet had attained the rank of corporal in 1792, prior to the fall of the monarchy. Elected captain in 1793, he became aide-de-camp to General P Lefebvre in 1794, and thenceforward enjoyed rapid promotion. General of Division in 1803, he was created Comte (Count) D'Erlon by Napoleon in 1809. He served in Bavaria and Spain and was promoted lieutenant general in 1813. Under the first restoration of Louis XVIII in 1814 he was appointed commander of the 16th military division but conspired against the regime. Joining Napoleon, he was made a peer of France and given command of an army corps, but during the Waterloo campaign he divided his forces, on 16 June, between Ney at Quatre Bras and Napoleon at Ligny, and failed to support either as required.

On the second restoration of the Bourbons, Drouet fled to Bavaria where, as Baron Schmidt, enjoying King Maxilian I's protection, he established a brewery close to Munich. The death sentence passed on him in France in 1816 was revoked in 1825. Returning to France in 1830, he was reinstated on the active list by Louis Philippe's regime. In July 1834 Drouet was appointed governor general of Algeria. He was recalled to France in 1835 and, after some years at Nantes, was appointed a marshal of France in April 1843. Drouet died in Paris on 25 January 1844. *ed.*

(36) *Castlereagh*: Castlereagh, Robert Stewart, Viscount (afterwards 2nd Marquess of Londonderry) (1769-1822). He was the son of an Ulster landowner, Robert Stewart, who was elevated to the peerage in 1789 and later promoted earl (1796) and ultimately marquess (1816) of Londonderry. On his father's death Castlereagh became Marquess of Londonderry. He was educated at Armagh and at St John's College, Cambridge. Castlereagh entered the Irish Parliament (then separate) as an independent member (1790) but changed his political allegiance to the Tory party in 1795. As chief secretary for Ireland (1799-1801), under Lord Cornwallis (Lord Lieutenant of Ireland) he was instrumental in securing the passage of the Act of Union of Ireland with England, which abolished the distinct Irish Parliament. Castlereagh had become convinced of the need for union with England as the result of the Irish rebellion of 1797-1798 and the threat of French invasion. Castlereagh shared the view of Lord Cornwallis that a policy of lenienccy was the most practical response to the insurrection. He forced the measure virtually unaided through the Irish Parliament, in the face of bitter opposition from the Protestant members. King George III's veto on Pitt's concessions to Irish Catholics forced the resignation of both Cornwallis and Castlereagh, who realized that the success of the Union was dependent upon the removal of discrimination against Catholics. Castlereagh became secretary of state for war and the colonies (1805-1806). On Pitt's death in January 1806 he left office and became the chief opposition spokesman on foreign and military affairs. He returned to the war department in the Duke of Portland's ministry in 1807 and displayed his determination to engage in major warfare against

a continent now completely dominated by Napoleon. In this role, he was responsible for selecting Sir Arthur Wellesley (the future Duke of Wellington) for the Peninsular command. Equally, however, he must bear some responsibility for the selection of the Earl of Chatham as commander of the disastrous Walcheren expedition of 1809. In that year Castlereagh fought a duel with, and slightly wounded, his political rival, George Canning, who had been intriguing against him. He resigned in 1809 but returned to the government in 1812 to commence his great period as foreign secretary. Following the assassination of the Prime Minister, Lord Perceval, in 1812, Castlereagh became leader of the House of Commons, in the ministry of Lord Liverpool (1812 - 1822).

In his role of foreign secretary Castlereagh was responsible for forming and maintaining the great anti-French alliance in the later stages of the Napoleonic Wars. Following the French defeat in 1814 he represented England at the Congress of Paris and the signing of the Treaty of Paris (30 May 1814). Castlereagh opposed vindictive peace terms and was instrumental in France's retention of Alsace Lorraine. Under the terms of the Treaty of Paris France retained the boundaries of 1792, which included Avignon, Venaissin, parts of Savoy, and parts of the German Empire and Belgium; all of which had not been held by France in 1789. The Allies also abandoned all claims to indemnities. These concessions were intended to strengthen the prestige of the newly reinstated Bourbon regime. Castlereagh was later the main English representative at the Congress of Vienna (cf note (37) below). Castlereagh also attached fundamental importance to the regular consultation by the great powers on matters of common concern; and the peace treaty contained specific provision for periodic meetings of the contracting parties. These meetings became known as the 'Congress system'. Castlereagh's objective was to facilitate diplomacy through conference rather than to establish any system of international regulation or interference in the internal affairs of other states. The Congress of Aix-la-Chapelle (1818) readmitted France to the concert of powers.

He later became opposed to the Holy Alliance (consisting of a coalition of Austria-Hungary, Prussia and Russia) being exploited as a medium for suppressing liberal movements in Europe. The Holy Alliance was formed in response to the liberal movements in Germany, organized after 1818; and the revolutions in Spain and the Kingdom of the Two Sicilies in 1820. After the Congress of Laibach (1821) he openly repudiated the principle formulated at the meeting at Troppau (October 1820) (which he refused to attend) of intervention and coercion. He decided to attend the Congress of Verona (1822), in order to discuss the Greek War of Indpendence (which had broken out in 1821) and the rebellion of the Spanish colonies in South America; both issues directly affecting British interests. The instructions which he compiled clearly indicated that he was not prepared to sanction forcible interference in either Greece or Spain; and that Britain would ultimately be prepared to recognize de facto governments created by successful revolutionary movements. It was clearly apparent that Castlereagh was preparing for the detachment of Britain from the reactionary continental governments.

Little interested in domestic politics, as leader of the House of Commons, he had to defend and bear censure for the government's repressive policies orchestrated by the Prime Minister, Lord Liverpool, which characterized the period 1815-1822. His unpopularity escalated as the result of the Cabinet's unsuccessful introduction, in 1820, of a bill to dissolve the marriage between George IV and Queen Caroline. Castlereagh was savagely attacked by liberal Romantics such as Byron and Shelley. In 1821 he began to reveal symptoms of paranoia and was perpetually armed. These pressures, combined with the strain induced by overwork, and threats of blackmail relating to alleged homosexual practices, eventually resulted in his suicide. One of the ablest statesman of his time (in fact a distant precursor of the 'Europhiles' in the current controversy concerning the European Common Market), and a man of strong character, he was very far from being a bigoted reactionary; in which light he was popularly presented (and which, indeed, finds an echo in Pattison's observations). This extreme unpopularity was graphically expressed in the fact that his coffin was waylaid and danced upon; whilst cheering accompanied the funeral obsequies at Westminster Abbey, where he is buried. *ed*.

(37) *Congress*: ie the Congress of Vienna, which met between September 1814 and June 1814. The Congress was an extension of the Congress of Paris, and intended to resolve the question of the general distribution of the conquered territories among the victorious Allies. It was one one the most brilliant international assemblies of the 19th Century. Most of the rulers of Europe attended; in addition to a host of lesser potentates, ministers, etc. The principal negotiators were: Prince Metternich (reprenting the Habsburg Empire); Hardenburg and William von Humboldt (Prussia); Lord Castlereagh and the Duke of Wellington (Great Britain); the Tsar Alexander I and his many advisers (Czartoryski, Stein, Razumovsky, Capo d'Istries, Nesselrode and others) representing Russia; Talleyrand (the French delegate); and Cardinal Consalvi representing the Papacy. The main decisions were made by the chief representatives of the four major allied powers; Great Britain, Austria, Prussia and Russia. The various settlements were ratified by the Act of the Congress of Vienna (8 June 1815). Its chief provisions were:

(i) Restoration of the Austrian and Prussian monarchies.

(ii) Austria received, in addition to her former domains, the Italian provinces of Lombardy and Venetia (to be designated the Lombardi-Venetian kingdom); the Illyrian provinces (the former French territories of Illyria and Dalmatia); Salzburg and the Tyrol (taken from Bavaria); and Galicia.

(iii) Prussia received part of the Grand Duchy of Warsaw (Posen) and Danzig; Swedish Pomerania and Rugen (in return for the latter Denmark being ceded Lauenburg); the former Prussian possessions in Westphalia (somewhat enlarged); Neuchatel; the greater part of Saxony, as compensation for the loss of her former possessions (eg Ansbach and Bayreuth (ceded to Bavaria), East Friesland (ceded to Hanover) and part of Polish territory (ceded to Russia).

(iv) Formation of the Kingdom of the Netherlands. This united the former republic of Holland and the territory now known as Belgium (then designated the Austrian Netherlands). The new kingdom was ruled by the head of state of Holland (the hereditary stadtholder).

(v) Britain returned the former Dutch colonies (with the exception of Ceylon and the Cape of Good Hope).

(vi) The Kingdom of Poland: Most of the former Grand Duchy of Warsaw, created by Napoleon, was ceded to Russia, and became a Polish kingdom, with the Russian Tsar as king. Alexander granted Poland a liberal constitution. Polish was to be the official language and Poland maintained her own separate institutions (including its own army). Cracow became a free state under the protection of Prussia, Austria and Russia.

(vii) Great Britain retained Malta, Heliogoland, some the French and Dutch colonies (ie the Cape of Good Hope and Ceylon; cf above) and assumed a protectorate over the Ionian Isles. [Treaty of 5 November 1815].

(viii) Sweden retained Norway, which had been procured in terms of the Treaty of Kiel (January 1814). Norway was granted a separate constitution. Denmark, which had formally possessed Norway, received Lauenburg as compensation.

(ix) Creation of the Germanic Confederation: This new political entity replaced the 1 000 year old Holy Roman Empire, which had been formally declared defunct in 1806. The Confederation comprised 39 states and four free cities. The new federation was essentially a mutually defensive alliance. The princes who remained outside the federation retained their independence. The Act of Federation was signed on 8 June 1815 and later supplemented by the Final Act of Vienna (15 May 1820). Arguments for a unified German state presented by nationalists were dismissed.

(x) Switzerland was re-established as an independent confederation of 22 cantons. Geneva, Wallis and Neuchatel (a principality formerly controlled by the King of Prussia) were included within the confederation.

(xi) Restoration of the legitimate dynasties in Spain, Sardinia (which received Genoa and the Papal states). ed.

(38) *Saxony*: cf note (37) above. Saxony had been ceded to Prussia in terms of the Act of Vienna. *ed*.

(39) *Belgium*: cf note (37) above. *ed*.

LETTER II

(1) *pickets (or piquets)*: A picket is essentially an outlying infantry sentinel or sentry. The term refers to a small group positioned at a considerable distance from the main force (as opposed to the sentry proper) in order to procure intelligence of enemy movements. *ed*.

(2) *flying field artillery*: Pattison is referring to the Royal Horse Artillery. This formation was created in 1793, with the object of furnishing fast-moving fire support for the cavalry. All the gunners were either mounted, or rode into combat on the limbers and battery vehicles. Whilst the foot artillerymen, who deployed the same 6 pr and 9 pr guns (cf below), had to walk behind their pieces on the march, and to manhandle them on drag ropes once they had been positioned for battle, the horse gunners were enabled to accompany the forward cavalry units as they made contact with the enemy, then withdraw and re-appear anywhere on the battlefield where artillery support was required. The three drivers would ride postillion fashion on the six-horse gun team; the eight gunners on their own horses.

The basic organisational structure of the horse artillery was that of the brigade (most commonly referred to by the cavalry term 'troop'; cf **Letter I**, note (15)). These troops were commonly identified by a letter (eg A). Each was divided into three divisions; each division consisting of two guns. Each division, in turn, was further subdivided into a subdivision. Each subdivision consisted of one gun and its attendant ammunition waggon and gun crew. Each division was commanded by a lieutenant; each right subdivision by a sergeant and each left subdivision by a corporal. A full brigade thus comprised six guns. When divided into 'half brigades' (each of three guns), one was commanded by the captain and one by the second captain. The concept of the division was obviously based upon the principle of the guns operating in pairs; enabling one to be fired whilst the second was being reloaded. The establishment of a troop of horse artillery comprised the following: 1 captain; 1 second captain; 3 subalterns; 2 staff sergeants; 3 sergeants; 3 corporals; 6 bombardiers; 80 gunners; 60 drivers; 1 farrier; 1 carriage-smith; 2 shoeing-smiths; 2 collar makers; 1 wheelright; 1 trumpeter; 56 saddle-horses; 108 draught horses. However, the strength of such establishments fluctuated. For example, at Waterloo, Mercer's troop (cf below) consisted of 84 drivers and a surgeon, in addition, with 120 draught and 100 saddle horses, and six mules. By 1806 12 horse brigades had been formed. They regarded themselves as the elite of the artillery arm. The association with the cavalry was reinforced through the medium of uniforms and equipment. Whilst the foot artillery were uniformed in infantry style, the Horse Artillery adopted a uniform reminiscent of the Hussars; with pelisse (short fur trimmed cloak), dolman (braided tunic) and 'Tarleton' helmets in the manner of light dragoons. In addition, officers wore the Pattern 1796 light cavalry officer's sword.

As in the foot artillery, each basic formation (ie the troop of Royal Horse Artillery, the counterpart of the foot artillery's battery, or brigade) was armed with five guns and one howitzer. Intially the Horse Artillery was equipped with the 6 pr gun, and latterly with the 9 pr; but even by 1815 9 prs were by no means universal. The armament of the Horse Artillery Troops at Waterloo was as follows:

Lt Col Sir H Hew Ross's Troop (A Troop)
(4 x 9 prs and 2 x 5½" howitzers)
Lt Col Sir Robert Gardiner's Troop (E Troop)
(5 x 6 prs and 1 x 5½" howitzer)
Capt A Cavalie Mercer's Troop (G Troop)
(5 x 9prs and 1 x 5½" howitzer)
Lt Col J Webber Smith's Troop (F Troop)
(5 x 9 prs 1 x 5½" howitzer)
Maj George Beane's Troop (D Troop)
(5 x 6 prs and 1 x 5½" howitzer)
Maj Norman Ramsay's Troop (H Troop)
(5 x 9 prs and 1 x 5½" howitzer)
Maj Robert Bull's Troop (I Troop)
(6 x 5½" howitzers)
2nd Rocket Troop (better known by its later title of O Troop).
(Maj E C Whinyates; 6 x 6 prs plus a supply of 12 pr rockets with carts and launchers)

Following the practice with foot artillery, the Horse Artillery was distributed throughout the army; ie it did not serve as an independent force. At Waterloo, all were attached to the cavalry; with the exception of A and G Troops, which were attached to the artillery reserve.

The French formed their horse artillery in 1791, and the Imperial Guard included a corps of horse artillery; viz Napoleon's Horse artillery of the Guard. It was one of the most brilliant units under the Emperor's command. The uniforms of the French and British horse artillery closely corresponded in so far as both were heavily influenced by the hussar uniform. The Prussians were the first to introduce horse artillery, in 1759.

Horse artillerymen of all armies were to pride themselves upon their ability to gallop up to a startled enemy, unlimber, load, fire, sponge, repeat, and then limber up again and whirl away in a cloud of dust before the enemy could initiate an effective response. *ed*.

(3) *1st Dragoon Guards*: It is curious that Pattison should at first refer to this regiment, and then describe an action which featured the 1st Life Guards. One gains the impression that he had confused the 1st Dragoon Guards with the 1st Life Guards. One should note that the 1st (King's) Dragoon Guards served with the Household Cavalry Brigade (in which the two regiments of Life Guards and the Royal Horse Guards were included). *ed*.

(4) *Life Guards*: In 1639 a number of Royalists formed themselves into a bodyguard

to protect King Charles I. After his execution in 1649 they crossed the Channel and transferred their loyalty to his son, the future King Charles II. In 1656 he formed them into a corps of Life Guards under Lord Gerard. In the same year Parliament established a body of horse to be called General Monck's Troop of Life Guards; Monck then being commander-in-chief of the army of the Commonwealth. On 3 June 1660 Parliament established the Duke of York's Life Guards, raised in Flanders. On 26 January 1661 Charles II established the Household Cavalry, which amalgamated all three forces - the original Royal Bodyguard, the Life Guards of General Monck (afterwards the Duke of Albermarle) and the Duke of York's Life Guards. In 1788 the Life Guards were divided into the 1st and 2nd Regiments of Life Guards. In the Waterloo campaign the two regiments each contributed two squadrons. *ed*.

(5) *the cloud...top of Carmel*: Elijah was a Hebrew prophet who lived during the 9th Century BC. He is mainly featured in the Old Testament Books *Kings I* and *II*. Elijah was, arguably, the greatest and certainly the most colourful of the Old Testament prophets. The name means 'My God is Yaweh'. He preached under the kings Ahab and Ahaziah; and was the focal point of opposition to the Canaanite and Phoenecian cults, especially that of Baal, which were flooding into Israel at that time. These had been propagated and greatly popularized in part by Jezebel, the Phoenecian wife of Ahab. To Elijah and his supporters such worship of heathen gods involved the severance of the divinely ordained covenant with God. In the Biblical account Elijah challenged the priests of Baal to a trial of spiritual strength, which occurred on Mount Carmel. Elijah won the contest, thereby convincing the people of Israel of the superiority of their God.

According to Biblical tradition, Elijah did not die but ascended to Heaven in a whirlwind (*Kings II*: 1-15). Hence, it was claimed in the Book of *Malachi* that Elijah would return to earth as a messenger of the Messiah's advent; and Christ claimed that this had in fact occurred, Elijah's role being personfied in the figure of John the Baptist. Immediately before his ascent into Heaven, Elijah transferred his role as a prophet to his disciple, Elisha.

The specific reference in this instance relates to the episode in which Elijah ended the drought which had plagued Israel, following his victory over the priests of Baal, recounted in *Kings I*; Chapter 19, verses 41-45:

'And Elijah said unto Ahab, Get thee up, eat and drink, for *there* is a sound abundance of rain. So Ahab went up to eat and drink. And Elijah went up to the top of Carmel; and he cast himself down upon the earth, and put his face between his knees. And said to his servant, Go up now, look towards the sea. And he went up and looked, and said, There is nothing. And he said, Go again seven times. And it came to pass at the seventh time, that he said, Behold, there ariseth a little cloud of the sea, like a man's hand. And he said, Go up, say unto Ahab, Prepare *thy chariot*, and get thee down, that the rain stop thee not. And it came to pass in the mean while, that the heaven was black with clouds and wind, and there was a great rain.'

LETTER III

(1) *General officer*: A general officer is senior in rank to a colonel. At the time of Waterloo the term encompassed the following ranks (in ascending order of seniority): brigadier general, major general, lieutenant general, general and field marshal. The rank of brigadier general was superseded in 1920 by that of brigadier, formerly denoting a staff appointment. *ed*.

(2) *Picton*: Picton, Sir Thomas, Lt General (1758-1815). He was the younger son of Thomas Picton, Esq, of Poyston, Pembrokeshire, and was born in August 1758 at Poyston. On 14 November 1771 he was gazetted as an ensign in the 12th Regiment of Foot, then commanded by his uncle, Lt Col (later Gen) William Picton, a distinguished officer. He joined his regiment in Gibraltar in 1773, and employed the leisure of garrison life in learning Spanish and studying professional works, with the assistance of his uncle. In March 1777 Picton was promoted to the rank of lieutenant in the 12th Regiment of Foot. After three years of inactive service at Gibraltar, Picton pressed his uncle to facilitate the former's exchange into a regiment more likely to see active service. Accordingly, on 26 January 1778 Picton was promoted captain in the 75th or Prince of Wales's Regiment of Foot, and returned to England. During the succeeding five years, however, his ambition to see active service was not realized, and he served in various provincial towns and home garrisons. In 1783 he played a leading part in quelling mutinous behaviour by the troops, who reacted violently to news of the regiment's impending disbandment, whilst stationed in Bristol. The King's personal commendation was communicated to Picton; but the promise of a majority was not fulfilled. Thereafter Picton spent 12 years on half-pay. Despite numerous applications for meaningful military employment, his appeals went unanswered. However, when hostilities with France broke out in 1793, he was determined to take action himself.

Towards the end of 1794, without holding any appointment, Picton embarked for the West Indies, on the strength of a slight acquaintance with Sir John Vaughan, who had been despatched to that theatre as commander-in-chief. Vaughan immediately recognized Picton's abilities and appointed him to the 17th Regiment of Foot, making him also an extra aide-de-camp to himself. Picton, now seeing active service for the first time, so distinguished himself that Vaughan obtained for him a majority in the 68th Foot, appointing him a quartermaster general to the force, with the temporary rank of lieutenant colonel. Picton's patron, however, died at Martinique in August 1795 and Picton was superseded by Maj Gen Knox. However, the new commander-in-chief, Sir Ralph Abercromby (who had known Picton's uncle) induced Picton to remain as an extra aide-de-camp.

Picton bore a distinguished role in the attack upon the French based on the island of St Lucia. A force of 1 700 men, commanded by Maj Gen Campbell, was landed off Longville Bay, St Lucia, after a strong defence by the French. As a result of his service in these operations, Picton was recommended by Abercromby for a lieutenant colonelcy in the 56th Regiment; his commission being antedated from

22 June 1795.

Picton next accompanied Abercromby in the attack on the island of St Vincent, which capitulated to the British on 10 June; three days following the latter's landing. Thence Picton served in the force which journeyed to Martinique near the end of January 1797; being present at the surrender of Trinidad by the Spaniards on 17 February in that year. Abercromby appointed Picton, who was fluent in Spanish, as commandant and military governor of Trinidad.

Picton vigorously applied himself to the remedy of the civil disorder and corruption prevailing within the island, but his efforts were hampered by the extremely limited size of his force; the garrison consisted merely of 500 men, of whom only 300 were British. However, by making an early example of mutineers among the coloured troops, he succeeded in enforcing discipline. Picton established a police force, not only in Port of Spain (the capital) but throughout the island. The roads which, prior to his arrival, were in a chaotic state of disrepair, were developed into the finest in the West Indies. His administration was highly commended by Abercromby, when the latter revisited the island in June 1797. In the autumn of 1797 Picton overcame an attempt at rebellion on the part of the coloured inhabitants of Trinidad and in January 1798 received the thanks of the king. When the peace of 1801 was under consideration, the Spanish inhabitants of the island, in a letter to Picton, expressed their strong disapproval of the transfer of Trinidad to Spain; and it was mainly due to Picton's despatches that when peace was declared, Trinidad remained a British possession. On 22 October 1801 he was promoted to the rank of brigadier general and, in June 1801, was entrusted with the civil administration of the island; with judicial powers as were formerly exercised by the Spanish governor. However, following allegations of cruelty, Picton resigned. On 30 May 1803 he learned that his resignation had been accepted, and on 11 June of that year he was superseded in the military command by Brig Gen Frederick Maitland. (The extent of Picton's popularity with the islanders may be gauged from the fact that on 23 April the inhabitants of Trinidad presented Picton with an address; a sword of honour purchased by them at their own expense and subsequently presented by the Duke of York; and also petitioned the king to reject Picton's resignation.

Between 1804 and 1808 Picton fought a protracted battle in the law courts to refute the allegations of cruelty - centred upon the interrogation of a woman of dubious character, named Luise Calderon. In actual fact, no conclusive judgement was ever returned; although judgements of 8 June 1808 and 10 February 1810 effectively vindicated Picton of any imputation of malice.

On 25 April 1808 Picton was promoted to the rank of major general. In July 1809 he was appointed by the Duke of York to the staff of the Earl of Chatham in the ill-starred Walcheron expedition. He was subsequently appointed commandant of Flushing and its environs, with a force of four regiments. After the departure of Lord Chatham with the greater part of the troops for England on 14 September 1809, Picton was appointed governor of Flushing, but was attacked by the epidemic of malarial fever and invalided home.

In January 1810 he received orders to join the army in Portugal where, upon his arrival, he was placed in command of the 3rd Division, situated close to Celerico. This division comprised:

1 Bn/45th Foot; 74th Foot; 1 Bn/88th Foot; Maj Gen Lightburne's Brigade (5th Foot, 2 Bn/58th Foot, 2 Bn/83rd Foot, and 5 Bn/60th Regiment).

The total army numbered under 24 000 men, organized in four divisions. In mid-September 1810 Massena suddenly concentrated his entire army, and marched rapidly along the right bank of the Mondego river in order to secure Coimbra before he could be effectively opposed by Wellington's force. Wellington, throwing his army across the river, took up a position, on 20 September 1810, in the rear of the Busaco ridge. Picton was posted to defend the ridge extending from San Antonio de Cantara to the hill of Busaco. The French attacked before daylight on 27 September and the assault was mainly directed on the pass of San Antonio, defended by Picton's force. Fourteen enemy guns directed their fire upon the pass, and a large column attempted to effect a forcible entry. However, Picton's attenuated 3rd Division maintained such an incessant and destructive fire that the French were ultimately compelled to abandon the assault. However, simultaneously a heavy enemy column penetrated to the left of Picton's division, close to the hill of Busaco; at which point the 88th Regiment and four companies of the 45th Regiment were positioned. With the assistance of a Portuguese regiment, which opportunely arrived, Picton's force succeeded in driving the enemy across the ravine in great disorder

On 2 May 1811 Massena advanced on the besieged French garrison of Almeida. The battle of Fuentes D'Onor followed on 5 May, and the principal role in the fighting once more devolved upon Picton's force. The defeat of the French was followed by their almost immediate evacuation of Almeida. Early in January 1812 Picton was directed to initiate the siege of Cuidad Rodrigo. On the evening of 19 January Picton's division assaulted the right, or great breach, whilst Craufurd's division stormed the left or smaller breach. Both assaults proved successful. Wellington, in his despatch, observed that the

> 'conduct of the 3rd Division in the operations which they performed with so much gallantry and exactness on the evening of 19 January, in darkness, afforded the strongest proof of the abilities of Lt Gen Picton and Maj Gen Mackinnon, by whom they were directed and led.'

In March 1812 Badajoz was invested, and Picton was entrusted with the conduct of the siege. The assault was made on 6 April 1812. The 3rd Division, led in person by Picton, who was wounded, stormed the castle. As he lay disabled in the ditch, he continued to urge on his men until the castle was taken. Subsequently, Picton expressed the warmest admiration of his men's conduct. He sent his aide-de-camp, Capt Tyler, to report the capture of the place to Wellington, who directed Picton to hold the castle at all costs. The final effort of the enemy was an attack upon the castle, which Picton's men repulsed with great slaughter. Picton's wound incapacitated him during the subsequent shameless sack of Badajoz, which so tarnished the conduct of the besiegers. A few days later Picton gave one guinea to each survivor of his division as a mark of his approval. Lord Liverpool, in the debate in the House of Lords of 27 April 1812 observed:

> 'The conduct of General Picton has inspired a confidence in the army and exhibited an example of science and bravery which have been surpassed by no other officer. His exertions in the attack of the 6th cannot fail to excite the most lively feelings of admiration.'

Picton accompanied his division to Salamanca but was too ill with fever to take part either in the attack on the forts or to participate in the battle itself. In August 1812 he was invalided to England, where a sojourn in Cheltenham restored his health.

On 1 February Picton was made a Knight of the Order of the Bath (KB). In the spring of 1813 he returned to the Peninsula. On 16 May 1813 the allied army, nearly 100 000 strong, was again in motion. Picton's force crossed the Duoro river on 18 May, and on 15 June the Ebro. On 21 June the French, numbering some 65 000 men, held a strong position in Vittoria. The battle began early in the morning of 21 June. Picton rapidly extirpated the enemy from their positions, forced them to abandon their guns, and drove the French in confusion towards the city of Vittoria; until darkness intervened to screen their disorderly flight. The 3rd Division was the most severely and permanently engaged sector of the allied army, and sustained casualties of almost 1 800 men killed and wounded; more than a third of the total allied losses in the battle.

Picton's division then moved slowly towards Pamplona, whence the enemy retreated across the Pyrenees. Picton subsequently rendered valuable services in the fastnesses of the Pyrenees, helping to repulse the French attempts to relieve Pamplona. There being no immediate prospect of major operations, Picton went to England on leave of absence, and took his seat in the House of Commons as member for Carmathen. On 11 November, in accordance with a resolution of the House of Commons, the Speaker delivered a unanimous vote of thanks to Picton for his great services at Vittoria on 21 June; and also in repelling the repeated assaults made on the allied army by the entire French forces under Soult between 25 July and 1 August 1813. In the December of 1813 Picton once again rejoined the Army of the Peninsula, resuming his command of the 3rd Division. On 27 February 1814 Picton's division played a prominent part in defeating the French at the battle of Orthez. Soult covered his retreat with large masses of infantry and for some time fell back in good order; but as he became increasingly pressed towards evening the French retreat disintegrated into a rout. On 10 April (Easter Day) 1814 the battle of Toulouse was fought, characterized by desperate courage and extremely heavy losses on both sides. The victorious allies entered Toulouse on 13 April, Soult having evacuated the city on the previous evening. An armistice was soon after agreed upon receipt of the news that Napoleon had abdicated.

Picton retired to his country seat in Wales, where he devoted himself to the improvement of his estate. At the beginning of 1815, upon the reorganization of the Order of the Bath, he was elevated to a Knight Grand Cross (GCB) of that order.

When Napoleon escaped from Elba, Picton was called to the colours once again and requested to join Wellington in the Netherlands. There Picton was appointed to the command of the 5th Division and the reserve (the latter force numbering some 10 000 men). On 16 June the 5th Division marched to the support of the army of the Netherlands, and on the same day was engaged in a fierce contest with Ney's columns at Quatre Bras. After repulsing the French infantry Picton barely had time to form squares when the French cavalry impacted upon his force. Another furious onslaught was launched by the French lancers, which was also repulsed. When Picton saw that the enemy were on the point of retiring, he himself led his men in the charge. The French cavalry were in superior numbers, both in his front and rear; but, showing contempt for the enemy force in his rear, he charged and routed those in front, creating such a panic among those in his rear that they galloped back through the intervals in his division's ranks, seeking only their own safety. During the battle Picton was hit by a ball which broke his ribs; but, determined to lead his division to a final victorious conclusion, he kept the knowledge of the wound a secret to all but his servant, who assisted in binding it up.

On the morning of 17 June, in consequence of the defeat of the Prussians at Ligny, the previous day, Wellington's force fell back on Waterloo; and by night the allied army was formed on the ground of Waterloo, sleeping on their arms. On the morning of 18 June, Picton's wound had assumed a serious aspect, but it nevertheless remained a close secret. He positioned his division on the Wavre road, behind the broken ridge between La Haye Sainte and Ter la Haye. Attacked by dense masses of French infantry, a desperate struggle ensued. Picton, summoning his second brigade, placed himself at its head and, waving them on with his sword, cried 'Charge! Hurrah! Hurrah!' At this moment a ball struck him on the temple and he fell dead. Capt Tyler, his aide-de-camp, placed Picton's body beneath a tree, where the former could rapidly retrieve it when the battle had ended.

Picton's remains were conveyed to Deal, where they were landed amidst extensive public mourning. In accordance with a resolution of the House of Commons, a public monument was erected to his memory on the west side of the north transept of St Paul's Cathedral. The monument, sculptured by Sebastian Gagahan, consists of a bust of Picton on a marble column, with a symbolic group of figures representing fame, genius and courage. In 1828 a costly monument was erected to his memory at Carmathen by public subscription (the king, George IV, contributing 100 guineas). A portrait of Picton, painted by Sir M A Shee, was exhibited at the National Portrait Gallery; and another portrait, by Sir William Beechey, is contained within the Duke of Wellington's collection.

The Dictionary of National Biography summarises Picton's personality and career in the following terms:

> 'In private life Picton was warm in his friendships and strong in his enemies. He had a very strong sense of honour which would not brook the petty deceptions of society. His manners were brusque, and his speech blunt without respect of persons. He was a capable administrator. As a soldier, he was a stern disciplinarian, calm in judgement, yet when excited overwhelmed in passion. With the foresight of a born commander, possessing considerable power of concentration, strong nerve, and undaunted courage, he proved himself Wellington's right hand in the

Peninsula.'

The above summation of Picton's character and career suggests a somewhat brittle, uncompromising character; possibly the source of his lack of professional advancement during the early years of his career. *ed.*

(3) Captain James Drummond Elphistone [*sic*], on being taken prisoner, was brought before Napoleon, and interrogated by him. I need hardly say his answers were appropriate; keeping the emperor in the shadows of ignorance and by no means administering comfort to his troubled mind. After this he was given in charge to a guard and imprisoned in the upper part of a house in Genappe, where he was kept 'in durance vile' but treated with politeness and consideration due to his rank as a British officer. One Sabbath evening his ears were assailed by an unusually confused and excited noise, caused by the French making speedy preparations to evacuate Genappe. On hearing that the British cavalry were approaching in pursuit (a characteristic phase of French character was developed here) [ie the French adopted the posture of flight, a trait in their behaviour that was to characterize the Waterloo campaign. ed.], the officer in charge of Captain Elphistone [*sic*], not being able to leave his prisoner without bidding him adieu, called aloud from the foot of the stair, 'Mon capitaine, je vous souhaite bon soir'. ['My captain, I will bid you good evening'. *ed.*] Vive le France pour les manieres! *auth.* [Hooray for France for its manners. *ed.*]

MEMORANDUM

It cannot be denied by anyone who has visited France, and mingled much in its society, that the French are a nation pre-eminently distinguished for politeness and suavity of manners. In fact, from the scavenger to the peer of the realm, they are a nation of ladies and gentlemen. I have no hesitation in saying that in all my intercourse with them (and at one period of my life it was pretty extensive), I invariably found among all classes of society an attention and delicacy of feeling towards 'l'etrangers' [foreigners], which, speaking generally, will be sought for in vain in similar strata of British society. To illustrate this, let me here describe my march from Brussels to Paris in command of a detachment of men from different regiments, who, like myself, had been under medical care, but who had now been discharged from the hospital. It so happened that on halting for the night at a small hamlet (I forget its name), my billet was on the dwelling of an old Imperial Guardsman. The sole menage [guest] of the veteran's chaumiere [humble cottage] was committed to the care of his only daughter Marie, her mother having been dead some years, and she herself, although still very young, a widow. The old man had also had two sons but 'they were not' [ie dead]. Joseph, however, philosophized and consoled himself for his bereavement, saying it was the will of Le Bon Dieu [the good God], and that his boys had fought for the Empire, and died for the glory of France; while he himself, old and maimed as he was (having been shot through the body, lamed by a Cossack's spear (a) [ie lance], and scarred on the face by a sabre), was still willing to take sword in hand, and, like his gallant sons, fight and die for Napoleon. The emphatic voice and energetic flush of indignant passion which spread over his fine countenance as he made this declaration were deeply interesting, being the outcome of an irrepressible emotion evoked no doubt from being in the presence of a Waterloo officer who had witnessed the defeat of his beloved Imperial Guard. (b)

Soldiers are a peculiar people, and like children they are soon at home with one another. Thus Mon Hote [my host], the hero of Vienna and Moscow, and 'le capitaine Anglais' [the English captain] fraternized admirably, and passed an agreeable and social evening. Joseph was an acute and intelligent fellow, and although born and reared in the humbler walks of life was, like most Frenchmen, in manner and address quite a gentleman. The history of his daughter was romantic and affecting. Her acquaintance with her first and only love dated from infancy. The consummation of their nuptial happiness had hardly taken place when that diabolical institution - the conscription - dragged Edmonde from the arms of bliss, and carried him with the French army to the icy regions of Russia, where, along with tens of thousands of his countrymen, his body became a prey either to the vultures or the wild beasts which infest those howling wastes. Marie was not, strictly speaking, beautiful, but nevertheless she was most attractive and interesting, and her manners gentle and engaging. She was yet at that time of life when the peach-like bloom which overshadows virgin cheeks - the betrayer of secrets - still lingered there. As her father was describing the appalling scene of retreat from Moscow, her heart, no doubt full of tender memories of the past, gave way, and raising her beautiful blue pensive eyes from her needle, which she was plying most assiduously, I saw they became suffused with tears; she rose and sought relief in her own apartment. Joseph and 'le capitaine Anglais' dined together, Marie presiding with as much ease and self-possession as if she had been an eleve [scion] of the higher circles of Parisian society. The table furnishings were scrupulously clean and comfortable; napkins and dinner-forks - articles then almost unknown in Glasgow society - being in daily use in this humble dwelling. Bouillie [boiled meat] and a delectable ragout [meat stew], proving Marie to be an excellent cook, composed our dinner, and I never remember enjoying a repast more. Our table-talk was truly exciting and interesting, and to me very instructive, developing French character in a marked degree - my host being a fine type of a French soldier, and his daughter possessing all the ease and manner peculiar to her countrywomen. Joseph, in referring to his military career, exhibited a most intense hatred of the Prussians, averring that the British were the only troops who could contend with his nation; and that were they only united they could conquer the world. I thought this pretty near the truth. During the evening an incident occurred which portrayed the good breeding of this household. As we conversed together, sitting in the kitchen, the servant-girl found it necessary to put fuel on the fire. In passing between us to perform this duty she turned to me, and making a graceful curtsy said, 'Monsieur mon Capitaine, je vous demande pardon mille fois' ['My good captain, I beg your pardon a thousand times'. ed.], and on retiring she made a similar obeisance. My bed was in a recess in the salle-a-manger [dining room]. On retiring for the night, I had a difficulty in parting the curtains, and to my surprise found the obstacle was occasioned by a beautiful bouquet pinned between them, placed there no doubt by Marie's fair hands. When I spoke of this to her in the morning Marie blushed. Before marching, which we had to do early in the morning, coffee was prepared for le Capitaine, and on bidding adieu to this engaging household, most lively and agreeable feelings were awakened in my mind, mingled with deep regret that creatures endowed with rational minds, and formed in the image of God, should have been capable of performing such deeds of bloodshed and devastation as had taken place at Waterloo. *auth.*

Editorial observations on above addendum

(a) *Cossack's spear*: The Cossacks originated in a nomadic Tartar people scattered throughout Russia: on the steppes along the lower reaches of the Rivers Don and Dnieper; in southern Siberia; and the Far East. The word is of Turkish origin and means 'free fighters'. The word became associated with various peoples; mainly peasants who had fled from Muscovite control and religious oppression in various parts of Russia, and even emanating from Poland and Lithuania. The original ethnic base of the Cossacks was thus considerably attenuated by this infusion of other refugee peoples. They were grouped in communities with a religious-type organization; in which the various sub-divisions or social groupings were under the authority of an ataman or hetman. Although the Cossacks formed the backbone of numerous rebellions against Tsarist rule, their main function was to man the frontier in defence against Tartar incursions. In 1650 the Russian government began to found military colonies from men described as 'Cossacks', and eventually some of these were converted into regiments of regular light cavalry. From this time state subsidies were an increasingly important source of revenue and the election of Cossack leaders had to be approved by Moscow. Economy and administration became dependent on the central government and the Cossacks, as a result, never achieved the same sort of self-sufficient mobility characteristic of true nomadic peoples. Unlike the Tartars, the Cossacks were not archers but relied upon muskets and lances.

(b) *Imperial Guard*: The Napoleonic Imperial Guard, which features extensively in Pattison's memoirs, should not be identified as a regiment or brigade. Indeed, it constituted an army within an army and by 1814 it had expanded to no less than 112 500 men of all arms. Such an increase made it necessary to form new regiments, consisting of conscripts. A distinction was thus made in the Imperial Guard between the 'old guard' - formed of veterans - and the 'young guard', recruited from conscripts. The Imperial Guard infantry regiments included such elite units as the Grenadiers-a-pied (originally the Consular Guard, formed in 1799 and elevated to the Imperial Guard in 1804). The cavalry of the Imperial Guard included: the Empress's Dragoon Regiment; the 1st Chevaulegars Lanciers (a lancer regiment recruited exclusively from Poles, formed in 1807); the Chasseurs-a-Cheval (light cavalry), a squadron of which was formed in 1800 and expanded into a regiment in 1801, its nucleus being Napoleon's Corps of Guides; the *Grenadiers-a-Cheval* (the horse grenadiers) (heavy cavalry). The Imperial Guard was organized into seven corps. In the closing stages of Waterloo, Napoleon mustered nine battalions of his veteran Old Guard and Ney led them in yet another futile assault. When the Prussian troops, whose late arrival decided the battle, pursued the broken French line, the discipline of the old guard survived and they withstood being ridden down and annihilated. The Grenadiers of the Old Guard were never broken and marched out in perfect order; whilst the remainder of Napoleon's army disintegrated into leaderless fugitives.

(4) *7th Hussars*: The 7th Queen's Own Hussars (formerly the 7th or Queen's Own Light Dragoons) was the senior hussar regiment, having been converted to hussars in 1805; cf note (12) below. The regiment was severely mauled by the French lancers at the engagement at Genappe (cf **Letter I**/note (7) (d)). *ed.*

(5) *French lancers*: The French lancer regiments at Waterloo were in the main manned by Poles. Several Polish cavalry regiments had served with the Imperial armies at an early date, but it was only in 1809 that two of the regiments were re-equipped with the lance, their native weapon (cf below). Prior to this Polish units were simply known as *chevaux legers*. In 1811 Napoleon converted six dragoon regiments to lancers also, in addition to adding two more such regiments to the cavalry of the Imperial Guard. Lancers were valued as shock troops against enemy squares, when the extra length of their weapons enabled them to outreach the infantryman armed with musket and bayonet. They proved their worth on many occasions; as at Dresden (1813), when the cuirassiers were supplemented by a front rank of lancers, which helped pierce the Austrian squares, although the latter had repulsed the cuirassiers alone with little difficulty. However, the lancers proved indifferent soldiers in wholly cavalry engagements, in which the lance revealed itself as a greater hindrance than an asset. Speaking of his role in the battle of Carpio (1811), an officer of the 16th Light Dragoons referred to an engagement with the Lancers of Berg:

> 'They looked well, and were formidable till they were broken and closed by our men, and then the lances proved an encumbrance; they caught in the appointments of other men and actually pulled them off their horses.'

Lancers wore distinctive uniforms, as did cuirassiers and hussars. Officers and men of lancer regiments wore the czapska, the strange shaped helmet that was curiously Polish; and also the short jacket and overalls.

The lance had been rendered obsolescent during the 14th and 15th Centuries; embodying the obsolescence of the mailed cavalryman in the face of the missile (the arrows of the longbow and crossbow bolts), the infantry pike and ultimately firearms. However, the lance survived as a weapon of war in the hands of Lithuanians, who originally occupied a spacious territory between Poland and Russia. The Lithuanians found the lance to be an effective weapon against the lightly armed Moslem and Tartar cavalry, their former enemies. The term 'uhlan', derived from the Polish term for cavalryman, was applied to the Lithuanian lancers.

When Lithuania was absorbed into Poland, the Polish cavalry adopted the lance. In 1717 Augustus III of Poland took into his service two *polks* (regiments) of *uhlan voluntaires*. Marshal Saxe recruited an uhlan regiment into the French army and the practice was soon imitated by other armies (but not by the British until the close of the Napoleonic Wars (cf below). The Germans retained the name 'uhlan' for their lancer regiments, and the term became the general designation for German cavalry. The *modus operandi* of the uhlans was similar to that of the hussars (cf below); viz traversing the countryside in small groups, until coalescing to trap the enemy. The lance enjoyed increasing popularity as the French Revolutionary and Napoleonic Wars progressed. The Austrians maintained three regiments of lancers, and uhlans formed an important arm in the reorganized Prussian army of 1813; there being six uhlan regiments in the Prussian service. *Landwehr* (militia) cavalry regiments in the Prussian army were armed with the lance.

Following the close of the Napoleonic Wars virtually every European army adopted the lance, and lancer regiments became very fashionable. In the British Army the 9th, 12th, 16th, 17th and 19th Light Dragoons were converted into lancer regiments following the end of the Napoleonic Wars; and the 5th and 21st Lancers were added at later points in the 19th Century. The vogue for the lance during the 19th Century derived from two main factors. The first was the distinguished service of the Polish lancers in the French service at Waterloo (cf above). The second was the hope that the lance would effect a new ascendancy on the part of the cavalry; overcoming the subordinate position into which it had been relegated as the result of concentrated infantry fire directed from the square. It was hoped that the lance would enable cavalry attacking a square to penetrate beyond the defensive barrier formed by the hedge of bayonets. (Inevitably, it proved a vain hope, as the lance proved a cumbersome and inefficient weapon; whilst the square became an obsolescent tactical formation by the mid-19th Century. In any event, any form of cavalry had been totally irrelevant on European battlefields by the last quarter of the 19th Century, as the result of vastly improved technology with regard to rifle fire and breech loading artillery. (Such was the deeply ingrained conservatism of the British Army, however, that, although Lord Roberts (then commander-in-chief) had decreed that the lance should be abolished, in a memorandum of 1903, it stealthily re-emerged in 1909 (following Roberts's retirement) and was not finally abolished until 1927)). *ed.*

(6) *Brown Bess*: Pattison is here referring to the flintlock musket. The method of ignition was as follows: A flint was fitted into the jaws of the hammer. The trigger propelled the flint forward, so that it struck an L-shaped steel plate facing the hammer. Directly beneath the plate was a pan fitted with a sliding cover activated, when the gun was fired, by the cock. (The combined steel plate and pan cover was termed the 'frizzen'). The latter action produced a safety factor; for, unless the steel plate was in position, any accidental tripping of the hammer or cock would not discharge the weapon. The pan was primed with fine powder which, when ignited by the sparks generated by the flint striking the plate, despatched a flame into the touch hole. This ignited the charge and sped the ball from the barrel. The method

of loading was common to the preceding flint mechanisms (ie the miquelet and snaphaunce), and, indeed, also applied to the succeeding percussion system. A measured charge of powder was poured down the barrel and ball rammed on top. The ball was encased in wadding in order to ensure that it fitted tightly into the smooth bore barrel.

The inventor of the true flintlock was a Frenchman named Martin Bourgeoys, who was also a sculptor, painter and maker of musical instruments, in addition to being a gunsmith and maker of crossbows. He worked during the early decades of the 17th Century, and was a member of a renowned family of gunsmiths. By 1700 every major European power had adopted the flintlock musket. It was first adopted by the French army during the 1670s, and was universally employed by the armies engaged in the War of the Spanish Succession (1701-1714). It supplanted the matchlock as the standard military arm. The flintlock eliminated the hazards and unreliability of the lighted match, avoided the expense of the wheel lock, and overcame the crudities of the earlier flint arms. For more than a century (up to circa the 1830s) it was the standard infantry arm, and thus dominated the battles of Europe, India and North America during the 18th Century.

The term 'Brown Bess' was an affectionate nickname accorded to the flintlock musket by the British soldiers of the time, probably derived from the browned or dulled barrel of the musket, combined with 'Bess'; the latter either a term of endearment or a corrupt form of the German busche ('gun'). The barrels were browned, or dulled, in order to prevent rusting and also to avoid the glare of the bright sun. Although this represented sound practice, the injunction to dull their musket barrels was frequently ignored by the soldiers; many of whom felt that the browned tubes did not accord with their scarlet coats and bright buttons (although this consideration applies more to parade ground scenarios than the battlefield).

In actual fact, the term 'Brown Bess' encompassed many different patterns. Prior to the outbreak of the wars with France in 1793, the British infantry was armed with the 'Land Pattern musket'. It was thus named in order to distinguish it from the similar 'Sea Service' musket; and was designated either as the 'Long Land Pattern' or 'Short Land Pattern', according to the length of the barrel (in the former case 46 inches and in the latter instance 42 inches, this shortening of length rendering the weapon more manoeuverable). The first fully developed and dateable specimens date from the 1720s. At the outbreak of the French Revolutionary Wars in 1793 the Board of Ordnance was confronted with an enormous dearth of muskets; in 1794 there were only 110 000 muskets with which to arm 250 000 men. As a result, an attempt was made to remedy this deficiency by importing muskets from abroad, many of a markedly inferior quality. The quality of the imported muskets improved, however, when the East India Company was persuaded by the British Government to transfer its arsenal, intended for use by the Company's troops in India, to the Ordnance. This Indian source supplied the government with over 30 000 muskets and 2 600 pistols. The East India muskets proved so efficient that from 1797 Ordnance gunsmiths were ordered to produce only 'India Pattern muskets'. These had simplified 'furniture' (ie fittings) and a 39 inch barrel. They were quicker to produce, although slightly inferior in quality to the Short Land Pattern. It remained the standard infantry weapon throughout the duration of the Napoleonic Wars; the sole modification being the introduction of a reinforced cock in 1809. Between 1804 and 1815 some 1 603 711 East India Pattern muskets were manufactured. Many were exported to allied nations (Prussia alone received 113 000). Other subsequent patterns were produced (eg the New Land Service Pattern, with a 42 inch barrel length and a special version for the light infantry, with a 39 inch barrel and backsight). These, however, enjoyed only limited use.

The musket fired a spherical lead ball weighing one ounce. Its impact inflicted a horrendous wound (as may be imagined by such a large calibre weapon; viz .75). Its greatest deficiencies were those of range and accuracy. As the barrel of the musket was smooth, and not rifled (or grooved) the ball followed a flat trajectory, a major factor in its limited range and inaccuracy. George Hanger, a somewhat eccentric but experienced officer, and himself an expert marksman, commented on this aspect of the flintlock as follows, in his work, *To all sportsmen* (1814):

> 'A soldier's musket, if not exceedingly ill-bored (as many are), will strike the figure of a man at 80 yards; it may even at a hundred; but a soldier must be very unfortunate indeed who shall be wounded by a common musket at 150 yards, provided his antagonist aims at him; and as to firing at a man at 200 yards with a common musket, you may as well fire at the moon and have the same hope of hitting your object. I do maintain and will prove that no man was ever killed at 200 yards, by a common musket, by the person who aimed at him.'

In actual combat conditions, when the smoke blanketing the battlefield would obscure targets that were moving, the effectiveness rate of musketry fired at approximately 100 yards was estimated to be 5%; declining to 2% or 3% at greater distances. It was also estimated that during the Peninsular War the British inflicted only one casualty for every 459 rounds fired.

The extremely limited range and inaccuracy of the musket shaped the tactics of the armies engaged during the 18th Century and Napoleonic Wars; pivoting upon dense volleys of musket fire and the manoeuvre of compact masses of troops, engaging one another at extremely close range (cf **Introduction - Military/ Historical Context**: *Tactics and drill*).

Pattison's deprecatory observations regarding the Brown Bess were written when the flintlock had been obsolete for some four decades. It had been superseded initially by the percussion cap (cf note (7) below). However, one should view the flintlock in correct perspective and recognize its outstanding attributes, within the context of its time. The flintlock possessed four major assets: strength, or durability; reliability; speed of loading; and the bayonet. With reference to reliability, or dependability in ignition, if the shooter took good care to see that his flint was sharp, his frizzen in good condition, the touch hole open and the priming powder fresh and dry, he had no real problems with regard to misfires. (Conversely, should the touch hole between the pan and the bore become clogged, the priming powder could flash brilliantly in the pan without detonating the charge. This phenomenon has bequeathed an expression to the English language which remains in vogue to the present day; viz 'flash in the pan', denoting a spectacular performance but leading to no result. Moreover, if the flint were dull, or the frizzen worn and greasy, the priming powder could not be ignited). Provided that the flints were replaced regularly and the powder kept dry, the flintlock musket proved to be an extremely dependable weapon. The flint was obviously a far more compact accessory than the matches upon which the musketeer had formerly relied, and which festooned his person. As a result both the equipment of the infantryman and his weapon became lighter; greatly facilitating the mobility of armies. Speed was the third most important attribute of the flintlock's performance. Loading became a very quick process during the 18th Century; especially with the advent of the paper cartridge, containing the priming powder, which became universal during the 18th Century. A military treatise of 1768 states that recruits were not to be released from practice until they were sufficiently skilled to load and fire 15 times within three-and-a-quarter minutes; ie a sustained rate of fire of one shot every 15 seconds. In the actual battle scenario this rate of fire might somewhat decelerate; but there is no truth whatever in the popular fallacy that it took minutes to prepare each shot. Admittedly four shots a minute left little time for aiming; but it bears reiteration that this was a very low priority in 18th Century warfare. The line of battle and square formation discussed at several earlier points in this work pivoted upon dense concentration of fields of fire. (Curiously, the wheel has come full cycle, for the same principle applies to modern automatic weapons, in which accuracy is virtually a nil consideration).

With regard to the flintlock musket's fourth major asset - the bayonet - this obviously extended the infantryman's capability. Probably its greatest effectiveness lay, not in personal contact (there being very few instances of bayonet charges in the Napoleonic Wars) but in the deterrent to horsemen which a hedge of bayonets presented when troops were formed in a square. According to tradition, the bayonet derived its name from its birthplace in southern France, Bayonne. Daggers from that region were called bayonets during the 16th Century, and the earliest reference to the use of daggers with firearms emanated from Bayonne during the 1640s. Initially the bayonet was a simple dagger with tapering hilts that could be driven into the gun muzzles. These plug bayonets, as they were termed, possessed serious defects. If they were rammed into the muzzle too tightly, they were difficult to remove; conversely, if they were not pushed in tightly enough they might fall from the weapon or remain in the body of the enemy. In any event, whilst the bayonet remained in place, it was impossible to fire. Nevertheless, the plug bayonet enjoyed some popularity. A few British weapons were equipped with them as early as 1663 and they were carried by the French fusilier and grenadier regiments raised in 1671. Methods were soon experimented with to improve the bayonet; especially with a view to removing the impediment to firing. First, loose rings were fastened on the hilt to loop over the barrel, but this technique did not prove successful. Eventually, at approximately the end of the 17th Century, the socket bayonet was developed and quickly adopted throughout European armies. It consisted of a sleeve which fitted over the barrel and locked in place with a stud or slot; an elbow at right angles, and a straight blade, usually triangular in section. It could not be used for cutting, but was a magnificent stabbing instrument. The appendage of the bayonet rendered the flintlock extremely versatile; for the infantrymen could now combine the functions of musketeer and pikeman.

The renowned adversary of the British Brown Bess was the French Charleville musket, model 1763, named after the Royal Armoury at Charleville (although the armouries at Maubeuge and St Etienne also produced it). It was a lighter weapon than the Brown Bess, firing a smaller calibre ball (.69) and possessing a lighter, more graceful stock. *ed.*

(7) *detonating the caps*: Pattison is referring to the percussion cap method of propelling the charge from the barrel of a musket or rifle (the former being a smooth bore weapon, whilst the latter was distinguished by the rifled groove of the barrel). Alexander John Forsyth (1768-1843), a Scottish minister, is generally credited as the inventor of the percussion method of ignition. The patent was granted on 11 April 1807. His system was based on a pivoted magazine, shaped in the form of a scent bottle, which deposited a small amount of fulminate in a channel leading to the bore, and a hammer which closed all other avenues for the flame. However, his magazine (popularly known as the 'scent bottle' because of its shape) was soon found to be inadequate. The Forsyth lock was expensive, as a result of the careful finishing required to make the magazine, and assure its safety; and the lock alone cost as much as a complete, good quality flintlock. Moreover, the fulminates were highly corrosive and the lock had to be carefully cleaned after each use. The scent bottle lock was eventually superseded by the percussion cap.

The percussion cap, of thin metal casing, was shaped somewhat like the top hat, so characteristic of the male headdress of the mid-19th Century. Within the bottom of the cavity, a small amount of fulminate of mercury or potassium chlorate was covered with a disc of tin foil and sealed with a drop of shellac to make it waterproof. In use, the cap was placed on a tube or nipple leading directly to the charge in the bore. The hammer, acting like the cock of a flintlock, struck it a sharp blow when the trigger was pulled; and the resultant explosion sent a spurt of flame into the propellant charge. The system was impervious to the elements and, providing that the charge in the barrel remained dry, a percussion cap gun could be fired even in the driving rain. The technique was obviously an advance upon the flintlock (cf note (5) above), which it had rendered obsolete and superseded by the 1840s. *ed.*

(8) *out-pickets*: These were infantry scouts who were furthest removed from their main lines, and thus closest to those of the enemy. *ed.*

(9) *commissary*: At the time of Waterloo the Commissariat (a distant ancestor of the Royal Army Service Corps) was a civilian department under the direct control of the Treasury (cf **Introduction - Military/Historical Context**: *Organization of the British Army*). It had existed since the 18th Century, and its officials wore uniforms when on active service (although not holding the king's commission). As the Commissariat was controlled by the Treasury, and its members thus not subject to

military discipline, many were inefficient and corrupt; especially as appointments were heavily subject to 'patronage' by Treasury officials. Not until 1810 were any qualifications required for the post; and these then only consisted of a minimum age of 16 with one year's clerical experience. Each infantry bridgade and cavalry regiment had attached to its establishment Assistant Commissaries, Deputies and clerks; and these were supervised by the Commissary General and his staff of Assistant and Deputies. Many of these were no more efficient than their subordinates. The Commissariat's fundamental duty was the provision of the ordinary soldier's daily ration. In the British service any form of plundering or illegal foraging was strictly forbidden; and, although it undoubtedly occurred, it entailed heavy punishment. Any supplies taken from the countryside had to be paid for (either by cash or docket), and in the vast majority of cases this was done. (Only private 'scavenging' by individuals was unpaid). The British procurement of produce was in marked contrast to the French practice of living off the land and the forcible requisition of produce. *ed.*

(10) *Geneva*: a popular term for liquor. *ed.*

(11) *cap-a-pie*: literally 'from head to foot'. The phrase is, in actual fact, an anachronism. The term relates to the mailed cavalry of the Medieval period, who were encased in chain mail, and latterly in plate armour from head to foot. The sole survivors of this practice were the breastplates of the cuirassiers and carabiniers. *ed.*

(12) *cuirassiers ... light dragoons*: Pattison is referring to the different components of the French cavalry. AT Waterloo, Napoleon's heavy cavalry comprised two regiments of carabiniers and 12 regiments of cuirassiers. His medium cavalry consisted of 10 regiments of dragoons. The French light cavalry comprised eight regiments of chasseurs and four of hussars. In addition, the Imperial Guard possessed its own cavalry. The I, II and VI corps each had its own division of light cavalry; the III, IV and V corps each had a brigade of cavalry. Further, the reserve of cavalry comprised seven divisions: two of heavy cavalry (cuirassiers and carabiniers); four medium (dragoons); and one of dismounted dragoons. The establishment of a cuirassier or carabinier regiment consisted of some 1 040 men in four squadrons (each squadron comprising two companies). A dragoon regiment had five squadrons, each of two companies (totalling some 1 200 men). (From 1812 onwards there were sometimes two dismounted squadrons in a dragoon regiment). Light cavalry regiments also had four squadrons, each of two companies. The cavalry was organized in divisions, brigades and regiments, but the basic tactical unit was esssentially the squadron. This consisted of two companies, each of two platoons (a platoon being composed of 36-40 men). A squadron formed in line, or column, by platoons. It was a comparatively simple matter for a properly drilled column to form line of battle from columns, or to reassume column formation. The charge was made at the gallop, and usually in echelons of squadrons, regiments or brigades.

Pattison delineates four main types of French cavalry; viz cuirassiers, lancers, heavy dragoons and light dragoons.

(i) *Cuirassiers*: cf **Letter I**/note (20) above.

(ii) *Lancers*: cf note (4) above. The reference to 'lancers with their gay flitting penants' relates to the penants which were tied to the shafts, close to the spear point, of the lances in order to render their appearance more awe-inspiring. This practice, which originated in the original Lithuanian lancers, was certainly decorative (if serving no other purpose).

(iii) *Dragoons*: The earliest dragoons, of the late 16th and 17th Centuries, were mounted infantry armed with a type of rifle termed the 'dragon'. (Hence their name). They were organized and trained as infantry and were mounted on horses which, generally speaking, would not have passed muster as cavalry mounts. In the manner of British mounted infantry of the Anglo-Boer War (1899-1902) they dismounted to fight. The original dragoons thus corresponded to the modern rifleman in motorized infantry or mechanized infantry battalions. They rode to battle, rather than into battle, using the speed of their horses to deploy rapidly in order to seize a position or reinforce a threatened one. The dragoons thereupon dismounted and served on foot as musketeers. Since their horses were intended purely for transport, and not as fighting platforms, the dragoons could be mounted chaeaply on lower quality horses; not requiring the heavy expensive war horse of the true cavalryman. However, there appeared to be a marked reluctance on the part of dragoons to fight in a dismounted role if they had the opportunity to fight in the saddle and the officers and men of the dragoon service increasingly sought to display their capability to fight as mounted men, to the gradual exclusion of their infantry role. Governments were not averse to the emergence of a cheaper form of cavalry; capable of taking their place in the line of battle without demanding the expensive equipment, powerful horses and higher wages of true cavalrymen. (However, inevitably, the deployment of dragoons as regular cavalrymen involved as much expense as the horse regiments that they began to supplement.

In Britain the original regiments of horse of the line cavalry (as distinct from the Household Cavalry) were designated Dragoon Guards in 1746. These were placed next in precedence to the Life Guards (formed into two regiments in 1788) and the Royal Horse Guards (the 'Blues') (the Life Guards and Royal Horse Guards constituting the Household Cavalry). The regiments of Dragoon Guards were numbered 1 - 7. The remaining six regiments of heavy cavalry were all styled 'Dragoons' (although there was, in fact, no real difference between them and the Dragoon Guards, apart from precedence. At the time of Waterloo there were five regiments of dragoons, these being numbered 1-4 and 6. [There was then no 5th Regiment of Dragoons. In fact, the number 5 was absent from both cavalry and infantry lists. The omission derived from the fate of the 5th (Royal Irish) Dragoons. It served with credit during the Irish Rebellion of 1797-1798 but unfortunately enlisted a number of recruits were disguised rebels. These planned a massacre of the officers and loyal soldiers. The plot was discovered before it could be executed, but the regiment was disbanded at Chatham in 1799, its officers and men being transferred to other corps. As a mark of official disapproval for what was interpreted as disloyalty (albeit restricted only to a segment of the corps), the number 5 remained unoccupied until a new 5th regiment was formed in the line cavalry (this being a lancer unit).]

It is, however, important to bear in mind that, although dragoons were common to both the French and British cavalry, the dragoons of the latter were not the exact equivalents of their counterparts in the Napoleonic army. Whilst the British regiments of Dragoons and Dragoon Guards constituted the heavy cavalry, the French heavy cavalry was represented by the cuirassiers and carabiniers; the latter wearing a lighter armour than the former. The reference to the French 'heavy dragoons' thus applies to these two armoured arms of the heavy cavalry.

The similarity between the French and British dragoons was emphasized by the uniforms, those of the British closely resembling the French. In 1812 peaked leather helmets with a brass comb, from which depended a horsehair mane, was introduced; replacing the former bicorn hat. The new uniform, French in style, also included a new single breasted tunic. Wellington protested at this change in the heavy cavalry's uniform in 1812; mainly on the grounds that the French style helmet could only lead to confusion in a scenario in which headdress, rather than tunic, was the most useful criterion in recognition. The new French style uniform was worn in the later phases of the Peninsular War and at Waterloo. (The 2nd Dragoons was the only regiment to escape the French style helmet, continuing to wear their traditional fur grenadier caps throughout the period).

Dragoons were frequently employed in policing duties (especially the control of riots) in the absence of a police force. This role has bequeathed to the English language the term 'dragoon', meaning to force or coerce.

(iv) *light dragoons*: The designation 'light dragoons' did not exist in the French cavalry, being a peculiar British title, referring to a light cavalry regiment. The light dragoons originated in the British Army during the late 1750s, and early 1760s, when the services of the 'light horse' began to be valued. These units were intended to maintain the 'shock' impact of the charge but in addition were theoretically capable of acting as the mounted equivalent of the light infantry; viz serving as scouts, skirmishers and the army's 'outposts' or vedetttes. These light dragoon regiments were numbered 7 and upwards. It is doubtful as to whether their training different in any real sense from that of the heavy cavalry regiments. The counterpart of the light dragoons in the French army would have been the hussars and chasseurs. As they wore the braided tunics characteristic of light cavalry regiments, they would have been identified as 'light dragoons' by Pattison.

– *Hussars*: The original hussars had been raised by the Hapbsburgs; the guardians of Christian Europe's south eastern flank against the Turks. To populate and guard these distant marches they established a broad military frontier (*Militargrenze*), and granted land to the settlers on a system of military tenure. The frontiersmen, in return for these direct grants of land from the monarchy, undertook to provide a type of militia service. Their primary role was the immediate defence of their own provinces against border raids and to support regular troops in a major war by their knowledge of local conditions. This force (the *Grenzer*) formed a frontier 'police' defending the borders from the Adriatic to Poland, and were hardy, frugal and independent. They continued in being throughout the 18th and 19th Centuries.

They included a number of German settlers, but in the main consisted of Hungarian, Rumanian or Slav communities. The nature of their contingents differed according to the terrain they inhabited. The men of the hilly or forested regions took the field as light infantry; the men of the plains deployed as light cavalry, the hussars. The term 'hussar' derives from the Hungarian word, 'husz', meaning 20, as every 20th household had to furnish a recruit for the corps. The first hussars were raised by Matthias I in 1458.

Both the hussars and light infantry possessed the main characteristics of light troops; viz the ability to operate independently or in small bands in broken country, in which they waged guerrilla warfare against the serried and disciplined ranks of the enemy's line formations.

The hussar units manifested a high esprit de corps and a powerful sense of historical continuity; combined with a strong sense of loyalty to the Austrian monarchy. The Austrian commanders were quick to recognize that these attributes could readily be exploited in conventional warfare, as well as border skirmishes; with the result that the frontier cavalry soon became absorbed into the regular forces. They were principally deployed in the conventional duties of light cavalry; viz outpost work, scouting, raids and pursuit. The success of this arm in the Habsburg service caused its adoption in the major European armies; initially as mercenary and latterly as regular regiments. Hussars were taken into regular service in France in 1702, in Prussia in 1721, and in Britain in 1805 (in the last named instance emerging from the light dragoon regiments; cf above). The association between the light dragoons and hussars is reinforced by the fact that, in 1805, the first conversions of British light dragoon regiments into hussars were effected; the regiments in question being the 7th, 10th, 15th and 18th Light Dragoons. In 1822 the 8th Light Dragoons was converted into a hussar regiment; followed by the 11th, 14th and 20th Light Dragoons during the course of the 19th Century. (The remaining light dragoon regiments were converted into lancers; cf note (5) above).

Hussars of all armies were distinguished by certain characteristic items of uniform: notably the fur trimmed jacket (or pelisse), worn over the left shoulder; and the fur busby (kalpak). The remainder of the uniform consisted of the ribbed dolman (tunic) worn by light cavalry regiments; short boots; a barrel sash worn across the waist; and a decorative sabretache (pouch suspended from the sabre scabbard). The British discarded the tall fur hussar cap in favour of the shako during the later phases of the Peninsular War. The Magyar/Croatian origins of the hussars are clearly evident in their distinctive dress. The flayed skins of wolves were worn across the shoulders by Hungarian herdsmen, and from this garment evolved the elegant pelisse.

– *Chasseurs*: These were attired in a similar manner to the hussars, and performed similar roles.

In a curious fashion the French cavalry embodied both the past and the (extremely limited) future of the British mounted arm. The cuirassiers and carabiniers looked backwards to the 'Ironsides' of Cromwell's cavalry. The hussars and lancers exemplified future developments in the British cavalry. The light cavalry was to remain more relevant and meaningful than the heavy cavalry; the latter of which had become totally obsolescent by the second half of the 19th Century. The role of the light cavalry in scouting and reconnaissance retained its significance prior to the advent of the aeroplane. *ed*.

(13) *Maitland's Guards*: ie the 1st Brigade of Guards (consisting of the 2nd and 3rd Battalions of the Grenadier Guards).

The commander of this brigade was Gen Sir Peregrine Maitland (1777-1854). He was the son of Thomas Maitland of Shrubs Hall, New Forest. On 25 June he was appointed ensign in the 1st Regiment of Foot Guards; in which regiment he became lieutenant and captain in 1794; and captain and lieutenant colonel in 1803. He commanded the 1st Brigade of Guards in course of Peninsular War and in the succeeding invasion of France. He was appointed a major general in 1814. Maitland was made a Companion of the Bath (CB) on 4 June 1815 and received the Army Gold Medal. At Waterloo, to reiterate, he commanded the 1st Brigade of Guards once again and continued to command the brigade during the occupation of Paris. He was subsequently made a Knight Commander of the Order of the Bath (KCB). Maitland was appointed a lieutenant governor of Upper Canada (1818-1828); lieutenant governor of Nova Scotia (1828-1834); and commander-in-chief of the Madras army (1836-1838). He resigned owing to disagreements with the East India Company with regard to the Company's religious policy. Maitland subsequentlly served as Governor and commander-in-chief of the Cape of Good Hope (1844-1847). The native war (known as the kaffir war) of 1846-1847 broke out during his tenure of governor. He became a full general in 1846 and was colonel successively of the 76th and 17th Regiments. He was made a Knight Grand Cross of the Order of the Bath (GCB) in 1852. Maitland died at his London residence on 30 May 1854. *ed*.

(14) *Keilmansegge's Hanoverian Brigade*: Maj Gen Count von Keilmansegge commanded the 1st Hanoverian Brigade, consisting of six battalions; cf also **Letter V**, note (15). *ed*.

LETTER IV

(1) *Lord Uxbridge*: Henry William Paget, 1st Marquis of Anglesey (1765-1854). He was the eldest son of Henry Paget, Earl of Uxbridge, who died in 1812. Born in London on 17 May 1768, he was educated at Westminster School and at Christ Church College, Oxford. In 1790 he entered Parliament as member for Carnarvon borough; and was afterwards MP for Milborne Port in 1796, 1802-1804, 1806 and 1807-1810. He served in the Staffordshire Militia, which was commanded by his father. In September 1793 he raised a regiment of infantry, the Staffordshire Volunteers, primarily recruited from his father's tenantry. This was one of 12 regiments added to the establishment of the Regular Army on the outbreak of war with Revolutionary France in 1793, becoming the 80th Regiment of Foot. He was given the temporary rank of lieutenant colonel on 12 September 1793 (at the age of only 25). Three months later he took his regiment to Guernsey and in June 1794 joined the army in Flanders, commanded by the Duke of York.

The French successes in this campaign compelled the Duke of York's force to retreat across the Rhine and re-embark for England. For a considerable part of this period Lord Paget (although a soldier of only 12 months service) was in command of a brigade. In 1795, to provide him with a permanent commission in the army, Paget was commissioned as a lieutenant in the 7th Royal Fusiliers on 11 March. Between 25 March and 15 June of this year he was promoted to the rank of lieutenant colonel. He was accorded the brevet rank of colonel on 3 May 1796 and on 6 April in the following year became lieutenant colonel of the 7th Light Dragoons.

Paget commanded the cavalry brigade (consisting of his own and three other regiments) in the expeditionary force (half English, half Russian) despatched to Holland in 1799, under the command of the Duke of York. The operations were confined to the promontory north of Amsterdam, which provided scant scope for cavalry action. Nevertheless, in the battle of Bergen (2 October) Paget fully exploited the opportunity presented to his cavalry brigade. The French commander, Vandamme, who was engaged on the sandhills by the coast, seeing that some British guns were unsupported, charged at the head of his cavalry and captured them just before nightfall; but he was charged in his turn by Paget, at the head of the 15th Light Dragoons; the guns were recovered, and Vandamme's force was pursued for almost a mile to Egmont-op-Zee. Four days afterwards, in the engagement at Kastricum, the British cavalry once again distinguished itself, taking 500 prisoner. However, the expedition proved a failure, hostilities ceased, and the force re-embarked for England.

Paget thenceforth devoted himself to his regiment (the 7th Light Dragoons), of which he became colonel on 16 May 1801, transforming the corps into one of the most efficient in the British Army. He was appointed major general on 29 April 1802 and lieutenant general on 25 April 1808. In the latter part of 1808 he was given command of the cavalry division which was sent out to join the army of Sir John Moore in Portugal. He landed at Corunna and, in spite of great difficulties generated by the extreme dearth of supplies, succeeding in joining Moore at Salamanca. At the engagement fought at Sahagun he led the 15th Light Dragoons (only 400 strong) in an attack against 600 French dragoons drawn up in line to receive him. Paget charged the enemy and routed them, taking some 167 prisoners. The retreat to Corunna commenced three days later. All involved in Moore's retreat suffered severely, but the privations endured by the cavalry mounts was especially severe and half of the horses were lost; whilst the remainder had to be destroyed when they reached Corunna, as there was no room for them in the transports. Nevertheless, the cavalry played its part well in covering the rear of the retreat. Moore wrote:

'The only part of the army which has hitherto engaged with the enemy has been the cavalry, and it is impossible for me to say too much in their praise. Our cavalry is very superior in quality to any the French have, and the right spirit has been infused in them by the example and instruction of their two leaders, Lord Paget and Brigadier-General Stewart.'
[Quoted by *Dictionary of National Biography*].

Paget saw no further service in the Peninsula. He commanded an infantry division in the Walcheren expedition of 1809 and remained on that island until 2 September of that year. Paget was unemployed for the ensuing five years. He became Earl of Uxbridge on the death of his father (13 March 1812) and was made a Knight Grand Cross of the Order of the Bath (GCB) on 2 January 1815.

A few months later, in the spring of 1815, he was ordered to Flanders and appointed to the command of the entire cavalry and horse artillery in Wellington's army; although until the morning of Waterloo the Prince of Orange retained the control of the Dutch and Belgian horse. The Duke of Wellington allocated total discretion to Uxbridge. At Waterloo, when the English left was attacked by d'Erlon's corps, at approximately 13h30, Uxbridge directed Gen Ponsonby to charge the French columns, already shattered by the fire of Picton's division. Whilst the Union Brigade (comprising the 1st, 2nd and 6th Dragoons), was dealing with the infantry, Uxbridge himself led forth Somerset's heavy brigade (consisting of the two regiments of Life Guards and Royal Horse Guards - the Household Cavalry - and 1st (King's) Dragoon Guards) against a brigade of Milhaud's cuirassiers, who were upon the left of d'Erlon's corps, and who had routed a Hanoverian battalion which was advancing to support the garrison at La Haye Sainte. Gen Shaw Kennedy states that this was

'the only fairly tested fight of cavalry during the day. It was a fair meeting of two bodies of heavy cavalry, each in perfect order.'
[Quoted by *Dictionary of National Biography*].

The French brigade, which appears to have been numerically weaker, was completely defeated; but the English horsemen swept on despite all the efforts of Uxbridge to halt the cavalry by voice or trumpet. He then went back to bring up the second line, in order to cover the retirement of the first, but the latter was too far to the rear. The Household Brigade, like the Union Brigade, whilst brilliantly successful, lost almost half its strength; mainly as a result of having to defend itself, when scattered and exhausted, against French cavalry. He received a wound in the knee from one of the last shots fired in the battle, resulting in the amputation of the leg.

In recognition of his services at Waterloo, Uxbridge was created Marquis of Anglesey on 4 July 1815. He was subsequently made a Knight of the Garter (KG) in 1818 and acted as lord high steward at the coronation of King George IV in 1821. Anglesey was appointed a general of the army when Canning formed his short-lived ministry in 1827, and when Wellington resigned his posts of master-general of the ordnance and commander-in-chief, Anglesey succeeded him in the former post, which bestowed a seat in the cabinet. He served as master general of the ordnance between 30 April 1827 and 29 January 1828. He then succeeded Lord Wellesley as Lord Lieutenant of Ireland (27 February 1828). However, his tenure as lord lieutenant coincided with an intense agitation for Catholic emancipation, and the resultant tension eventually led to Anglesey's recall, in March 1829. He served for a second time as Lord Lieutenant of Ireland, during the period 1830-1833. When Lord John Russell formed his ministry in 1846, Anglesey became for the second time master general of the ordnance (8 July), and continued in this post until 27 February 1852. He was appointed Field Marshal on 9 November 1846 and Lord Lieutenant of Staffordshire on 9 November 1849; as well as having been Lord Lieutenant of Anglesey since 21 April 1812. After holding the colonelcy of the 7th Light Dragoons for more than 40 years, he exchanged it for that of the Royal Horse Guards on 20 December 1842. He died at the age of 86, on 24 April 1854. His portrait was painted by Sir Thomas Lawrence. *ed.*

(2) *heavy Brigade*: ie the brigade of heavy cavalry, consisting of the Household Cavalry (the two regiments of Life Guards and Royal Horse Guards) and the 1st (King's) Dragoon Guards). This brigade was officially known as the Household Brigade. *ed.*

(3) *fractured shells and cannon-balls*: Pattison is referring to two types of ammunition employed by the artillery of the period; viz the rounds known as 'common shell' and 'round shot'. Common shell is referred to as 'fractured shells' and 'round shot' is denoted by the term 'cannon balls'.

Common shell formed the main ammunition for howitzers. This consisted of a hollow iron ball containing a fuse and bursting charge. The fuse was ignited by the explosion of the charge that propelled the shell. If the detonation was faultless, the fuse's ignition would cause the bursting charge to explode after the shell had landed. The fuse had to be trimmed by the gunner to sufficient length so that the charge would burst among the enemy ranks. It was intended that the exploding shell would fragment upon impact (hence 'fractured shells'). To achieve this desired result it was necessary that the shell should have thin walls and convey a large bursting charge, so that the casing broke up into numerous fragments; these fragments then being propelled with a lethal velocity. As a result, the shell was too large and too fragile to be fired from a field gun. However, this problem was overcome as the shell did not demand the high muzzle velocity demanded by round shot (cf below); and consequently a lighter piece, with a shorter barrel, could accommodate the shell. The piece in question was the 5½ inch howitzer, which accordingly became the standard field piece for firing shell. It could accommodate a 24 lb ball; whilst its light construction and short barrel (only 33 inches compared with 72 inches for the light 6 pr, 96 inches for the heavy 6 pr, and 84 inches for the 9 pr) enabled the howitzer to keep pace even with the cavalry. Thus, as field guns could not fire shells (being restricted to round shot and case shot), every battery included a howitzer. Experiments sought to develop all-howitzer batteries, but these proved to be too specialized to be adapted to the dispersed positioning in which Wellington generally deployed his guns. The common shell was effective at ranges between 300 and 1 000 yards, but only if the target was reasonably stationery.

An especially effective variation of common shell was shrapnel. This was named after its inventor, Lt Gen Sir Henry Shrapnel. His ammunition was initially termed 'spherical case' but later became popularly named shrapnel. Its inventor sought to render field guns more effective at ranges above 300 yards by facilitating their use of shell. Shrapnel resembled common shell, but the casing was thinner and the shell was filled with gunpowder and musket balls. With careful fuse trimming this payload could be timed to burst above the heads of the enemy, when it rained down like case shot. (Hence its official designation of 'spherical case'). Shrapnel was issued to all field guns and was first employed in 1804. Technical problems, however, prevented its being fully effective at that time. The principal problem was imperfect timing of the fuse, which caused Wellington to doubt its efficacy after Busaco (1810), when he noted that the shrapnel did not cause formidable wounds. (The French general, Simon, had pieces extracted from his face like duck shot). Nevertheless, when correctly timed, shrapnel proved both effective and demoralizing to the enemy. It represented up to 15% of gun ammunition, and up to 50% of howitzer ammunition.

Round shot was deployed for striking moving men and demolishing targets. Entire files of men could be swept away. When fired, a round shot fell steadily to earth until it touched ground (providing that it did not strike an absorbent surface, such as swampy earth). It then bounced from this initial impact ('first graze') and the ricochet propelled it to its 'second graze'; whereupon it bounced a second time. Anything in its path would be struck down. Rolling along the ground in the manner of a cricket ball, limbs would be lopped off any man who came in contact with its path. Due to the gun's low trajectory, virtually any object between the cannon's muzzle and the final resting place of the shot would be struck. Although all cannon possessed similar muzzle velocities, the heavier the shot the greater the velocity when the target was struck. Thus, the heavy round shot was considerably more effective than its light counterpart. Hence, a 6 lb shot was 50% more effective than a 3 lb shot.

The third main type of ammunition employed in this period was grape shot (cf **Letter I**/note 30 (f)).

(4) My first acquaintance with Dr. Pagan, F.R.C.S., Edinburgh, dates from my return from India with the head-quarters of the 33rd, the Duke of Wellington's Own Regiment, in 1812. I found him then an Ensign with the depot of the

regiment at Hull, and from that period, now more than fifty years, our esteem and affection for one another knew no diminution. Dr. Pagan was a brave man and a distinguished officer, exhibiting at all times that coolness and presence of mind which alone enables a soldier to perform his duty under *fire* [author's italics]. In 1821 the 33rd, having been ordered to Jamaica, Dr Pagan with a number of officers retired on half-pay. After this he turned his attention to the study of medicine, and his success in this profession is well known to many of the citizens of Edinburgh, where he attained to a large practice, and died esteemed and deeply regretted by a large circle. *auth*.

(5) In order to illustrate what I have said, let me give two interesting anecdotes regarding two brave men, both royal personages. It is recorded of that great warrior, Charles XII of Sweden (a), that the first time he was in action, being then only a boy of fifteen years, on hearing the whistling of musketry, he inquired of his staff whence the sound proceeded, and on being informed of the cause, he exclaimed with exulting voice, 'I like it! It shall be my music henceforth'. I state this interesting historical fact from the affinity it bears to a similar occurrence that happened to another illustrious personage, in whose company I had the honour to be in action; I refer to H.R.H. the Duke of Clarence (b), who afterwards became William IV of England. Old people will recollect, after the revolution in Holland (c) that in 1814 an attempt was made by the British Army to burn the French shipping at Antwerp. This attempt would no doubt have succeeded but for the genius of Carnot (d), that distinguished Engineer and French general, who, in order to save the fleet, moored the ships at relative distances, and, shutting down the hatches, wheeled soil so as to form conical figures on their decks, covered these figures with Beunos Ayres bullocks' hides, so that, from the spiral character of the protection and the elasticity of the hides, when our shells reached their destination they rebounded into the Scheldt. Preparatory to erecting our batteries, we must needs eject the French from Merxem, and drive them into Antwerp. The attack to accomplish this was led by Colonel Brown, an old Peninsular officer. My position was next to the Grenadiers, the leading company of attack. On advancing, and when the music which Charles XII loved so well commenced its strains, I was struck with seeing a gentleman, attired in a blue coat with gilt buttons and a light coloured cashmere waistcoat, walking by the side of Colonel Brown's horse, and conversing in a very animated manner with him, and still more astonished to discover this individual to be no less a personage than H.R.H. the Duke of Clarence.

Old as I now am, I still look back to this occurrence as a cherished moment in my military career, beholding as I then did a member of our Royal Family and the heir to the throne of England giving such a noble example of intrepidity and encouragement to the British Army by this voluntary exposure of himself to such imminent danger. But bravery has always been a characteristic of our Royal Family, and the father of our beloved Lady Queen (d) was much distinguished for this virtue. [William IV was the uncle, not the father, of Queen Victoria. ed]. I may here notice that the only time I was ever hit in all my fighting was during this little affair - a spent musket ball grazed my right thigh, but the wound being of a very slight nature I peremptorily refused that Thain the adjutant should return me. *auth.*

Editorial observations on above footnote

(a) *Charles XII*: King of Sweden (1682-1718). He ascended to the throne in 1697, at the age of only 15. He was an absolute monarch, who defended his country for 18 years in the great Northern War (1700-1721), fought against Peter the Great's Russia. Charles launched a disastrous invasion of Russia (1707-1709), resulting in the total collapse of the Swedish armies and the eclipse of Sweden's status as a great power.

In 1700 the Great Northern War was initiated when a coalition of powers - Russia, Denmark and Saxony - attacked Sweden. The speedy success hoped for by the three allied powers did not materialize, whilst rumours of rebellion against the absolutist monarchy, in the event of war, proved groundless. The early campaigns in the war involved: the descent on Zealand (August 1700) which forced Denmark out of the war; the battle of Narva (November 1700) which drove the Russians away from the Swedish trans-Baltic provinces; and the crossing of the western Dvina river (1701), which scattered the troops of Augustus II (Elector of Saxony and ruler of Poland). Charles decided to fight Augustus II and transform Poland from a divided country - where Augustus experienced opposition to his rule - into an ally and a base for the envisaged final campaign against Russia. The transformation was to be effected by dethroning Augustus and substituting a Polish-born king willing to co-operate with the Swedes. Swedish troops accordingly invaded Poland and Augustus was eventually forced to accede to the enthronement of Stanislaw Leczcynski as the elected king of Poland by a Swedish invasion of Saxony in September 1706.

However, the Swedish involvement in Poland had been advantageously exploited by Peter I, Tsar of Russia, who had taken the opportunity afforded by Charles's distraction in Poland to train his army and navy on modern European foundations; and to undertake a piecemeal conquest of the Swedish east Baltic provinces. Charles's troops left Saxony to invade Russia in the late Autumn of 1707. The Swedish army won the battle of Holowczyn in July 1708; but Russian scorched earth tactics forced Charles to abandon his route to Moscow, and turn instead into the Ukraine. Thereafter, the Russians disrupted the Swedish lines of communication; and by the summer of 1709 Charles had no choice between the two alternatives of accepting battle with the Russians or withdrawing once more into Poland. Although wounded in the foot and unable to lead his army in person, Charles chose battle and attacked the Russian fortified camp at Poltava on 8 July (modern calendar dating) 1709. The attack proved to be a disastrous failure and three days later the bulk of the Swedish army surrendered to the Russians at Perevolochna. Charles at that point in time was already en route to Turkish-held territory, where he hoped to find allies.

Charles spent five years in the Ottoman Empire (1709-1714). Turkey's desire to reconquer Azov from Peter the Great augured well for Charles XII, but such hopes proved unavailing; as the Swedish army never arrived. Charles became the object of Ottoman intrigues and, in February 1713, had to fight a regular battle in order to avoid his capture and deliverance to Augustus of Saxony (now restored in Poland). The determination of the anti-French alliance in the War of the Spanish Succession (1701-1714) to prevent Sweden from using its bases in Germany to attack its enemies further restricted Charles XII's freedom during these years; as also did the closing of the Turkish-Habsburg frontiers due to plague. The Swedish Council, virtually in charge of affairs at home during his absence, was preoccupied with Danish threats to Sweden. The administrative and financial reforms that Charles promulgated from Turkey in order to distribute the burden of the war more equably, and to increase the nation's resources and efficiency, were largely sabotaged and put into effect only after his return to Swedish Pomerania in November 1714 (having ridden incognito through Habsburg and German territory in 14 days and nights).

He was shot dead in the course of the siege of Frederikshald (Halden), at an early stage in the invasion of Norway, on 11 December 1718. ed.

(b) *Duke of Clarence*: HRH the Duke of Clarence (1765-1837), later King William IV, who reigned during the period 1830-1837. He was the third son of King George III and Queen Charlotte. At the age of 13 he was entered as a midshipman on board the *Prince George*, a 98-gun ship. In 1786 he was appointed captain of the *Pegasus*, and in 1787 sailed for the West Indies as commander of the frigate, *Andromeda*. He was appointed a rear admiral in 1790. On 20 May 1789 he was created Duke of Clarence and St Andrews, and Earl of Munster; and on 8 June in the following year took his seat in the House of Lords. In 1811 he was appointed Admiral of the Fleet, and in 1814 conveyed Louis XVIII of France to his restored kingdom. During the earlier part of the same year he was present, as an observer, in the operations before Antwerp, in which he distinguished himself by his coolness and courage. [This is the episode referred to in Pattison's footnote in which the Duke of Clarence is paired - somewhat incongruously - with Charles XII of Sweden].

A marriage was negotiated for him with the Princess Adelaide Louisa, of the house of Saxe-Coburg Meiningen, and they were married at Kew in 1818; shortly afterwards proceeding to reside in Hanover. The duchess had two daughters, both of whom died almost immediately (and thereby paved the way for the accession of Queen Victoria in 1837). On the death of his elder brother, the Duke of York, in 1827, he became the heir-presumptive to the English throne. He was appointed lord high admiral on 17 April 1827. His conduct in this office was eccentric, and after much friction with the lords of the admiralty resigned his office on 11 August 1828. At the death of George IV the Duke of Clarence succeeded to the throne on 26 June 1830, emerging from a position of comparative obscurity.

The major event in William IV's reign was, of course, the passage of the Parliamentary Reform Bill of 1832. Initially, he was favourable to Parliamentary reform, but the deposition of Charles X in France in 1830, by a revolutionary movement, entrenched his conservatism. In the crisis of May 1832, when the House of Lords was preparing to reject the bill for a third time, he would not consent to create new pro-Reform Bill peers (who would thus block the Lords' rejection of the Bill) and allowed the Grey ministry to resign. However, the failure of Wellington to form a ministry convinced him that the feeling of the nation was emphatically in favour of reform. Accordingly, he used his personal intercession with the peers to induce them to consent to the bill; and was even prepared to 'swamp' the House of Lords with new peers if his advice were rejected. The bill, however, was carried, and followed by the other reforming statutes which have made William IV's short reign an eventful period in English history. The king liked neither the Whig ministers nor their policy; and on 15 November 1834 exercised his prerogative and suddenly dismissed Lord Melbourne and his ministers. However, the succeeding ministry under Peel was hopelessly weak, and in the April of 1835 the King found it expedient to recall Lord Melbourne and his ministers.

William IV, although not greatly distinguished in terms of either talent or character (being chiefly memorable for bequeathing the eponym 'Silly Billy' to the English language) was a kindly, good natured man. In his *History of England from 1815* (1879), the author, S Walpole, commented: 'He would have passed in private life for a good natured sailor.'

(c) *revolution in Holland*: Pattison is referring to the rebellion against French rule and the extirpation of the Napoleonic forces, which commenced in late 1813.

(d) *father of our beloved Lady Queen*: Pattison is mistaken on this point. William IV was not the father, but the uncle, of Queen Victoria. Victoria was the only child of Edward, Duke of Kent (the fourth son of George III) and Princess Louisa Victoria of Saxe-Coburg.

(e) *Carnot*: Carnot, Lazare. His full name was Lazare-Nicolas-Marguerite Carnot (1753-1823). He was a French statesman, military engineer and administrator in successive governments of the French Revolution. As a leading member of the committees of General Defence and Public Safety, and of the Directory (1793-1797) he helped to mobilize the revolutionary armed forces and materiel. He withdrew from public life in 1807 but the allied invasion of 1814 forced him out of retirement. Napoleon appointed him governor of Antwerp, and this is the post that he occupied when Pattison speaks of him. Carnot remained in this post until after the fall of the Empire. He lent his support to Louis XVIII at the time of the restoration of the Bourbons, but in July 1814 published his *Memoire au roi en juillet 1814*, in which he denounced the excesses of the reaction under the Bourbon king. During the Hundred Days, in which Napoleon sought to re-establish his power, Carnot served as minister of the interior. After Napoleon's defeat at Waterloo, Carnot vainly encouraged the former emperor to continue his resistance. The Second Restoration marked the end of Carnot's political career. In July 1815 he was exiled from France and settled in Warsaw in January 1816. In August 1816 he left Warsaw for Magdeburg in Germany, where he died in 1823.

LETTER V

(1) *old Colonel*: The Duke of Wellington had been Officer Commanding the 33rd Regiment during the period 1793-1806; and subsequently colonel (1806-1813); cf **Letter 1**/note (13). *ed*.

(2) *French rifles*: The term 'rifles' is a misnomer within this context. Neither the French line infantrymen nor the skirmishers were armed with rifles (in contrast with the use of this weapon by the British and allied rifle corps; cf **Introduction - Military/Historical Context**: *Organization of the British Infantry*). The French army universally employed the Charleville musket, which fired a lighter calibre ball (.69 as opposed to the British .75) and was generally lighter in weight; cf **Letter III**/note (6). The principal distinction between the rifle and musket lay, not in the method of ignition, ammunition or loading (identical in all instances) but in the grooving of the barrel with regard to the rifle; which despatched the ball in a spinning trajectory, facilitating far greater range and accuracy. *ed*.

(3) *rifle practice ... proficiency*: Pattison is referring to the enormous enhancement in the power of small arms; in terms of rate of fire, range and accurancy. Important landmarks in these developments since Waterloo were:

– The advent of the percussion cap system (cf **Letter III**/note (7)). This implied a self-ignition system for detonating the charge; thereby dispensing with the need for flints and the application of a spark. The most renowned percussion rifle employed by the British was the Enfield rifle of 1851, and the legendary pattern 1853.

– The invention of the cylindro-conical projectile with a hollow base. The loose fitting projectile was self-sealing in so far as the lead was forced outwards and into the rifled grooves by the force of the explosion. Two notable inventors in this regard were French army officers; Capts Devigne and Minie (the latter of whom bequeathed his name to the renowned Minie ball). This development, which had been refined by the 1850s, automatically implied the total obsolescence of the smooth bore musket and the complete, unchallenged ascendancy of the rifle. For henceforth the rifle could be loaded with a speed equal to that of the musket. (A major disadvantage of the British Baker rifle - employed during the Napoleonic Wars - had been the far slower rate of loading vis-a-vis the 'Brown Bess'. This was due to the additional pressure and time required to ensure that the ball fitted tightly into the rifled bore. If this were not effected, the ball would follow a widely careering trajectory and accuracy would be sacrificed in the interests of speed of loading). Henceforth, all infantrymen could attain hitherto unprecedented feats of marksmanship at ranges totally denied to the musket (especially with the advent of the telescopic sight, which emerged during the American Civil War of 1861-1865). At this point in time - the 1850s - the loading was still directed from the muzzle, the ball rammed home with the ramrod, and the load still depended upon powder for its discharge.

– The next major phase was the development of the combustible cartridge, combined with the firing pin. The system operated on the principle of a percussion compound that was lodged at the base of the bullet, the priming compound being detonated by the firing pin, which passed straight through the powder charge. The combustible cartridge was in every sense a self-contained fixed round, in the sense of a modern cartridge. It was invented by Johann von Dreyse. In 1837 he developed a breech loading rifle which incorporated his needle gun principle. His weapon became officially designated the needle gun, and was officially adopted into the Prussian army in 1848. The rifle was instrumental in the Prussian defeat of the Danes in 1864 and the rout of the Austrian forces in 1866.

– A major landmark in the development of the breech loading mechanism was the American Sharps rifle, the patent for which was granted in 1848. Invented by Christian Sharps, it had a simple but strong mechanism; known as the falling breechblock. The trigger guard acted as a lever, and when this was pulled down the block was lowered, exposing the chamber for the insertion of the cartridge. It fired a .52 calibre cartridge. (The term 'sharpshooter' is an adaptation of 'Sharps Shooter', a famed regiment led by Col Berdan which performed prodigious feats of marksmanship with the Sharps rifle during the American Civil War). The hinged breechblock system was adopted by the Spencer carbine, a .52 calibre weapon also employed during the American Civil War. The trigger guard was depressed to eject spent cartridges and, when closed, fed a fresh round into the breech from a magazine or tube contained within the butt. It was followed by the Henry rifle (a 16-shot weapon) and finally, in 1866, by the famed Winchester repeating rifle (the Model 73 being the most renowned of these weapons). Whilst the Sharps rifle operated on the percussion cap principle, its successors adopted the rimfire cartridge (ie a copper or brass case containing bullet and powder, the base of which was covered with a fulminate). The British adopted the Snider-Enfield rifle, based on the hinged breechblock, in 1865. This was the weapon of the British infantryman when Pattison's letters were published. It was succeeded in 1871 by the Martini-Henry rifle which, until the advent of smokeless powder and the bolt action rifle during the 1880s, was the British infantryman's main long arm.

When Pattison compiled his memoirs, therefore, the Brown Bess of Waterloo had been replaced by the breech loading rifle firing self-contained metallic cartridges. *ed.*

(4) *dress of officers ... private soldier.* The uniform of infantry officers had undergone a marked transformation between the battle of Waterloo and the publication of Pattison's memoirs over half a century later.

At the time of Waterloo the infantry officers' uniform (scarlet rather than red, the latter being the colour of other ranks' coats), was distinguished by long skirts at the rear and epaulettes. (This conformed to the *Regulations* of 1797). (Light infantry officers, however, wore short skirts in the manner of other ranks). During the period 1855-1867 epaulettes were abolished; being replaced by a crimson silk twisted cord (on the left shoulder only, to retain the sash on the right shoulder, which was transferred from the waist). In 1867 the shell jacket and double breasted blue frock were abolished. These were replaced by a dark blue patrol jacket, fastened with loops and olivets, and distinguished by a rounded collar. It was in these garments that officers fought the majority of colonial campaigns (the 'small wars') during the final quarter of the 19th Century. (Today this patrol jacket forms part of the officer's 'undress uniform'; ie the dress worn on semi-formal occasions, such as mess nights (where it forms an alternative to mess dress). It is thus apparent that, during Pattison's lifetime, the uniforms of the officers were sharply distinguished from those of other ranks; viz by the long skirts and epaulettes of the Napleonic period, and the blue patrol jacket after 1867; this jacket being rifle green in the case of officers serving in the rifle corps.

Pattison's observations relate to the escort of the Colours, and his comments communicate a curiously prophetic note; in so far as the transformation of tactics occasioned by the advances in military technology resulted in the abandonment of the carrying of Colours into battle (cf note (5) below). This prophetic note also applies to the Western Front of World War I (1914-1918). For in that conflict the extreme vulnerability of infantry officers to snipers occasioned the former to eradicate the distinctions between their uniforms and equipment and those of the rank-and-file (ie riding boots, Sam Browne belts, revolvers) and to transfer their rank insignia from sleeve cuffs to shoulders.

Underlying Pattison's observations is a sensitivity to the need for camouflage, in the light of the revolution in weapons technology that had occurred since Waterloo. In this respect, Pattison's remarks anticipated the developments of the succeeding decade. Khaki (the Persian word for 'dust' had first been introduced into British Army uniform during the Indian Mutiny of 1857-1858. Clothing in this colour - usually of a greyish hue as opposed to the greenish brown now associated with it - was widely adopted during its operations. Despite its popularity, khaki was abandoned after the Mutiny and the traditional uniform colours - red and rifle green - were resumed. Thus, in the First South African War of 1880-1881 and the Egyptian campaign of 1882, the home service undress uniform (red or rifle green) were worn with white foreign service helmets (the latter usually dyed). The red serge uniform was worn on the battlefield for the very last time in the Sudan, at the battle of Ginniss (1885). Overseas experience in India and the Sudan had proved the advantage of khaki. Khaki drill uniforms were adopted in India in 1885 and in 1896 an all-khaki uniform of cotton drill was approved for all foreign service. This was first worn in action in the Sudan campaign of 1897-1898 and one year later it was worn on an even wider scale in the South African war. The Anglo-Boer War of 1899-1902 was the first major conflict in which a substantial British field army was entirely clothed in khaki. The lessons of the war relegated to full dress (ie that worn for ceremonial purposes) the rifle green and scarlet formerly worn in battle. ed.

(5) *standard bearers of the regiments*: The extremely hazardous nature of the role performed by the escort to the Colours has been commented upon in an earlier note; cf **Letter I**/note (22) above.

In actual fact, Pattison is revealing an instinctive grasp of the radically transformed character of warfare at the time that his memoirs were compiled, in relation to his own experience of warfare. The advent of breech loading rifles and rifled artillery had rendered the dense tactical formations (column, line and square) characteristic of Waterloo clearly obsolescent by the final quarter of the 19th Century. As such, the role of Colours on the battlefield, functioning as a rallying point, was clearly anachronistic by 1870. In point of fact, the battle of Laing's Nek (1881), which occurred during the First South African War of Independence of 1880-1881, proved to be the very last occasion on which Colours were carried into battle. *ed*.

(6) *Canova*: Antonio Canova (1757-1822). He was an Italian sculptor who was a foremost figure in the neo-classical school of the late 18th and early decades of the 19th Centuries. The son of a stonemason, he established his own studio in Venice in 1775. In 1779 he sculpted *Daedalus and Icarus*, which had been commissioned by Pisani, procurator of Venice. It was Canova's first important work. Somewhat roccoco in style, the figures were considered to be so realistic that the sculptor was accused of making plaster casts from live models.

Canova visited Rome in 1779 and 1780. In 1781 he again visited Rome, where he commenced his residence in that city; spending most of the remainder of his life there. In the ensuing decade he acquired the reputation of being the most technically accomplisheed neo-classical sculptor in Europe. His bent towards neoclassicism (an aesthetic based on classical Greek precepts) was fully developed following his contact with leading artists of the period. These included Johann Winckelmann and Anton Mengs (both German expatriates and the leading apostles of German classicism); and the Scottish painter-dealer George Hamilton. Under the influence of these figures Canova strove to synthesize his own tendencies towards naturalism with the strict canons of classical art. He also gained Papal patrongage. In 1783 Canova received an important commission to sculpt the tomb of Pope Clement XIV in the Roman church of SS Apostoli. When displayed in 1787 crowds flocked to see it. The same year he was commissioned to execute a tomb in St Peter's for Pope Clement XIII. Completed in 1792, its general treatment reveals a more developed understanding of the classical aesthetic of antiquity than his monument to Clement XIV. Subsequent tombs were increasingly neo-classical in style. Other works of this 'Roman' period included the *Cupid and Psyche* and *Hebe*.

In 1802, at the instigation of the Pope, he accepted Napoleon's invitation to reside in Paris, where he became court sculptor and considerably influenced French art. Some of his most expressive and ambitious works of this period included *Perseus with Medusa's head* (1801) and the *Pugilists* (1802). In 1806 Joseph Bonaparte (then king of Sicily) commissioned an equestrian statue of Napoleon. In circa 1807 Canova completed one of his most renowned works; a sculpture which depicts Napoleon's sister, Pauline Borghese, reclining almost nude on a couch as 'Venus Victrix'. The fusion of classical art and contemporary portrait embodies the cold, somewhat inhuman idealism that is characteristic of his work. In 1811, Canova completed two colossal statues of Napoleon, in which the Emperor is presented as a heroic, classical nude.

Canova was appointed inspector general of fine arts and antiquities of the Papal state in 1805. He was also appointed president of the Accademia di S Luca in Rome in 1810 (a position that he was to hold for life). After having visited Paris to organize the return of art treasures plundered by the French, he visited London in 1815 to give his opinion on the Elgin marbles. The success of his mission in Paris led to his being accorded the title of Marquis of Ischia by the Pope. Whilst Canova was in London the Prince Regent (later George IV) commissioned a life size group of *Venus and Mars*. His other works of this late period included the Stuart monument in St Peters (1819) and an idealized statue of George Washington in Roman costume (1820) (destroyed by fire in 1830).

Canova was as important in the development of the neoclassical style in sculpture as was Jacques-Louis David in the sphere of painting. That aesthetic sought to substitute moral grandeur and classical sobriety for roccoco 'flippancy'. Canova's domination of European sculpture at the end of the 18th and dawn of the 19th Centuries is reflected in countless eulogies in memoirs, letters, poems and newspapers. 'Sublime', 'superb' and 'marvellous' are adjectives that recur in descriptions of Canova's work during his lifetime. However, his reputation as a sculptor declined considerably during the course of the 19th Century. *ed.*

(7) *Foy*: Maximilian Sebastien Foy (1777-1825). Foy served in the Peninsular War under Junot, Soult and Massena. He received his 15th wound on the field of Waterloo, where he commanded the 9th Division within Reille's II Corps. Subsequently he became a prominent member of the Chamber of Deputies. In 1827 his widow published *Histoire de la guerre de la Peninsule* on the basis of Foy's papers. *ed.*

(8) *Donzelot*: General Francis Xavier Donzelot, Comte (1764 -1843). He became a soldier in 1783, and was first commissioned in the 21st Cavalry in 1792. He fought at Neerwinden; and between 1793 and 1797 saw much service on the Rhine in various staff appointments. In 1798 he was transferred to the Army of the Orient and served on Desaix's staff, fighting in many engagements in Egypt. He recaptured Cairo from the rebels in April 1800 and was confirmed as *general de brigade* in March 1801. He unwillingly ratified the surrender of Cairo to the British on 27 June 1801. After his eventual return to France he held a number of staff posts, was promoted to *general de division* on 6 December 1807, and was made a Baron of the Empire in 1808. This was followed by service in Corfu and the Ionian Islands, ending in 1814 when he surrendered the former to the British. In 1815 he joined D'Erlon's I Corps and fought as a divisional commander (2nd Division) at Waterloo. Although relieved of duty in August 1815, he was eventually made governor of Martinique in August 1817, a post he held until 1828. He finally retired in 1832. *ed.*

(9) *Byng's Guards*: Pattison is referring to the 2nd Brigade of the 1st (Guards) Division. The brigade was commanded by Gen Sir John Byng, Earl of Strafford (1772-1860). He was the son of Maj George Byng of Wrotham Park Middlesex, the MP for that county, and grandson of Admiral Sir George Byng, 1st Viscount

Torrington. Sir John Byng was born in 1772, and entered the army as an ensign in the 33rd Regiment on 30 September 1793; being promoted to lieutenant on 1 December 1793 and captain on 24 May 1794. Accompanying the 33rd Regiment (then commanded by Sir Arthur Wellesley, the future Duke of Wellington), Byng served in the disastrous campaign in Flanders of 1793-1795; being wounded in a skirmish in the course of that campaign. In 1797 he was appointed aide-de-camp to Gen Vyse, then commanding the southern district of Ireland; and was heavily involved in the suppression of the Irish rebellion of 1798, in the course of which he was wounded. In 1800 he was appointed lieutenant colonel of the 29th Regiment, and in 1804 he exchanged into the 3rd Regiment of Foot Guards. He served with the latter regiment in Hanover (1805), Copenhagen (1807) and in the Walcheren expedition of 1809. In 1810 he was promoted to colonel and in 1811 ordered to join Wellington's army in Portugal. Shortly after Byng's arrival in Portugal in September 1811 he was appointed to the command of a brigade in the 2nd Division, commanded by Gen Hill; retaining this command until the end of the Peninsular War. At the conclusion of the war he was made a Knight Commander of the Order of the Bath (KCB). Byng commanded the 2nd Brigade of the 1st (Guards) Division under Gen Cooke at Waterloo; consisting of the 2nd Battalion of the 2nd Regiment of Foot Guards (Coldstream Guards) and the 2nd Battalion of the 3rd Regiment of Foot Guards (Scots Guards). For his services at Waterloo he was made a Knight of the Thistle of Scotland (KT), a Knight of Maria Theresa (Austria) and a Knight of St George (Russia). Following the battle his brigade formed part of the army of occupation.

Byng saw no more active service. In 1819 he received the command of the northern district. He was appointed colonel of the York Infantry Volunteers (1815-1816); of the 10th West India Regiment (1816-1819); and of the 2nd West India Regiment (1822). In 1825 he was promoted to lieutenant general and in 1828 received the colonelcy of the 29th Regiment. Byng became commander-in-chief of the forces in Ireland in 1828 and was sworn a privy councillor of that kingdom. In 1832 he was appointed governor of Londonderry and Cudmore, but resigned his Irish command in 1831 to enter the House of Commons as MP for Poole. As one of the very few distinguished generals who supported the Reform Bill of 1832 he was regarded with especial favour by Lord Melbourne, who created him Baron Strafford of Harmondsworth, county Middlesex (1835). His elder son held office under Lord Melbourne and Lord Russell, and Gen Byng was elevated to the Earldom of Strafford and Viscount Enfield in 1849. He was made a Knight Grand Cross of the Order of the Bath (GCB) in 1828 and a Knight Grand Cross of the Order of Hanover (GCH) in 1831. Byng was promoted to full general in 1841 and in 1850 succeeded the Duke of Cambridge as colonel of the Coldstream Guards. In 1855 he was appointed a field marshal and on 3 June 1860 died at his residence in London. *ed.*

(10) *Lord Hill's division*: Rowland Hill, 1st Viscount Hill, general (1772-1842). He was the son of John Hill, later 3rd Baronet of Hawkstone, Shropshire. On 21 July 1790 he was appointed an ensign in the 38th (Staffordshire) Regiment of Foot, then

based in Ireland. Hill subsequently transferred to the 86th (Royal County Down) Regiment of Foot. Thomas Graham, Lord Lynedoch, was favourably impressed by Hill, and obtained a majority for him in the newly raised corps titled the Perthshire Volunteers (later the 90th Foot). Hill was appointed a major in the 90th Foot on 10 February and lieutenant colonel on 13 May 1794. He accompanied his regiment to Gibraltar and served in its garrison during the period 1796-1798, and in the capture of Minorca in 1798. He later commanded the regiment in the expedition to Egypt in 1801. Hill was incapacitated by a serious wound sustained in the course of these operations, but rejoined the 90th Regiment at El Hamed on 13 April and commanded the regiment in the advance upon, and surrender of, Cairo; as well as in the siege and capitulation of Alexandria. After its return home, the regiment narrowly avoided disbandment; its escape being due to the renewed threats of war with France.

Under his command, the 90th Regiment had emerged as a particularly efficient corps. His impress upon the regiment had included a separate mess for the sergeants (then a novelty) and a regimental school. He was promoted to brigadier general in 1803 and to major general on 30 October 1805. Hill commanded a brigade in the Hanover expedition of December 1805.

In 1808 he was given command of a brigade in the force despatched to Portugal under Lt Gen Sir Arthur Wellesley, and served at Rolica and Vimeiro. When Wellesley returned home Hill remained in Portugal. He commanded a brigade in the division under the Hon John Hope during Moore's campaign in Spain. His brigade (comprising reformed battalions of the 1st (Royal Scots), 5th, 14th and 32nd Regiments) was the last to embark at Corunna. The people of Plymouth presented Hill with an address in recognition of his active efforts on behalf of his own and other brigades disembarked from that port. After Wellesley had been reappointed to the command of the British troops in the Iberian Peninsula, Hill commanded a brigade in the operations against Oporto, which drove Soult from Portugal. When Gen Edward Paget (the brother of Lord Henry Paget, Lord Uxbridge) was wounded, Hill succeeded to the command of the 2nd Division, which he led at the battle of Talavera (27-28 July 1809). In January 1810 Hill commanded a detached corps (including his own division) and was entrusted with the defence of the Portuguese frontier between Guadiana and the Tagus. Hill was promoted to lieutenant general in January 1812 and invested with the Order of the Bath on 10 March in the same year. He commanded the right of the army in the great battle of Vittoria (21 June 1813); which commenced with an attack by one of Hill's brigades and concluded with the utter rout of the enemy, commanded by Jourdan and Joseph Bonaparte, King of Spain. Hill was subsequently entrusted with the defence of Pamplona, and for several months repelled the determined French attempts to dislodge him from his Pyrenean fastnesses. When the allied army was reorganized on French soil into three army corps (under Hill, Beresford and Hope), the right was assigned to Hill (to whose force was attached the 2nd and 4th British divisions, a Portuguese division and a corps of Spaniards). Hill rendered valuable services at the battle of Nivelle (10 November 1813), in which Soult's triple line of defences was turned, and in the operations on the Nive during the following months.

After the close of the war Hill was raised to the peerage. On 17 May 1814 he was created Baron Hill of Almarez and Hardwicke. He was also awarded a pension of £2 000 per year.

Following Napoleon's escape from Elba, the Allied Army of the Netherlands was formed into two large army corps; the command of one being given to the Prince of Orange and that of the other to Hill, whose command included: the 2nd and 4th British divisions, with the artillery attached; a cavalry brigade of the King's German Legion; a Dutch East Indian contingent; and a Dutch-Belgian division of all arms. Some Hanoverian *landwehr* (militia) were also added. At Waterloo Hill's corps was posted on the right of the Nivelle road. The brigades actually engaged were: Adam's light brigade (3rd Brigade) (52nd, 71st and rifle battalions), near which Hill was posted during the greater part of the day; Mitchell's Brigade (4th Brigade) (14th, 23rd and 51st Regiments); and Duplat's brigade (the King's German Legion and some Hanoverian *landwehr* brigades. When the Imperial Guard launched their final assault, and before the famous charge of Adam's brigade (led by Sir John Colborne, who succeeded to the command of the brigade after Adam had been wounded), Hill's horse was shot from under him, was knocked over and badly contused. For more than half an hour he was believed by his staff to have been killed. His horse was afterwards found to have been hit in five places. Following the battle Hill advanced with the army to Paris and commanded the troops who took over the defence of the city. Wellington wrote in his Waterloo Despatch: 'I am particularly indebted to General Lord Hill for his assistance and conduct on this as on all other occasions'.

Hill returned to France and was second-in-command of the army of occupation under Wellington; until the final withdrawal of the allied troops in November 1818. He then returned to his estate at Hardwicke Grange, where he resided for some years. In 1820 Oxford University conferred upon him the honorary degree of Doctor of Civil Law (DCL). When the Duke of Wellington became Prime Minister in 1828 Hill (who attained the rank of full general on 27 May 1825) was appointed to the command of the army (16 February 1828). He held this post for 14 years. Failing health at length compelled him to resign, when he was succeeded as commanderin-chief by the Duke of Wellington. He was raised to the dignity of a Viscount. Hill died on 10 December 1842. He had been awarded numerous orders: Knight Grand Cross of the Order of the Bath (GCB); Knight Grand Cross of the Order of Hanover (GCH); Grand Cross of St George (Russia); William the Lion (Netherlands); the Tower and Sword (Portugal); and the Order of the Crescent (Turkey). In addition he received the Army Gold Cross with clasps and the Waterloo medal. *ed.*

(11) *Shepherd boy of Bethlehem*: David (died circa 961 BC) was the second, and probably the most renowned, king of Israel. His long career, beginning with his tortuous climb to power, is related in *Samuel I* (16-31), II and *Kings* (1-2). David entered the service of Saul, Israel's first king.

He attracted the attention of Saul when, as a shepherd boy, the latter struck down the giant Goliath, the Philistine champion, with a pebble hurled from a slingshot. David (the Hebrew term for 'leader') became Saul's son-in-law. Saul's jealousy finally forced David to flee and he sought refuge, first as a bandit leader, and latterly as a mercenary in the service of the Philistines. David returned to Hebron following Saul's death. There he was anointed king over Judah; and several years later, following a long civil war with Saul's heir, king over Israel. David consolidated his power in Jerusalem, which he made the political and religious capital of his kingdom. Although God did not permit David to build a temple, he promised David an eternal dynasty in Jerusalem. This promise, combined with the religious ideology that informed David's successful imperial expansion, were the sources of Israel's later hopes for a Messiah. The latter part of David's reign was marked by family squabbles and numerous revolts; two of which were led by his own sons. The Bible portrays these events as the bitter fruit of his adulterous relationship with Bathsheba. David was forgiven, however, and the son who succeeded him, Solomon, was Bathsheba's child.

David was an accomplished musician. A later tradition credits him with organizing the temple choirs and accords to him the authorship of many of the Psalms. *ed.*

(12) *Philistines*: The Old Testament people who were the traditional enemies of the Israelites. On the basis of Old Testament sources (specifically *Amos* and *Jeremiah*) the original homeland of the Philistines is regarded as being the island of Caphtor, which appears as Captara (modern Crete) in ancient cuneiform tablets. However, the location Crete should not be interpreted in terms of the confines of that island, but should rather be applied to the Aegean islands and the coast of Ionia (modern Turkey). The Philistines were probably a splinter group of the Dorian invaders who swept through the Cretan-Mycaenaean world. These invaders were known generically as the 'sea peoples'. The Philistines introduced iron into Palestine-Syria, which they invaded in the 13th Century BC. Their skill as metal workers in both bronze and iron is reflected in the armour furnished for their giant and champion, Goliath. They held the Hebrews in subjection until the reign of David (cf note (11) above)), who conquered them in the 10th Century BC. Conquered in turn by the Babylonians, Persians and Macedonians, and the Ptolomies of Egypt, within a few centuries the Philistines had merged completely with the local Semitic peoples. Nevertheless, although they quickly vanished as a people, they bequeathed their name to Palestine (the original name for the territory now known as Israel). *ed.*

(13) *Sir John Colborne*: Gen Sir John Colborne (1778-1863). He was the only son of Samuel Colborne, of Lyndhurst, Hampshire, being born at that place on 16 February 1778. He was educated at Christ's Hospital and entered the army as an ensign in the 20th Regiment of Foot on 10 July 1794. He subsequently won every step in the ladder of promotion without purchase. He was promoted to lieutenant on 4 September 1795. Colborne accompanied his regiment to Egypt; being promoted captain on 12 January 1800, shortly before the expeditionary force sailed. From Egypt the 20th Regiment journeyed to Malta, and thence to Sicily. Shortly afterwards Colborne distinguished himself at Maida, attracting the attention of Sir

John Moore, who secured Colborne's promotion to the rank of major on 21 January 1808, and his appointment as military secretary.

Colborne accompanied Moore to Sweden and Portugal and was by his side throughout the retreat to Corunna. Moore's dying request was that Colborne's faithful and meritorious service be rewarded with a lieutenant colonelcy. The request was duly granted, and in February 1809 Colborne was granted a lieutenant colonelcy in the 5th garrison battalion; whence he exchanged into the 66th Regiment on 2 November 1809, and into the 52nd Oxford Light Infantry on 18 July 1811.

In August 1809 Colborne joined Wellington's army in the Peninsula. He was present at the battle of Busaco (1810), serving with the 66th Regiment; and in the following year temporarily commanded a brigade of the 2nd Division, as senior colonel at the battle of Albuera. Directly following that battle, he assumed the command of the 52nd Light Infantry; one of the three famous regiments which formed the Light Brigade and the nucleus of the famous Light Division. He first took them into action in storming the fort of San Francisco, an outwork of Cuidad Rodrigo (1812), where he was so severely wounded that he was absent from any engagements which followed. He returned to the army in July 1813 and in September of that year assumed temporary command of a brigade within the Light Division, as a result of the illness of Maj Gen Skerrett; and commanded it through the great battles of the Nivelle and the Nive. In January 1814 he reverted to the command of his old regiment, leading it in the battles of Orthes and Toulouse.

On the conclusion of the peace he was promoted to colonel (4 June 1814). On the extension of the Order of the Bath, was made one of the first Knights Commander (KCB). He was also appointed aide-de-camp to the Prince Regent in June 1814. When Napoleon escaped from Elba the 52nd Regiment, under Colborne's command, was ordered to Belgium; and brigaded with the 71st and 95th Regiments under Maj Gen Adam, within Lord Hill's division. This division was posted on the extreme right of the English position. When it was perceived that Napoleon was attempting to force his way through the English line, the brigade gradually moved forward in order to be able to pour in a flank fire on any charge in column that might be effected within its reach. This opportunity arrived when the old guard advanced to the charge; at which point Colborne suddenly fired a volley into the flank of the dense column, and then charged and routed it. This episode is graphically described by Pattison, who is of the opinion that this manoeuvre was a decisive factor in the French defeat, as it routed the old guard. The matter remains a moot point, but is strenuously argued in Colborne's favour by Pattison. It is, however, certain that Colborne defeated a section of the Guard; either the main body or a detached portion, and most probably the second line. In any event, the Duke of Wellington (very rarely readily forthcoming) never acknowledged Colborne's contribution to the victory. However, the latter received the distinguished orders of Maria Theresa (Austria) and St George (Russia); and was promoted major general in 1825.

He became lieutenant governor of Guernsey in 1821. There he made himself both useful and popular, especially by the restoration of the Elizabeth College to its legitimate purpose. In 1828 Colborne was appointed lieutenant governor of Upper Canada. He vacated this appointment upon his promotion to the rank of lieutenant general in 1838. However, at the moment that he was preparing to leave Canada, the Canadian rebellion broke out. Colborne was at once ordered, if he had not yet embarked, to assume the offices of governor general and commander-in-chief. He quelled the rebellion so speedily, and so judicially, that his elevation to the peerage (as Lord Seaton of Seaton in Devonshire) met with universal approval. During the period 1843-1849 he served as lord high commissioner of the Ionian Islands. In 1842 he was made a Knight Grand Cross of the Order of St Michael and St George (GCMG). Colborne was promoted full general in 1854 and transferred from the colonelcy of the 26th Regiment to that of the 2nd Life Guards. Between 1855 and 1860 he served as commander of the forces in Ireland and was sworn as a privy councillor of that country. Upon his retirement in March 1860 he was created a field marshal. Thereafter his health began to decline and he died on 17 April at Torquay, aged 85. ed.

(14) *black hole of Calcutta*: Pattison is referring to the notorious incident which occurred in 1756, in India. When the ruler (Nawab) of the Bengal region captured Calcutta on 20 June, he imprisoned the Europeans who had not escaped in a small storeroom in the fort (later called the 'black hole'). There over 100 perished from suffocation, thirst, heat and wounds. ed.

(15) *Hanoverian friends*: Pattison is referring not to the King's German Legion, but to the recently reformed Hanoverian army, occasioned by the collapse of French influence in Germany as the result of the 1813 campaign. This army contributed a considerable number of units to the Anglo-Allied army in the Waterloo campaign. The Hanoverian contingents present in the Waterloo campaign were: three regiments of hussars; two foot artillery batteries; seven 'field battalions' (ie infantry consisting of regular troops); and 15 *landwehr* (militia) battalions. The militia battalions comprised some 13 000 infantry and 1 600 cavalry; with one field battalion and 12 *landwehr* battalions in reserve (totalling 9 000 men). The reference to their commander being Lt Col Hugh Halkett (cf note (16) below) confirms this identification; as his command consisted of the *landwehr* battalions. ed.

(16) *Colonel Halket*: As is the case with his brother - Sir Colin Halkett - the name is misspelt in the text. The Colonel Halkett referred to by Pattison was (then) Lt Col (later Baron von) Hugh Halkett (1783-1863) who was, to reiterate, the brother of Sir Colin Halkett. He was the second son of Maj Gen Frederick Godar Halkett, born on 30 August 1783. On 19 April 1794 he was appointed ensign in his father's battalion of the Scotch Brigade, in the Dutch service, then being raised. In 1803 he was nominated senior captain in the light battalion being raised in Hanover by his brother (cf **Letter I**, note (3)), which became the 2nd Light Battalion of the King's German Regiment; and in which Hugh Halkett became major before the age of 22. He served with this battalion in the north of Germany under Lord Cathcart in 1805-1806; serving in the Isle of Rugen, at the siege of Stralsund (1807) and in the

expedition against Copenhagen later in the same year. His promptitude and iniative, whilst on outpost duty, in seizing a Danish redoubt without waiting for orders won the approval of Sir David Baird. He accompanied his battalion to Sweden in 1806 and thence to Portugal. Hugh Halkett served in the retreat to Corunna (although he was not present at the battle itself); in the Walcheren expedition of 1809 (serving in the siege of Flushing); and in 1811 joined the Peninsular army, commanding his battalion in the battle of Albuera of that year. He commanded it again during the following year; at the siege of the forts of Salamanca and at the battle of Salamanca; and in the retreat to Burgos, in which the Light Brigade (composed of the 1st and 2nd Light Battalions of the King's German Regiment, formed the rear guard of the army). On 22 October 1812 these battalions distinguished themselves in the gallant repulse of the French cavalry at Venta de Pozo.

Halkett was promoted to the lieutenant colonelcy of the 7th Line Battalion of the Legion, then in Sicily. In April 1813 Halkett, then on leave in England, was sent to North America, with some officers and men of the German Legion, to assist in organizing the new Hanoverian levies. In command of a brigade of these troops in Count Walmoden's army, Halkett distinguished himself at the battle of Gohrde (16 September 1813); and in the unsuccessful engagement with the Danes at Schestedt in the following December. On the latter occasion, when a Danish cavalry regiment was attacking a battalion of his brigade, Halkett dashed upon the standard bearer, seized the standard, and escaped by clearing a quickset hedge with double ditch, over which none of his numerous pursuers dared follow. He held command at the sieges of Gluckstadt and Harburg in 1814.

During the Waterloo campaign Halkett commanded the 3rd and 4th Brigades of the Hanoverian militia (*landwehr*), which accompanied the recently organized Hanoverian troops (not to be confused with the King's German Legion) into Belgium. On 18 June these brigades were deployed in the wood to the right of Hougoumont; where, at the close of the day, Halkett distinguished himself by taking prisoner the French general Cambronne, a commander in the Imperial Guard. The former observed a French general seeking to rally broken parties of the guard, which had already begun to fall back and were close to the British advanced skirmishers. Seeking to encourage his inexperienced soldiers, Halkett spurred his horse forward. The French thought that Halkett's horse had bolted until Halkett, approaching Cambronne, pointed his pistol at him and called upon the latter to surrender, which he promptly did. At that moment Halkett's horse was shot from under him and he saw Cambronne seeking to rejoin the French. Incredibly, Halkett managed to get his horse to rise again and with a desperate effort pursued Cambronne, caught him by his aiguillet, swung him round, and cantered off towards the British line again.

Following the peace the King's German Legion (in which Halkett was still a lieutenant colonel) was disbanded. Halkett was placed on half-pay, which he drew until his death. He and other former members of the German Legion received permanent commissions in the new Hanoverian army. He rose to be a general and inspector general of Hanoverian infantry (1848). In the Schleswig-Holstein war of

1848-1849 he commanded the 10th Army Corps.

He received numerous orders and decorations: the Companion of the Order of the Bath (CB); Knight Grand Cross of the Order of Hanover (GCH); the Order of the Black Eagle (Prussia); Order of Military Merit (Prussia); the Order of St Anne (Russia) (both the Prussian and Russian orders being awarded in the 1st Class); the Order of Dannebrog (Denmark); the Sword of Sweden, and other orders; together with the Spanish Gold Cross for Albuera, the Army Gold Medal (with clasps for Albuera and Salamanca); the Military General Service Medal 1793-1814, Waterloo and Hanoverian war medals. *ed*.

(17) *Egyptian locusts*: Pattison is here referring to one of the plagues of Egypt, which Moses visited upon the Egyptian Pharaoh, Ramses II, after the latter had refused to release the Hebrews from subjection to his rule. Moses, with Aaron as his spokesman, appeared before the Pharaoh in order to convey to him the divine command to permit the departure of the Israelites. As proof of the Israelites' divine sanction, Aaron cast down his rod before the Pharaoh, and it became a serpent. The miracle having being performed, or stimulated by his advisers, the Pharaoh hardened his heart and refused the desired permission. By so doing, he triggered the ten plagues, as recounted in *Exodus*.

The locusts were the eighth plague ordained by Jehovah *(Exodus* 10: 1-20). Moses lifted up his rod, and God brought an east wind, which the following day summoned the locusts. They appeared in such dreadful swarms as Egypt had never known before, or indeed experienced since:

'They covered the face of the whole earth, so that the land was darkened,
and they did eat every herb of the land, and all the fruit of the trees which
the hail had left; and there remained not any green thing in the trees or in
the herbs of the field through all the land of Egypt'.

The fact that the wind blew a day and a night prior to summoning the locusts indicated that they travelled from a great distance and thus proved to the Egyptians that the omnipotence of God extended far beyond the borders of Egypt and governed every land. A further miraculous feature of the plague was its unparalleled extent. It prevailed throughout the entire length of Egypt; whereas ordinary swarms were confined to particular districts. In return to the Pharaoh's entreaty 'the Lord turned a mighty strong west wind, which took away the locusts and cast them into the Red Sea.' (*Exodus*: 10, verse 21 et seq). Pharaoh's promise to liberate the Israelites proved, however, to be no more sincere than those that he had made before, occasioning the succeeding two plagues. *ed*.

(18) An appropriate illustration of this assertion is to be found in the early career of 'The Duke' himself. During the investment of Seringapatam, under command of General Harris (a) (afterwards Lord Harris), in 1799, a night attack to eject the enemy from a tope, (b) was entrusted to his Grace, then Lieutenant-Colonel Wellesley, commanding the 33rd. The undertaking proved a complete failure, and panic and confusion ensuing, 'The Duke' was not to be found, and the retreat was altogether disastrous. When in garrison there in 1810, I had often walked over the position where this untoward event took place. To substantiate the accusation

against wise men, (c) I have merely to point to those panics which so frequently take place in our stock exchanges. *auth.*

Editorial observations on above footnote

(a) *General Harris*: George Harris, first Lord Harris of Seringapatam and Mysore (1746-1829). He was one of several children of the Rev George Harris, BA (Cantab), curate of Brasted, Kent. George Harris jnr was educated at Westminster School and on 1 January 1759 was entered as a cadet at the Royal Military College, Woolwich. In 1760 he passed out of Woolwich as a lieutenant-fireworker in the Royal Artillery; in which he served until 1762, when he was appointed an ensign in the 5th Foot. He accompanied his regiment to America in 1774. As a captain in the grenadier company he served under Lord Percy at Lexington and at the battle of Bunker's Hill. In the latter engagement (17 June 1775), where the 5th Regiment incurred heavy casualties, Harris received a head wound which necessitated the extremely painful process of trepanning. He rejoined his regiment in July 1776 and from that point until November 1778 was present in every engagement in the American War of Independence (with the exception of Germantown). At Iron Hill he was shot through the leg.

As a major he accompanied the force despatched from New York to the West Indies under the command of Gen James Grant. At the capture of St Lucia in December 1778 Harris commanded a battalion of grenadiers. He served as second-in-command under Maj Gen Medows at La Vigie when the Comte de Grasse attempted to relieve that island. On this occasion the 5th Regiment won the distinction of wearing the tall white feather in their fusilier caps. He embarked with his regiment - then serving as marines - in 1779, and was present at the naval engagement at Grenada. Returning home later in the year in a neutral vessel, his ship was catptured by a French privateer and carried to St Malo; but Harris was released on parole and permitted to proceed to Dover. In 1780 he became lieutenant colonel of the 5th Foot. He commanded the regiment for some years in Ireland, where it enjoyed a high reputation and great popularity.

The next phase of his career was associated with India. The moving force in this regard was Maj Gen Medows, who dissuaded Harris from resigning his commission when the 5th Foot was ordered once again to America. Medows had been appointed to the Bombay command and arranged to take Harris onto his staff. Harris thereupon effected an exchange into the 76th Foot; one of the four regiments then being raised for service in India. He served as aide-de-camp and secretary to Medows during the latter's tenure of command at Bombay and later at Madras. Harris participated in the campaigns of 1790-1791 against Tipu Sultan; commanding the second line in the battle of 15 May 1791 and engaged in Lord Cornwallis' attack on Tipu Sultan's camp and the island of Seringapatam (6 February 1792), which ended the war. In 1794 he was appointed commandant of Fort William and promoted to major general. Harris was promoted to the local rank of lieutenant general in 1796, coinciding with his appointment to the staff of Fort St George. As senior military officer present he commanded the troops in the Madras presidency between 1796 and 1800; and administered the civil government also between October 1797 and February 1798.

In December 1798 Harris was selected by Lord Mornington (Richard Wellesley, brother of Sir Arthur Wellesley, the future Duke of Wellington) to fill the post of commander of the 50 000 men being assembled to take the field in anticipation of the hostile intentions of Tipu Sultan. The operations attained their climax in the storming of Seringapatam and the death of Tipu in the breach on 4 May 1799; followed by the annexation of the Mysore territory. Harris received the thanks of the government of India in council and of both Houses of Parliament; being offered an Irish title, which he declined. He was appointed colonel of the 73rd Highlanders in February 1800; in which year he returned to Great Britain.

He was appointed a lieutenant general in 1801; and general in 1812. On 11 August 1815 he was raised to the peerage of the United Kingdom, under the title of Baron Harris of Seringapatam and Mysore, and of Belmont, Kent. He was created a Knight Grand Cross of the Order of the Bath (GCB) in 1820, and governor of Dumbarton Castle in 1824. Harris acquired a very considerable fortune in the course of his career, but was nevertheless extremely generous. (He is said to have lent his prize money to the Madras government when the latter was subject to severe financial constraints; and distributed a great deal of money among various charities in Madras). In a passage in his will he ascribed his 'rise from nothing to affluent fortune to economy 'and willing privation from self-indulgence all through a long life.'

(b) *a tope*: The word 'tope' appears in both the Hindi and Tamil languages. In Hindi it refers to an ancient structure, in the form of a dome or tumulus of masonry. In Tamil the word refers to a clump, grove or plantation of trees.

(c) *To substantiate the accusation against wise men*: The meaning of this phrase is somewhat obscure. Its sense would appear to be that Pattison supporting the criticism of those who argue that the outcome of military engagements is subject to completely logical analysis; and overlook the influence of irrational, totally unpredictable factors.

(19) *Imperial eagle*: The eagle was the French counterpart of the British Colours. The image of the eagle surmounted the standard bearing the unit's honours. It ultimately derived from the standards of the Roman legions, and was introduced by Napoleon in order to reinforce his regime's symbolic association with republican Rome. ed.

(20) *seize the holy father himself ... political schemes*: It is difficult to ascertain as to which Pope Pattison is referring; for two Pontiffs - Pius VI and Pius VII - were subject to arrest and imprisonment by Napoleon, following upon the French invasions of the Vatican.

In February 1798 the French occupied Rome and proclaimed the Roman Republic. The Pope, Pius VI, was taken to southern France (Valence), where he died one year later. The conflict with the Papacy was concluded in 1801, by a concordat between France and the Holy See. This concordat provided that French archbishops and bishops should be appointed by the government but confirmed by the Pope; the clergy to be paid by the government. Pope Pius VII (elected in 1800) was given possession of the Papal states, but minus Ferrara, Bologna and the Romagna. The liberties of the Gallican Church were strongly asserted. However, the Pope's return to Rome in 1805 was followed by increasing tension between Napoleon and the Vatican. Difficulties concerning the operation of the concordat, the autocratic action of Napoleon in depriving the Pope of some of his territories and the Pope's refusal of Napoleon's demand that the former join the Continental System were major factors in this estrangement; which reached its climax on 2 February 1808 when a French army, under General Miollis, occupied Rome once again. On 17 May the Papal states were declared to be integrated into France. Pius VII responded to this action by excommunicating the Emperor (10 June); in reply to which Napoleon had the Pope arrested (6 July) and taken to Savona, near Genoa, where he was held prisoner. However, Pius continued in his defiant attitude towards Napoleon and in 1812 was removed to Fontainbleau. He was finally released in 1814 when Napoleon, faced with a disintegrating empire, sought to placate Italian popular opinion. *ed.*

(21) *betrayed him with a kiss*: A reference to Judas Iscariot (died circa 30 AD); one of the twelve apostles, notorious for betraying Jesus. Judas's name is probably a corruption of the Latin term sicarius ('murderer' or 'assassin') rather than denoting family origin; suggesting that he was a member of the Sicarri, an extremist Jewish faction dedicated to destroying Roman power in Palestine, many of whom were terrorists. Other than his apostleship, betrayal and death, the Gospels tell us very little concerning Judas. Although cited last on the list of apostles, he acted as their treasurer. *John* (12:6) introduces Judas's thievery by stating: 'as he had the money box he used to take what was put into it.' He disclosed the location of Jesus to the chief priests and their supporters for 30 pieces of silver. These members of the Sanhedrin (the council of Jewish elders, composed of the Sadducee sect) provided an armed guard that Judas accompanied to the Garden of Gethsemene, close to Jerusalem, where Jesus went to pray with the other 11 apostles following the Last Supper. There Judas identified Jesus with a kiss, addressing him as 'master'. In Biblical tradition *(Matthew* 27: 3-10) Judas repented after seeing Jesus being condemned to death, returned the silver and then hanged himself. *ed.*

(22) *stern and unrelenting jailer*: Pattison is referring to Lt Gen Sir Hudson Lowe (1769-1844), who was governor of St Helena between 1815 and 1821. Born on 28 July 1769, he was the son of army surgeon.
 At the time that Napoleon escaped from Elba, Lowe held the position of the Quartermaster General of the Army of the Low Countries, under the Prince of Orange. (In this capacity he received intimations that Napoleon, during the interregnum of the 100 days, had made proposals to the King of the Netherlands, to the effect that the former would relinquish all claims to Belgium, in return for indemnities levied on territories in northern Germany: Letter from Lowe to Lord Bathurst (18 March 1821)). Wellington assumed command of the allied forces of the Netherlands in April 1815 and Lowe remained for a few weeks as his quartermaster general but, having been nominated to command the troops in

Genoa designed to co-operate with the Austro-Sardinian armies, Lowe was succeeded in May by Sir William Howe de Lancey. Lowe assumed command at Genoa on the day following the battle of Waterloo.

At Marseilles, on 1 August 1815, Lowe received the intelligence that he would be responsible for the custody of Napoleon, who had taken refuge on board the *Bellerophon*, in Aix roads, a fortnight previously. On Lowe's departure from Marseilles the inhabitants presented him with a silver urn, bearing an inscription which referred to the fact that he had rescued the city from pillage. Lowe was appointed governor of St Helena at a salary of £12 000 pounds per year. St Helena was then a possession of the East India Company, and Lowe was informed of his new appointment by the company's court of directors on 23 August. Lowe received the local rank of lieutenant general and made a Knight Commander of the Order of the Bath (KCB). On 11 April 1816 the 'Act for more effectually detaining Napoleon Bonaparte' received the royal assent. Lowe reached St Helena on 14 April 1816. A warrant, dated 12 April 1816, addressed to Lowe as 'lieutenant general of His Majesty's army in St Helena and governor of that island' required him to detain and keep Napoleon as a prisoner of war, under such directions as would be periodically issued by one of the principal secretaries of state.

Pattison's depiction of Lowe as a 'stern and unrelenting jailer' is unjust, but he was voicing the popular image projected to his contemporaries. Lowe was, in actual fact, described by all who knew him as a kindly and humane man. This was clearly exemplified by one of his first acts upon his arrival on the island when, on his own responsibility, he increased the amount allowed by the government for Napoleon's establishment at Longwood (from £8 000 to £12 000 per annum). However, the ensuing five years of Lowe's custodianship was characterized by constant friction. Napoleon, whom he always approached with a studied politeness, speedily took the most violent dislike to him. In actual fact, they saw each other only five times; all within five months of Lowe's arrival. At the last two interviews Napoleon abused Lowe who, according to all trustworthy accounts, retained his self-command perfectly and refused to see or communicate with him again. Endless quarrels with various members of Napoleon's retinue ensued during the succeeding five years. Lowe was not without fault; exhibiting a consistent want of tact and pedantic obsession with trifles.

Napoleon died on 5 May 1821. At the end of July Lowe handed over the governorship of the island to Brig Gen John Pine and quitted St Helena. Peace was made, at the dying wish of Napoleon, between the exiles of his suite and Lowe just before the general exodus. At his departure the inhabitants of St Helena presented Lowe with an address acknowledging the justice and moderation of his rule and the public confidence felt in his administration, which featured the abolition of slavery (without compensation to the former slave owners). His services in 'giving the death blow to slavery in St Helena' were very warmly acknowledged by Sir Thomas Fowell Buxton in the House of Commons in May 1823. His administration of the island was further publicly commended by both the Crown and British Government.

Lowe's custodianship, however, was powerfully maligned by Barry Edward

O'Meara, a naval officer who had been Napoleon's medical attendant. He had resigned his post on St Helena in protest against restrictions imposed upon him by Lowe, and had been expelled from the island in 1818. In 1819 his book, *Exposition of affairs at St Helena during the captivity of Napoleon* was published. This was followed by *Napoleon in exile: a voice from St Helena* (published in 1822, in two volumes). O'Meara's books proved tremendously popular, passing through five editions in a few months. Lowe was dissuaded from taking legal action.

In 1823 Lowe was appointed governor of Antigua, but resigned for domestic reasons. He was afterwards appointed to the staff in Ceylon, as second-in-command, under Sir Edward Barnes. Lowe remained in Ceylon until 1828. However, his hopes of succeeding to the command were never realized, largely due to political conditions in the island, and he returned home in 1831. He was made a Knight Grand Cross of the Order of St Michael and St George (GCMG) and, in 1842, was elevated to the higher class of the Order of the Red Eagle. Lowe was appointed to the colonelcy of his old regiment, the 50th, in the same year, and died on 10 January 1844, aged 74. *ed*.

(23) *Lavater.* Johann Kaspar Lavater (1741-1801). He was a Swiss divine and poet, and a student of physiognamy. His studies of this science and his interest in 'magnetic trance' conditions had their source in his religious beliefs, which impelled his search for demonstrable traces of the divine in human life. Goethe enjoyed a warm friendship with Lavater, that was later severed by Lavater's zeal for conversion. Lavater was also a noted author of lyrical poetry. *ed*.

APPENDICES

(1) Pattison does not distinguish between lieutenants and captains in this appendix. Nor does he furnish Christian names. The following list, extracted from the *Waterloo Roll Call*, is provided, therefore, in order to supplement the details provided by the author.

Lt Col William Elphistone [sic]
Maj Edward Parkinson (w)
[Eventually attained the rank of lieutenant general and colonel-in-chief of the 93rd Highlanders. He was made a Companion of the Bath (CB) and died on 4 January 1858].

Captains
    William M'Intyre (w)
    Charles Knight (w)
    John Haigh (k)
    Joseph M Harty (w)
    [Afterwards Colonel; made a Knight of Hanover (KH)]
    Ralph Gore
    John Longden

Lieutenants
    Thomas Reid (w)
    Peter Barailler
    George Barrs
    Henry Rishton Buck (k)
    J Hart (k)
    James Murkland (w)
    Frederick Hope Pattison
    Arthur Gore (k)
    Richard Westmore (w)
    [became major in the 33rd Regiment in 1840 and retired on full pay with rank of Lt Colonel].
    Thomas D Haigh (k)
    James Gordon Ogle (w)
    Samuel Alexander Pagan (w)
    Edward Clabon
    Joseph Lynam
    John Archbold
    John Cameron (k)

Ensigns
    Henry Bain (w)
    James Forlong (w) [spelt 'Furlong' in Pattison's text].
    William Bain
    James Arnot Howard
    William Thain (adjutant) (w)

Andrew Watson
　　Charles Smith
　　William Hodgson
　　Gerald Blackall
　　George Drury (w)
Paymaster
　　Edward Stoddart
Quartermaster
　　James Fazarckley
Surgeon
　　Robert Leaver
Assistant Surgeons
　　William D Fry
　　D Finlayson *ed.*

(2) *Clinton's Division*: ie the 3rd Division, commanded by Sir Henry Clinton, which was positioned on the right centre at Waterloo.

Gen Sir Henry Clinton (1771-1829) was the son of Sir Henry Clinton, snr, KB, and was born on 9 March 1771. He entered the army as an ensign in the 11th Regiment of Foot on 10 October 1787, and between October 1788 and August 1789 served as a volunteer in the Brunswick Corps, then acting with the Prussian army in Holland. In March 1791 he was transferred to the 1st Regiment of Foot Guards, promoted captain in the 15th Regiment in April, and transferred back to the 1st Foot Guards in November 1792. In January 1793, at the commencement of the Revolutionary Wars with France, he was appointed aide-de-camp to the Duke of York and served on his personal staff throughout the disastrous campaign in Flanders. He was appointed to the brevet rank of major in April 1794 and was severely wounded at Camphin on 10 May 1795. Clinton continued to serve as aide-de-camp to the Duke of York until his promotion to the lieutenant colonelcy of the 66th Regiment on 30 September 1795. He joined his regiment in the West Indies and in the following year exchanged once again into the Guards; but, being taken prisoner by a French cruiser, did not reach England until January 1797. Clinton subsequently served as aide-de-camp to Lord Cornwallis (then commander-in-chief in Ireland); and later in the campaigns in Italy and Switzerland (the latter waged against Massena). On 25 September 1803 he was promoted to the rank of colonel. Between 1803 and 1805 he rendered valuable service in India, which he left in March 1805. He next served as military commissioner with the Russian general Kutusoff in the Austerlitz campaign.

In July 1806 he was placed in command of the flank companies of the Guards then based in Sicily; and between December 1806 and November 1807 served as commandant at Syracuse. Appointed a brigadier general, Clinton accompanied Sir John Moore (with whom he had formed an intimate friendship) as adjutant general; first to Sweden and subsequently to Portugal. He fulfilled this most important role throughout Moore's advance into Spain and the famous retreat to Corunna. Following his return to England, Clinton was the first to defend Moore's actions (in his *A few remarks explanatory to the motives which guided the operations of the British Army during the late short campaign in Spain*).

Clinton then served as adjutant general in Ireland, but, following his elevation to the rank of major general on 25 July 1810, he requested to be sent to the Peninsula for active service. His request was acceded to, and in October 1811 he joined Lord Wellington's army, in command of the 6th Division. Although not gifted with the military talents of Picton or Hill, Clinton proved a most efficient and successful divisional commander. His first feat of arms was the reduction of the forts of Salamanca in June 1812, when one of his brigadiers (Gen Bowes) was killed; and he also played a conspicuous part in the battle of Salamanca in the same year, when his division was brought up to capture the Arapiles following the failure of Pack's Portuguese force. In April 1813 he was made local lieutenant general and on 29 July 1813 was created a Knight of the Bath (KB), in recognition of his services at Vittoria, fought in that year. He commanded his division at the battles of Nive, Orthes and Toulouse. At the conclusion of the war he received numerous awards; including the Army Gold Cross with one clasp and Order of the Tower and Sword (Portugal). In addition, he was made colonel of the 1st Bn, 60th Regiment and was promoted to the rank of lieutenant general on 4 June 1814; being appointed inspector general of infantry.

When Napoleon escaped from Elba, Clinton was one of the former subordinates for whose services Wellington especially applied; and, to reiterate, took command of the 3rd Division. In this position, Clinton suffered as much from the French artillery as the other divisions positioned in the centre of the British line; as well as having to repulse numerous charges of cavalry. After the battle, Clinton was made a Knight of the Order of Maria Theresa (Austria), St George (Russia) and William The Lion (the Netherlands). On 9 August 1815 he was appointed colonel of the 3rd Regiment (the Buffs). In 1818 he resigned his seat in the House of Commons (where he had sat for Boroughbridgeshire) and totally retired to his country seat in Hampshire, where he died on 11 December 1829. ed.

(3) *La Belle Alliance*: The title of the appropriately named inn where Wellington and Blucher, on the evening of Waterloo, met, in the rear of Napoleon's former position. ed.

(4) *The Christian Year*: This was a collection of sacred poems by John Keble (1792-1866). The book (published in 1827) attained great popularity owing to its associations with the Oxford Movement. Keble was a Fellow and tutor of Oriel College, Oxford, and Professor of Poetry at Oxford. In 1833 he initiated the Oxford Movement, which interpreted the role of the Church of England in a mystical light, and sought to relate its doctrine more closely to Roman Catholicism. This corpus of thought became known as Anglo-Catholicism. Keble's poetry was encapsulated in *The Christian Year*. ed.

Biographical note on editor

Stanley Monick was born in England and educated at the University of Leicester, whence he graduated with a BA (Hons) degree in combined studies, majoring in English Literature. He subsequently attended the School of Librarianship, Liverpool Polytechnic (now Liverpool John Moores University), where he qualified as a Chartered Librarian (ALA). In addition, he holds a PhD degree from Columbia Pacific University (California, USA), having submitted a thesis entitled *The role of myth in contemporary English Literature*. He also holds qualifications in photography and drama.

Although he commenced his career with the Westminister Library Service, he has worked mainly in southern Africa. After service as deputy librarian at the National Free Library of Zimbabwe, he was appointed a professional officer at the South African National Museum of Military History (Johannesburg, South Africa); specializing in medals and numismatics. In 1979 he was appointed Chief Librarian of the *Star* newspaper (Johannesburg, South Africa), but returned to the South African National Museum of Military History in 1981, as senior professional officer, continuing to specialize in medals and numismatics. He left the Museum in 1995 to return to England, and between 1995 and 1997 was a records clerk at the Council Tax Office of the London Borough of Sutton, where he resides.

He is the author of several books, mainly dealing with the histories of South African regiments and South African awards. He is the editor of *Douglas's Tale of the Peninsula and Waterloo* (published by Leo Cooper, 1997); based on a manuscript containing the memoirs of Sgt John Douglas of the Royal Scots, who fought in the Peninsular War and at Waterloo.

His articles (principally related to military history, medals and English literature), have appeared in a variety of South African and British journals.

Memories of the Waterloo campaign

INDEX
compiled by S Monick

INTRODUCTORY NOTES

1 As is readily apparent, the index is structured under a number of headings, these being:
Awards;
Battles, Campaigns, Wars;
Casualties;
Great Britain;
Shipping/Ships;
Tactics;
Uniform;
UNITS AND FORMATIONS;
Weapons and Ammunition.

2 The reader will soon become aware that numerous terms are subject to sub-divisions, many of these, in turn, being broken down into further sub-headings. This is a particularly noticeable feature of the section heading, Units and Formations. The major sub-headings consist of countries (with the exception of those units and formations common to several nations). Under each nation, in turn, the formations are further divided (eg the term 'Army' is sub-divided into Brigades, Divisions, Regiments, etc, each of these terms, in turn, being subjected to further sub-division. This admittedly complex approach has been determined by the need for specificity within complex organisational forms.

3 The key terms on each page have been indexed; in order to produce a structured keyword index.

Index

A

Aaron, 160
Abercromby, Sir Ralph, 121,122
Academia di S Lucia,152
Act of Union (1801), 114
Adriatic, 99
Accoutrements, 101
Adam, Maj Gen Sir Frederick, 155,157
Adelaide Louisa, Princess, 146
Adriatic, 137
Aegean Islands, 156
Aeroplanes [see: Aircraft]
Afghanistan, 85
Afghans, 85
After strange gods (T S Eliot), 22
Ahab (King of Israel, 9th Century BC), 120
Ahaziah (King of Israel, 9th Century BC), 120
Aircraft, 139
Aix Roads, 164
Akbar Khan, 85
Albermarle, Duke of [see: Monck, Gen George]
Alcohol [see: Liquor]
Alexander I (Tsar of Russia, 1801-1825), 116,117
Allied powers (opposed to Napoleon), 115,116
Alsace Lorraine, 115
Alderson, Ensign J, 76
Algeria
  Governor General, 114
Almeida, 123
Alvinza, General, 104
America, 161
  [see also: North America; United States]
Amritsa (Treaty) (1809), 86
Amsterdam, 140
Anglesey, 1st Marquis, 142
  [see also: Uxbridge, Lord]
Anglican Church [see: Church of England]
Anglo-Catholicism [see: Oxford Movement]
Ansbach, 116
Anson, George, 83
Antigua
  Governor, 165
Anton, Quartermaster-Sergeant James, 17
Antwerp, 63,144
  [see also under: **Battles, Campaigns, Wars**]
  Governor, 147
Apostles, 163
Apprentices, 36
Archibald, Capt J, 76
Argyll, Marquis of, 108

Aristocracy, 14,16,19,68,106,109
Armagh, 114
Armistice
  1814, 124
  11 November 1918, 112
Armour, 8,54,95,135,137 [see also: Breast plate]
Army List, 1
Asia
  East, 85,86
  South, 86
    South east, 85,86
Augustans, 6,7,9,10
Augustus II (Elector of Saxony, King of Poland (1697-1733), 145,146
Augustus III (King of Poland, 1734-1763), 130
Austen, Jane, 17,18, 19
  Pride and prejudice, 19
  Sense and sensibility, 19
Australia, 102
  Botany Bay, 102
Austria-Hungary, 115,116,117
  Military frontier [*Militargrenze*], 137
    Police (*Grenzer*), 137
    Settlers, 137
      Germans, 138
      Hungarians, 138
      Rumanians, 138
      Slavs, 138
  Monarchy [see: Habsburgs]
Avignon, 115
Awards
  Army Gold Cross, 155,168
  Army Gold Medal, 139
    Clasps
      Albuera, 160
      Salamanca, 160
  Bath, Most Honourable Order of
    [see: Most Honourable Order of the Bath]
  Doctor of Civil Law (DCL), 155
  Garter, Most Noble Order of
    [see: Most Noble Order of the Garter]
  Gold Cross for Albuera (Spain), 160
  Hanover, Order of [see: Order of Hanover]
  Hanoverian War Medal, 160
  Military General Service Medal 1793-1814, 160
  Most Ancient and Most Noble Order of the Thistle: Knight (KTS), 153
  Most Distinguished Order of St Michael and St George
    Knight Grand Cross (GCMG), 106, 158,165

Most Honourable Order of the Bath, 154
  Companion (CB), 84,86,139,160
  Knight (KB), 105,124
  Knight Commander (KCB),
    99,104,139,153, 157,164,168
  Knight Grand Cross (GCB),
    83,106,124,139, 141,153,155,162
Most Noble Order of the Garter (KG), 142
Order of the Bath
  [see: Most Honourable Order of the Bath]
Order of the Black Eagle (Prussia) (1st
  Class), 160
Order of the Crescent (Turkey), 155
Order of Dannebrog (Denmark), 160
Order of the Garter
  [see: Most Noble Order of the Garter]
Order of Hanover
  Knight Grand Cross (GCH), 83,153,
    155,160
Order of Maria Theresa (Austria), 157,159
  Knight, 153,168
Order of Military Merit (Prussia), 160
Order of the Red Eagle (Prussia)
  1st Class, 165
Order of San Fernando (Spain), 106
Order of St Anne (Russia)
  1st Class, 160
Order of St George (Russia), 157
  Knight, 104,153,168
  Knight Grand Cross, 155
Order of the Sword of Sweden (Sweden),
  160
Order of the Thistle
  [see: Most Ancient and Most Noble Order
   of the Thistle]
Order of the Tower and Sword (Portugal),
  106,155,168
Order of William the Lion (Netherlands),
  106,155,168
St Michael and St George, Most
  Distinguished Order of
  [see: Most Distinguished Order of St
   Michael and St George]
Waterloo Medal, 155,160
Azov, 145

B

Baal, 120
  Priests, 120
Babylonians, 156
Badajoz, 105
  [see also under: **Battles, Campaigns, Wars**]

Badges
  Light infantry regiments, 39
    Bugle horn, 39
  Rifle regiments, 39
    Bugle horn, 39
Baggage, 52,113
Bain, Lt, 66,76 [referred to as Ensign on
  this page]
Baird, Sir David, 159
Balgowan, 104
Ball, Capt Alexander, 105
Barnes, Sir Edward, 165
Barnett, Corelli, 12
Baronets, 17
Barr, Capt G, 75
Bathurst, Lord, 163
Bathsheba, 156
Battle Honours, 22
Battles, Campaigns, Wars
  Afghan War (1839-1840), 85
  Albuera (1811), 33,83,97,157,159
  Alexandria (1801), 30,154
  America [see: North America]
  American Civil War (1861-1865), 148
  American War of Independence (1776-
    1783), 27,161
    [see also: individual battles; eg Lexington]
  Anglo-Boer War (1880-1881), 98,150,151
    [see also: individual battles; ie Laing's Nek]
  Anglo-Boer War (1899-1902), 136,150
  Anglo-Mysore War (2nd) (18th Century),
    101
  Anglo-Mysore War (3rd) (18th Century),
    101
  Antwerp (1814), 1,4,84,144,146
  'Arrow war' [see: China - 2nd Opium War]
  Assaye (1803), 87
  Austerlitz (1805), 167
  Austro-Prussian War (1866), 149
  Badajoz (siege) (1812), 23,83,105,123
    Castle, 123
  Balaclava (1854), 13
  Barossa (1811), 14,39,105
  Bastia (1794), 98
  Bergen (1799), 140
  Bergen-op-Zoom (1814), 1,5,53,84,96,98,
    103,104,106,107
  Bidassoa (passage) (1813), 84,105
  Borodino (1812), 96
  Bunker's Hill (1775), 161
  Burgos (siege/retreat) (1812), 83,159
  Busaco (1810), 39,87,123,143,157

Index

San Antonio de Cantara (pass), 123
Cadiz (1810), 105
Cairo (1800/1801), 152,154
Canada (1838), 158
Cape of Good Hope (1795/1806), 90
Cape St Vincent (1798), 98
Carpio (1811), 129
China
   1st Opium War (1839-1842), 86
   2nd Opium War (1857-1860), 86
Civil War (England) (1642-1649), 20
Colonial campaigns (19th Century), 150
Copenhagen (1807), 24,153,159
Corunna (battle) (1809), 87,105
Corunna (campaign (1808-1809)), 37,83, 105,110,141,157
Corsica (Revolutionary Wars, 1792-1802), 98
Crimean War (1854-1856), 12,23,110
   [see also: individual battles, campaigns; eg Balaclava]
Cuidad Rodrigo (siege) (1812), 87,105, 123,157
San Francisco, 157
Danish-Prussian War [see: Prussian-Danish War]
Dresden (1813), 129
Egypt (French Revolutionary Wars, 1792-1802), 152,154
   [see also: individual battles and campaigns]
Egypt (1882-1889), 150
El Bodon (1812), 33
El Hamed (1801), 154
Eylau (1807), 96
First South African War of Independence (1880-1881)
   [see: Anglo-Boer War (1880-1881), 98
Flanders (French Revolutionary Wars, 1792-1802), 103,153
   Camphin (1795), 167
Flushing (siege) (1809), 105,159
   [see also in general section]
France (1814), 89,139
   [see also: individual battles; eg Toulouse]
Freckenhald (siege) (1718), 146
French Revolutionary Wars (1792-1802), 7,36,87,90,103,130,131,140,167
Fuentes d'Onor (1811), 123
Garcia Hernandez (1812), 32
Genappe (1815), 86
Germany (1805-1806), 83,158
Gilboa (10th Century BC), 99
Genappe, 129

Germantown (1777), 161
Ginniss (1885), 150
Gluckstadt (siege) (1814), 159
Gohrde (1813), 159
Greek War of Independence (1821-1829), 115
Grenada (1779), 161
Halden [see: Freckenhald]
Hamburg (siege) (1814), 159
Hanover (1805), 153,154
Hohenlinde (1800), 89
Holland
   1799, 140
      [see also: specific battles; eg Bergen]
   1813-1814, 106,144,147
      [see also: individual campaigns; eg Antwerp]
Holowczyn (1708), 145
'Hundred Days'
   [see: Ligny, Quatre Bras, Waterloo]
India, 131,150
   [see also: individual battles/campaigns; eg Seringapatam]
   1790-1792 (Operations against Tipu Sultan), 161
   1798-1799 (Operations against Tipu Sultan), 162
Indian Mutiny (1857-1858), 86,150
Inkerman (1854), 51,110
Irish rebellion
   under Charles I and Cromwell, 108
   1797-1798, 12,102,114,136,153
Iron Hill (1777), 161
Isle Dieu (French Revolutionary Wars, 1792-1802), 104
Italy (French Revolutionary Wars, 1792-1802), 167
Jagdallak (pass) (Afghanistan) (1841), 85
Java (French Revolutionary Wars, 1792-1802), 90
Jena (1806), 112
Kastricum (1799), 140
Laing's Nek (1881), 98,151
La Vigie (French Revolutionary Wars, 1792-1802), 161
Leipzig (1814), 89,112
Lexington (1775), 161
Ligny (1815), 88,112,114,125
Mahratta Wars (18th/early 19th Century), 87
Maida (1806), 156
Malta (siege), (1799), 104
Mantua (1796), 104

Messina (1798), 104
Mexem (1814), 1,106
Minorca (siege) (1798), 104,154
Napoleonic Wars (1803-1815), 7,12,14, 17,22,27,28,30,33,36,99,115,130,132, 133,148
[see also: specific battles, campaigns; eg Peninsular War, Waterloo]
Narva (1700), 145
Neerwinden (French Revolutionary Wars, 1792-1802), 152
Netherlands [see: Holland]
Nive (1813), 83,154,157
Nivelle (1813), 92,154,157
North America (18th Century), 27,131
[see also: specific campaigns; ie American War of Independence]
Northern War (1700-1721), 145
[see also: individual battles (eg Narva, Poltava)]
Norway (1718), 146
Opium wars [see under: China]
Orthez (1814), 124,157
Pamplona (1813), 154
Peninsular War (1808-1814), 7,21,26,28,57, 58,60,83,87,89,91,92,94,95,103,105,132, 138,141,144,152,153
[see also: individual battles and campaigns]
Poltava (1709), 145
Porto Novo (1781), 101
Prussian-Austrian War [see: Austro-Prussian War]
Prussian-Danish War (1864), 149
Quatre Bras (1815), 8,10,28,32,33,34,49-52, 53,54,68,71,83,84,86,88,89,91,92,94,98, 100,103,114,125
[see also in general section]
Quiberon (French Revolutionary Wars, 1792-1802), 104
Rhine (French Revolutionary Wars, 1792-1802), 152
Rolica (1808), 154
Russia (1707-1709), 145
Russia (1812), 87,89,96,127
Sabugal (1811), 33
Sahagun (1808), 141
Saint/San...[see St...]
Salamanca (1812), 39,57,83,124,159,168
Arapiles, 168
Forts, 159,168
Salerno (1943), 88
Schestedt (1813), 159
Schleswig-Holstein War (1848-1849), 160

Sebastapol (siege) (1854), 110
Seringapatam (1791), 161
Seringapatam (1799), 87,100,101,160,162
[see also in general section]
Seven Years War (1757-1763), 95,112
South Africa
  Frontier War (1846-1847), 139
South African War (1880-1881)
  [see: Anglo-Boer War (1880-1881)
South African War (1899-1902)
  [see: Anglo-Boer War (1899-1902)]
Spain [see: Peninsular War]
Spanish Civil War (1936-1939), 73
Spanish colonies
  South America
    Rebellion (1820s), 115
Spanish Succession (1701-1714), 131,146
Stralsund (siege) (1807), 158
  Isle of Rugen, 158
St Lucia (French Revolutionary Wars, 1792-1802), 121,161
  Longville Bay, 121
St Sebastian (1813), 105
St Vincent (Revolutionary Wars 1792-1802), 122
Sudan
  1880s, 150
  [see also: individual battles; ie Ginniss]
  1897-1898, 150
Sweden (1808), 83,105
Switzerland (French Revolutionary Wars, 1792-1802), 167
Talavera (1809), 87,154
Tolosa (1813), 105
Torres Vedras (Peninsular War), 87
Toulon (Revolutionary Wars, 1792-1802), 98
Toulouse (1814), 87,157
Trafalgar (1805), 64
Venta de Pozo (1812), 159
Vimeiro (1808), 87
Vittoria (1813), 39,83,87,105,124,154,168
Wagram (1806), 94
Walcheren expedition (1809), 83,105,115,122,141,153,159
  [see also: individual campaigns; ie Flushing]
War of Liberation (1813-1814), 94
Waterloo campaign (1815), 1,5,10,11,12, 14,15,23,26,28,31,33,34,39,40,41,42,43, 48,50,55,56,57,61,67,68,69,71,72,73,77, 78,80,83,84,88,89,90,91,92,94,96,97,98, 100,102,104,107,108,111,112,113,114,11 8,119,120,126,127,128,129,130,134,135,

Index

136,137,139,141,148,149,150,151,152,
153,155,158,159,164,167
[*see also* in general section]
Hougoumont, 12,66,68,84,107,108
La Haye Sainte, 66,141 [*see also* in general section]
Model of battlefield, 93
Western Front (1914-1918), 4,23,150
West Indies (French Revolutionary Wars, 1792-1802), 98
[*see also*: individual campaigns; eg St Lucia, St Vincent]
Worcester (1651), 108
World War I (1914-1918), 23,96
[*see also*: individual campaigns; eg Western Front]
Zealand (1700), 145
Bathsheba, 156
Bavaria, 114,116
Bay of Biscay, 99
Bayonne, 105,133
Bayreuth, 116
Beane, Maj George, 119
Beaufort, Duke of, 13
Beatitudes, 113
Bedford (family), 17
Beechey, Sir William, 125
Belcher, - 97
Belgium, 47,53,89,90,115,117,157,159,163
    Austrian Netherlands, 90,116
    Rebellion against Dutch rule (1830), 90
    Spanish Netherlands, 90
Bell, William, 7
Bellange, Joseph Louis Hippolyte, 34
Bengal, 86
    Nawab (ruler), 158
Benjamin (Israelite tribe), 99
Bentham, Lt Col, 77,79
Bentinck, Capt C A F, 109
Berdan, Col, 149
Beresford, Lady Anne, 7
Beresford, Marshal William Carr, 7,83,154
Bernhard of Sax-Weimar, Prince, 92
Bexhill, 83
Bible, 9,43,102,156
    New Testament
        Gospels, 163
            John, 163
            Matthew, 163
    Old Testament, 120,156
        Amos, 156
        Exodus, 160

        Jeremiah, 156
        Kings, 1 & II, 120,155
        Malachi, 120
        Psalms, 156
        Samuel I, 99,155
Biddle, Col Sgt John, 12
Bismarck, Count von, 96
'Black hole of Calcutta', 67,158
Blackall, Ensign G, 76
Blakeney, Sir Edward, 93
Blucher, Marshal, 64,72,88,110,112,168
Board of Ordnance, 113,131
Bolingbroke, Viscount Henry St John, 6
    A Letter to Sir William Wyndham, 6
    Letter on the spirit of patriotism, 6
    Letters on the study and use of history, 6
Bologna, 163
Bombay, 86
Bonaparte, Joseph [*see*: Joseph Bonaparte]
Bonaparte, Napoleon [*see*: Napoleon Bonaparte]
Booth, Charles, 7
Booth, Henry William, 7
Bordeaux, 102
Borghese, Pauline, 151
Bossu (wood), 49,51,54,55
Bourbons, 89,111,114,115,147
    Second Restoration, 147
Bourgeoys (family), 131
Bourgeoys, Martin, 131
Boroughbridgeshire, 168
Bowes, Gen, 168
Bowles, Lt & Capt George, 7
Boyce, Lt J, 48,51,52,75 [referred to as Captain on this page]
Breast plate, 95,135
Brereton, Lt William, 7
Briscall, Rev Samuel, 7
Bristol, 121
Britain/British [*see*: Great Britain]
Brock (commander in King's German Legion), 32
Brotherton, Col, 80
Brown, Col, 144
Brune, Marshal [Guillaume-Marie-Anne], 89
Brunswick-Oels, Duke of, 94
Brussels, 53,107,112,113,126
Brydon, Dr, 85
Byron, Lord George, 116
Buck, Lt, 66
Bugle, 39,48
Bull, Maj Robert, 119
Bullard, Gen Robert, 7

175

Bulow, Friedrich Wilhelm von, 1,104,106
Burke, Edmund, 19
   First letter on a regicide peace, 19
Burnes (political officer in Afghanistan), 85
Busaco [*see also under:* **Battles, Campaigns, Wars**]
   Hill, 123
   Ridge, 123
Butler, Lady Elizabeth, 34
Buxton, Sir Thomas Fowell, 164
Byng, Admiral Sir George, 152
Byng, Maj George, 152
Byng, Gen Sir John, 66,78,93,103,108,152,153
Byron, Lord George Gordon, 7,34
   Childe Harold, 34

C

Caananites, 120
Cabul, 85
Cadiz, 102
Calcutta, 99
Calderon, Luise, 122
Cambridge, Duke of, 153
Cambridge University
   St John's College, 114
Cambronne, General, 159
Cameron, Lt J, 66,76 [referred to as Captain on this page]
Campbell, Maj Gen, 121
Canada, 103 [*see also:* specific regions; ie Nova Scotia]
   Commander-in-Chief, 158
   Governor General, 158
   Upper Canada
      Lieutenant Governor, 139,158
Cannandine, David, 17
Canning, George, 88,115,142
   Ministry (1827), 142
Canova, Antonio, 2,42,64,151,152
   Cupid and Psyche, 151
   Daedalus and Icarus, 151
   George Washington (statue), 152
   Hebe, 151
   Perseus with Medusa's head, 151
   The Pugilists, 151
   Stuart Monument, 152
   Venus and Mars, 152
   Venus Victrix, 151
Cape of Good Hope, 117
   [*see also under:* **Battles, Campaigns, Wars**]
   Commander-in-Chief, 139
   Governor, 139

Caphtor [*see:* Crete]
Captara [*see:* Crete]
Caribbean, 37,121,122,161,167
   [*see also:* **Battles, Campaigns, Wars** - West Indies]
Carlyle, Thomas, 9,10
   History of the French Revolution, 9
Carmathen, 124 [*see also under:* Monuments]
Carmel, Mount, 55,120
Carnarvon, 140
Carnatic, 101
Carnot, Lazare-Nicolas-Margeurite, 63,144,147
   Memoirs au roi en juillet 1814, 147
Caroline, Queen, 116
Carss, Lt John, 7
Carter, Webb-, B W [*see:* Webb-Carter, B W]
Casque, 95
Castlereagh, Robert Stewart (Lord), 53,88,114, 115,116
Casualties
   Albuera
      British
         1st Bn/3rd Regiment, 33
         2nd Bn/48th Regiment, 33
   Quatre Bras
      British
         5th Brigade, 75
         33rd Regiment, 51,76
   Waterloo
      British, 68
         5th Brigade, 75
            Officers, 75
         33rd Regiment, 66,76
Cathcart (9th Earl), 104
Cathcart, Lord, 83,158
Catholicism, 168
Catholics, 88
   [*see also:* Irish - Catholics]
   Church, 69
   Emancipation (Act) (1829), 88,142
Caton Woodville, Richard
   [*see:* Woodville, Richard Caton]
Celerico, 123
Ceylon, 117,165
Chain mail, 135
Chalmers, Maj, 71
Channel, 98,119
Charles I (King of England, 1625-1649), 108,120
Charles II (King of England, 1660-1685), 20,36,107,108,120
Charles X (King of France, 1824-1830), 146

Index

Charles XII (King of Sweden, 1682-1718), 4,63,144,145-146
Charleville (royal armoury), 134
Charlotte, Queen (consort to King William IV), 146
Chasse, General David, 91
Chatham, 136
Chatham, Earl of, 115,122
Chelsea, 84
   Hospital, 84
      Governor, 84
Cheltenham, 124
Chernaya (rivers), 110
Chesterfield, Earl of, 6
Childe Harold (Lord Byron), 34
China, 86
Christ, 113,120,163
Christ Church College (Oxford)
   [*see under*: Oxford Univerisity]
Christ's Hospital (school), 156
Christian Year, The (John Keble), 79
Chronicles of ancient sunlight (Henry Williamson), 4
Christie, Ensign, 97
Church of England, 168
Churches
   SS Apostoli, 151
   St Peter's, 151,152
Cintra [*see*: Convention of Cintra]
Clabon, Capt E, 76
Clarence, Duke of, 4,40,144,146
   [see also: William IV]
Clarissa Harlowe (Samuel Richardson), 6
Clarke, Christopher (Volunteer), 50,96,97
Clement XIII (Pope)
   Tomb, 151
Clement XIV (Pope)
   Tomb, 151
Clinton, Gen Sir Henry, 78,167,168
   A few remarks...operations of the British Army during the late campaign in Spain, 168
Clinton, Sir Henry, 167
Clubs, 106
Cock fighting, 87
Cocks, 87
Coclough, Maj G, 75
Coimbra, 123
Colborne, Sir John, 11,33,42,53,66,77,78,79, 155,156-158
Colborne, Samuel, 156
Colours, 11,22,31,32,50,65,66,73,74,96,97,98, 150,151
   Escort parties, 31,32,64,73,97,150

King's Colour, 96
Regimental Colour, 96
Column [*see under*: **Tactics**]
Commonwealth (1649-1660), 20,108,120
Confederation of the Rhine, 90
Congress of Aix-la-Chapelle (1818), 115
Congress of Laibach (1821), 115
Congress of Paris (1814), 116
Congress of Verona (1822), 115
Congress of Vienna (1815), 53,88,90,115,116
   Act of Federation (1820), 117
   Act of Vienna (1815/1820), 90,116,117
Congress of Troppau (1820), 115
Congress sytem, 115
Consalvi, Cardinal Ercole, 116
Conscription, 14,36,37
Continent [*see*: Europe]
Continental System, 163
Convention (3 July 1815), 111
   Article 12, 111,112
Convention of Cintra (1808), 87
Convention of the Elbe, 82
Cooke, Maj Gen George, 40,51,103,153
Corfu, 152
Cornwallis, Admiral Sir William, 98,
Cornwallis, Gen Charles (1st Marquess), 101,114,161,167
Corunna, 14,15,140,154
   [*see also under*: **Battles, Campaigns, Wars**]
Cotton, 86
Cotton, Sir Willoughby, 85
Courier, 84
Cracow, 117
Craufurd, Brig Gen Catlin, 7
Craufurd, Brig Gen Robert, 15,18,94,123
Cretan-Mycenaean civilisation, 156
Crete, 156
Criminal code, 138
Croations, 138
Cromwell, Oliver, 94
Cuba, 102
   [see also: specific locations; eg Havana]
Cudmore
   Governor, 153
Cuirass, 94
Cupid and Psyche (Antonio Canova), 151
Czak, 99
Czarytoryski, Adam George, 116

D

Daedalus and Icarus (Antonio Canova), 151
Daily Telegraph, 110
Dalmatia, 116
Danes, 159
Danzig, 116
Darcy, Mr (character in Jane Austen's
    Pride and prejudice), 19
David (King of Israel, 10th Century BC), 42,
    67,99,155,156
David, Jacques-Louis, 152
Dawes, Capt, 102
Deal, 125
Decken, Col Frederick von der, 83
De Lancey, Lady [*see*: Lancey, Lady De]
De Lancey, Sir William Howe
    [*see*: Lancey, Sir William Howe De]
De Medici, Catherine
    [*see*: Medici, Catherine de]
Denmark, 116,117,145,146
Derby (family), 17
D'Erlon, Marshal Jean-Baptiste Drouet,
    52,97,114,141,152
Desaix, General Louis Charles Antoine, 152
Devigne, Capt, 148
Devonshire (family), 17
Dickens, Charles
    A tale of two cities, 9
Dictionary of National Biography, 98,125,141
Dighton, Robert, 34
Dissenters, 36
D'Istries, Capo, 116
Don (River), 128
Dnieper (River), 128
Donzelot, General Francis Xavier, 66,68,152
Dorians, 156
Dost Mohammed, 85
Douglas, Sgt John, 15,18
Dover, 161
Dreyse, Johann von, 149
Drivers, 113
Drums, 39
    Calls, 113
        'Assembly' [*see*: 'General']
        'Gathering' [*see*: 'General']
        'General', 47,84
Duery, Ensign G, 76
Duke of Albermarle [*see*: Albermarle, Duke of]
Duke of Beaufort [*see*: Beaufort, Duke of]
Duke of Brunswick-Oels
    [*see*: Brunswick-Oels, Duke of]
Duke of Cambridge [*see*: Cambridge, Duke of]
Duke of Clarence [*see*: Clarence, Duke of]
Duke of Elchingen [*see*: Elchingen, Duke of]
Duke of Kent [*see*: Kent, Duke of]
Duke of Marlborough
    [*see*: Marlborough, Duke of]
Duke of Portland [*see*: Portland, Duke of]
Duke of Sussex [*see*: Sussex, Duke of]
Duke of Wellington [*see*: Wellington, Duke of]
Duke of York [*see*: York, Duke of]
Dumbarton Castle
    Governor, 162
Dundas, Gen Sir David, 26,28,29,30,31
    *Rules and regulations for the field formation
    exercise of movements of His Majesty's Forces*,
    28,28,30
Dundreary, Lord (character in play, *Our
    American cousin*), 49,87
Duoro (River), 124
Dvina (River), 145
Dyneley, Lt Gen Thomas, 7

E

Eagle (French standard), 14,69,162
Earl of Cathcart [*see*: Cathcart (9th Earl)]
Earl of Chatham [*see*: Chatham, Earl of]
Earl of Mornington [*see*: Mornington, Earl of]
Earl of Munster [*see*: Munster, Earl of]
Earl of Uxbridge [*see*: Uxbridge, Earl of]
East India Company, 84,85,86,101,131,164
    [*see also under*: UNITS AND
    FORMATIONS - *Great Britain*]
    Presidency, 101
        Bombay Presidency, 101
        Court of directors, 164
        Madras Presidency, 101
            Commander-in-Chief, 139
East Indies, 86
Ebro (River), 124
Edinburgh, 102,143,144
    University, 10
Edward, Duke of Kent [*see*: Kent, Duke of]
Egmont-op-Zee, 140
Egypt, 156,157
    [*see also under*: **Battles, Campaigns, Wars**]
    Pharoah, 160
    Plagues, 160
Elau, 89
Elba, 88,107,112,155,157,163,168
Elchingen, 89
Elector of Hanover [*see under*: Hanover]

Elgin marbles, 152
Elijah, 2,42,43,55,120
Elley, Col John, 13
Elchingen, Duke of [*see*: Ney, Marshal]
Eliot, T S
  After strange gods, 22
Elisha, 120
Elizabeth College, 157
Elphinstone, Capt (later Col) James Drummond, 5,40,58,84,126
Elphinstone, Lord, 84
Elphinstone, Hon William, 84
Elphinstone, Lt Col William George Keith, 5,40,48,57,58,66,70,71,73,75,84,85
Elvas, 105
England, 6,12,82,88,91,99,104,105,107,114, 121,122,124,140,144,159,167
  [*see also*: **Great Britain**]
  King, 83 [*see also*: names of individual kings]
Epsom, 106
Escutcheon, 112
Estates, 17
Europe, 47,69,86,115,116,137
  Liberal movements, 115
European Common Market, 116
Exposition of affairs at St Helena during the captivity of Napoleon (Barry Edward O'Meara), 165

F

Face of battle: a study of Agincourt, Waterloo and the Somme, The (John Keegan), 34
Farming, 106
  Husbandry, 106
  Stock breeding, 106
Ferrara, 163
Ferrars, Edward (character in Jane Austen's *Sense and sensibility*), 19
Few remarks...operations of the British Army during the late short campaign in Spain, A (Gen Sir Henry Clinton), 168
First letter on a regicide peace (Edmund Burke), 19
Fitzgerald, Lord Edward, 13
Fitzgerald, Lt Edward Fox, 13
Flanders, 120,140,141
  [*see also under*: **Battles, Campaigns, Wars**]
'Flash in the pan', 133
Flushing
  [*see also under*: **Battles, Campaigns, Wars**]
  Commandant, 122
  Governor, 122
Fontaibleau, 163

Forge, 113
Forsyth, Alexander, 134
Fort St George (India), 161
Fort William (India)
  Commandant, 161
Fowell Buxton, Sir Thomas
  [*see*: Buxton, Sir Thomas Fowell]
Fox under my cloak (Henry Williamson), 4
Foy, General Maximilian Sebastien, 66,68,152
  Histoire de la guerre de la Peninsule, 152
  Widow, 152
France, 36,37,69,87,88,89,90,102,104,105, 106,110,112,114,115,116,121,131,133, 147,152,154,162,163
  [*see also under*: **Battles, Campaigns, Wars**; UNITS AND FORMATIONS; specific locations (eg Paris); French Revolution]
  Chamber of Deputies, 152
  Church
    Archbishops, 162
    Bishops, 162
  Colonies, 117
  Empire (Napoleonic), 147
  Marshal, 114
  Monarchy [*see*: Bourbons]
  Republic (1792-1802), 102
    Committee of General Defence, 147
    Committee of Public Safety, 147
    Directory, 102,147
  Second Empire, 89
  Third Republic, 89
Franchise, 16
Fraser, Sgt John, 14
Frasne, 52
Frazer, Sir Augustus, 7
Frederick II (King of Prussia, 1740-1786), 95
Frederick Augustus II (Elector of Saxony)
  [*see*: Augustus III, King of Poland]
Frederick William I (King of Prussia, 1713-1740), 95
French, 27,39,57,58,87,94,97,98,101,104, 105,107,108,112,114,115,116,121,123, 126,135,140,144,152,157,158,162
  [*see also under*: UNITS AND FORMATIONS - France]
  Government, 112 [*see also under*: *France*]
  Surrender (1940), 112
French Revolution (1789-1799), 27,89,104, 147
Friedland, 89
Friesland - East, 116
Furlong, Lt James, 5,51,76 [referred to as Captain on this page], 103
Furlong, William, 103

Memories of the Waterloo campaign

G

Gagahan, Sebastian, 125
Galicia, 116
Garden of Gethsemene
  [*see*: Gethsemene]
Gardiner, Lt Col Sir Robert, 119
Gawlor, Col, 80
General Order (23 February 1800), 99
Gentleman, 18
Genappe, 55,57,58,86,126
  [*see also under*: **Battles,Campaigns,Wars**]
Geneva, 117
Geneva [*see*: Liquor]
Genoa, 117,163,164
Gentry, 17,19,106,109
George I (King of England, 1714-1727), 82
George III (King of England, 1760-1820), 82,114,121,122,146,147
George IV (King of England, 1830-1837), 85,95,116,125,146,152
  Coronation, 95,142
  Lord High Steward, 142
Gerard, Lord, 120
Germans/Germany, 28,94,115,146,147,158,163
  [*see also* specific regions; eg Hanover, Westphalia]
  Classical school, 151
  Germanic Confederation, 117
  Liberal movements, 115
  Nationalists, 117
Gethsemene, 163
Gibbons, Pte James, 49
Gibraltar, 99,104,121,154
  Straits, 99
Glasgow, 2,53,100,101,103,127
  Central Library, 101
  Ducanon Street, 101
  Grammar School, 102
  Sauchiehall Street, 101
  Trongate, 100,101
  University, 102
Glasgow Herald, 111
Glover, Michael, 12,16
  Wellington's army in the Peninsula 1808-1814, 16
Goethe, Johann Wolfgang von, 165
Golden virgin, The (Henry Williamson), 4
Goliath, 155,156
Gore (brothers), 23,40,98
Gore, Maj Gen Arthur, 98,99
Gore, Lt Arthur, 3,50,76,102
  [referred to as Captain on this page], 98
Gore, Vice Admiral Sir John, 40,98,99
Gore, Lt Col Ralph, 98
Gore, Capt Ralph, 71,75,102
Goya, 34
Graeme, Thomas, 104
Graham, Robert, 68
Graham, Sir Thomas, 27,42,103,104, 105,106,154
Graham, Lady (wife of Sir Thomas Graham), 104
Graham, Sgt, 108
Granby, Marquess of, 23
Grant, Gen James, 161
Grasse, Comte de, 161
Great Britain, 16,36,111,115,116,117,122, 127,133,152,162
  [*see also*: England; specific locations]
  Ambassador in France, 112
  Counties, 36,37
  Crown, 86,146,164
  [*see also*: individual kings/queens]
  Government, 37,57,82,86,102,115,131
    Cabinet, 116,142
    Treasury, 134,135
  Peerage, 106 [*see also*: Aristocracy]
  Police force, 137
  Royal Family, 144
  [*see also*: individual Sovereigns]
Greece, 115
  [*see also*: **Battles, Campaigns, Wars -** Greek War of Indpendence]
Grey, Earl, 147
Guidiana, 154
Guerrilla warfare, 138
Guernica (Pablo Picasso), 73
Guernsey, 140
  Lieutenant Governor, 157
Guide to Captain Siborne's new Waterloo model, A, 93
Gunsmiths, 131

H

Habsburgs, 94,95,116,137,138,146
  [*see also*: Austria-Hungary]
Haidar Ali, 101
Haigh (family), 23,50,100
Haigh, Capt G D, 75
Haigh, Quartermaster (father of Haigh brothers), 100,102
Haigh, Capt John, 3,5,10,13,50,53,72,75,100

Haigh, Lt Thomas D, 66,100
Halkett, Lt Gen Charles, 82
Halkett, Maj Gen Sir Colin, 40,42,47,49,52, 59,62,65,66,73,75,82,83,84,92,94
Halkett, Maj Gen Frederick Godar, 82,158
Halkett, Lt Col Baron von Hugh, 40,42,68, 84,158-159
Hamilton, Lt Col, 75
Hamilton, George, 151
Hamilton, Vereker M, 34
Hampshire, 168
Hangar, George (*To all sportsmen*), 132
Hanover, 82,116,146
   Elector [*see*: George III]
Hardenburg, Prince, 116
Hardwicke Grange, 155
Harris, Rifleman
   The Recollections of Rifleman Harris, 18
Harris, Maj Gen George, 101,160,161-162
Harris, Rev George, 161
Hart, Lt J, 48,62,76 [referred to as Captain on this page],103
Harty, Capt K, 66,75
Havana, 102
Haversack, 54
Hay, Lt Col, 15
Headdress [*see*: **Uniforms** - Headress]
Heathcote, Ralph
   Letters of a young diplomat and soldier during the time of Napoleon, 7
Hebe (Antonio Canova), 151
Hebrews, 99,156,160
Hebron, 156
Heliogoland, 117
Hill, John, 153
Hill, Gen Sir Rowland, 66,78,104,153-155, 157,168
Histoire de la guerre de la Peninsule (General Maximilian Sebastien Foy), 152
History of England from 1815 (S Walpole), 147
History of the French Revolution (Thomas Carlyle), 9
Hitler, Adolf, 112
Hodson, Ensign W, 76
Holborn, 13
Holland, 1,90,104,117,140,167
   [*see also*: Netherlands; specific regions]
   Batavian Republic, 90
   Colonies, 117
   Ministry of War, 90
   Rebellion against Napoleon (1813), 90
   United Provinces, 90

Holy Alliance, 115
Holy Roman Empire, 109,117
Holy See [*see*: Papacy]
Home Office, 36
Hong Kong, 86
Hope, Sir John, 106,154
Horse Guards (administrative centre of Commander-in-Chief), 23,37,64
Horses, 8,11,32,54,72,73,92,95,96, 111,113,118,136
Hougoumont, 60,159
   [*see also under*: **Battles, Campaigns, Wars** - Waterloo]
Houldsworth, 100
House of Commons [*see* under: Parliament]
House of Lords [*see* under: Parliament]
Howard, Ensign JA, 76
Hugo, Victor, 34
   Les Chatiments, 34
Hull, 144
Humboldt, William von, 116
Hungarians, 138
   [*see also under*: Austria-Hungary - Military Frontier - Settlers]
   Herdsmen, 138
Hungary [*see*: Austria-Hungary]
Hunter's Hill (farm), 102
Hussey, Sir R, 93
Hyderabad, Nizam of, 101
Hyeres, 104

I

Iberian Peninsula, 24,26,37,124,167
   [*see also*: Portugal, Spain; *see also under*: **Battles, Campaigns, Wars** - Peninsular War]
India, 2,56,85,86,87,98,100,101,131, 143,158,162,167
   [*see also*: individual place names; eg Bombay]
   Fortresses, 101
   [*see also under*: **Battles, Campaigns, Wars**]
   Government, 162
   Moghul empire, 85
India Act (1784), 86
Indigo, 86
Industrial Revolution, 16
Inn-keeper, 14
Inns, 14
Ionia,156
   Islands, 117,152
   Lord High Commissioner, 158

Memories of the Waterloo campaign

Instructions for civil and military surveyors in topographical plan-drawing...(William Siborne), 93
Interregnum [see: Commonwealth]
Ireland, 12,27,83,153,154,161
[see also: individual locations; eg Londonderry]
  Adjutant General, 168
  Chief Secretary, 114
  Commander-in-Chief, 167
  Lord Lieutenant, 114,142
  Privy Councillor, 153,158
Irish
  Catholics, 12,114
  Parliament, 114
    Protestant members, 114
  Peasantry, 12
  Rebels (Irish insurrection, 1797-1798), 136
Iron, 156
Iscariot [see: Judas Iscariot]
Israel, 43,99,120,156 [see also: Palestine]
  King, 155,156
Israelites, 99
Italy, 104,116
[see also: specific regions; eg Lombardy, Venetia]

J

Jails, 12
Jamaica, 97,144
James II (King of England 1685-1688), 1,6
Janssens, General, 90
Jeffey (prize colt), 106
Jellalabad, 85
Jena (bridge), 110,112
Jersey
  Lieutenant Governor, 83
Jerusalem, 156,163
Jesus [see: Christ]
Jezebel (wife of Ahab, King of Israel, 9th Century BC), 120
Johnson, Dr Samuel, 9
John the Baptist, 120
Jones, Lt Rice, 7
Jordan, 99
Joseph Bonaparte, 151,154
Jourdan, Marshal Jean-Baptiste, 154
Journal, 7
Journal of Army Historical Research, 2
Journeyman, 49,87
Judah, 99
  King, 156
Judas Iscariot, 163

K

Keats, John, 7,8
Keble, John, 168
  The Christian year, 168
Keegan, John
  The face of battle: a study of Agincourt, Waterloo and the Somme, 34
Keilmansegge, Maj Gen Count von, 59,139
Kempt, Gen, 61
Kennedy, Gen Shaw, 141
Kent, Duke of, 147
Kew, 146
King...[see under: name of king; eg James II]
Kingdom of the Two Sicilies
  [see: Two Sicilies, Kingdom of]
Kish (father of Saul, King of Israel), 99
Knight, Capt C, 58,75
Knighthood, 16
Knox, Maj Gen, 121

L

Labedoyere, Col, 111
Labedoyere, Comtesse de, 111
La Belle Alliance, 78,168
Lacy,-, 97
La Haye Sainte (farm), 78,93,125
  [see also under: **Battles, Campaigns, Wars - Waterloo**]
Lancey, Lady De, 95
Lancey, Sir William Howe De, 163
Last Supper, 163
Latham, Lt Matthew, 97
Lauenburg, 116,117
Laurence, Sgt, 98
Lavater, Johann Kaspar, 2,42,71,165
Lawrence, Sir Thomas, 142
Leach,- 94
Leczcynski, Stanislaw, 145
Lefebvre, General P, 114
Le Mesurier, Commissary General Havilland
  [see: Mesurier, Commissary General Havilland Le]
Les Chatiments (Victor Hugo), 34
Letters, 6,7,10
Letters of a young diplomat and soldier during the time of Napoleon (Ralph Heathcote), 7
Letter to Sir William Wyndham, A (Viscount Henry St John Bolingbroke), 6
Letter on the spirit of patriotism, A (Viscount Henry St John Bolingbroke), 6

Letters on the study and use of history (Viscount Henry St John Bolingbroke), 6
Lever, Dr, 49
Lightburne, Maj Gen, 123
Line [*see under:* **Tactics**]
Linzee, Rear Admiral, 98
Liquor, 135
Lithuania, 128,130
Little Selsey, 12
Liverpool, Lord, 115,116,123
Lloyd, Maj William, 52,113
Local Militia Act (1808), 36
Lombardy, 116
London, 93,106,107,139,140,152,153
  Pall Mall, 106
London Society, 102
Londonderry
  Governor, 153
Londonderry, Marquis of (1st)
  [*see:* Stewart, Robert]
Londonderry, Marquis of (2nd)
  [*see:* Castlereagh, Robert Stewart]
Longden, Capt J, 75
Lord Bathurst [*see:* Bathurst, Lord]
Lord Castlereagh
  [*see:* Castlereagh, Robert Stewart]
Lord Cathcart [*see:* Cathcart, Lord]
Lord Cornwallis
  [*see:* Cornwallis, Gen Charles (1st Marquess)]
Lord Dundreary [*see:* Dundreary, Lord]
Lord Gerard [*see:* Gerard, Lord]
Lord Liverpool [*see:* Liverpool, Lord]
Lord Melbourne [*see:* Melbourne, Lord]
Lord Mornington [*see:* Mornington, Lord]
Lord Perceval [*see:* Perceval, Lord]
Lord Raglan [*see:* Raglan, Lord]
Lord Seaton [*see:* Seaton, Lord]
Lord Seaton's regiment at Waterloo, 77
Lords Lieutenant, 36,37
Lorne, Lord, 108
Louis Napoleon, 90
Louis Philippe, 114
Louis XV (King of France, 1715-1774), 9
Louis XVI (King of France, 1774-1792), 102,114
Louis XVIII (King of France, 1814-1824), 89,114,146,147
Louisa Victoria, Princess, 147
Love and the loveless (Henry Williamson), 4
Lowe, Lt Gen Sir Hudson, 163-165
Lynam, Capt J, 76
Lynedoch, Lord [*see:* Graham, Sir Thomas]

M

Macdonell, Lt Col James, 108
Macedonians, 156
Mackinnon, Maj Gen, 123
Mack von Leiberich, General, 89
Macmillan, Rev Hugh, 8,53,73
Macnaghten, Sir William, 85
Madison, Philip [character in Henry Williamson's novels], 5
Madras, 86,161
  Government, 162
Madrid, 87
Magdeburg, 147
Magyars [*see:* Hungarians]
Maitland, Capt, 69
Maitland, Brig Gen Frederick, 122
Maitland, Gen Sir Peregrine, 59,66,74,78, 103,107,139
Maitland, Thomas, 139
Malaria, 122
Malta, 105,117,156
  [*see also under:* **Battles, Campaigns, Wars**]
Marches/marching, 31,118
Margate, 14
Marlborough, Duke of, 26,88
Marquess of Granby [*see:* Granby, Marquess of]
Marquess of Londonderry [*see:* Londonderry, Marquess of]
Marquess of Wellesley [*see:* Wellesley, Marquess of]
Marseilles, 164
Martinique, 122
  Governor, 152
Massena, Marshal [Andre], 89,123,167
Masterson, Sgt Patrick, 14
Matthias I, 138
Matthew (Gospel), 113
Mauberge (royal armoury), 134
Maximilian I (Holy Roman Emperor/Ruler of Austria, 1493-1519), 95
Maximilian I (Elector/King of Bavaria, 1799-1825), 114
McIntyre, Capt W, 66
Mcready, Maj Edward, 14
Mecklenburg, 112
Medici, Catherine de, 113
Medows, Gen, 161
Meikland, Lt, 66
Melbourne, Lord, 147,153
Memoirs au roi en juillet 1814 (Lazare-Nicolas-Margeurite Carnot), 147

Mengs, Anton, 151
Menshikov, Prince Aleksander, 110
Mercer, Capt A Cavalie, 118,119
Merxem, 144
  [see also under: **Battles, Campaigns, Wars**]
Messiah, 156
Mesurier, Commissary General Havilland Le, 7
Meuse (River), 89
Mexico, 102
Milborne Port, 140
Milhaud, General Edouard-Jean-Baptiste, 141
Miollis, General, 163
Minie, Capt, 148
Minister of Supply, 23
Mirkland, Capt J, 76
Moira, Lord, 104
Monck, General George, 120
Mondego (River), 123
Monuments
  Picton
    Carmathen, 125
    St Paul's Cathedral, 125
Moore, Lt Gen Sir John, 15,24,27,83,87,
  105,110,140,141,154,156,167
Morice, Col C, 75
Mornington, Earl of, 87
Mornington, Lord
  [see: Wellesley, Lord Richard]
Mornington, Lt the Earl of (6th Duke of
  Wellington)
  [see: Wellington (6th Duke)]
Moscow, 69,127,145
  [see also under: **Battles, Campaigns, Wars -
  Russia**]
Moses, 160
Moskwa, Prince de la, 111
  [see also: Ney, Marshal]
Mount Carmel [see: Carmel, Mount]
Muir, James, 102
Muir, Thomas, 100,101
Mules, 113,118
Munich, 114
Munster, Earl of [see: Clarence, Duke of]
Murray, Lt Gen Sir George, 93
Muscovite [see: Russia/Russians]
Mysore, 100,101,162
  Governor general, 87,101

N

Nantes, 114
Naples (Bay), 105

Napoleon Bonaparte, 5,9,47,52,53,59,60,61,
  65,66,68,69,70,72,73,88,89,90,95,96,107,
  111,112,114,115,117,119,124,126,127,
  129,135,137,147,151,155,157,162,163,
  164,165,168
Napoleon III, 89,111
Napoleon in exile: a voice from St Helena (Barry
  Edward O'Meara), 165
Nassau, 90
Nelson, Admiral Lord Horatio, 64,105
Nesselrode, Karl Robert, 116
Netherlands, 124 [see also: Holland]
  King, 163 [see also: William Frederick I]
  Kingdom of the Netherlands, 90,116
    North Netherlands, 91
    South Netherlands, 91
Neuchatel, 116,117
New Forest, 83
Newman, Sgt William, 14
Newmarket Craven, 106
New Statesman, 97
New York, 102,161
Ney, Marshal, 49,51,52,53,55,61,65,66,68,70,
  80,88,89,95,110,111,112,114, 125,129
Nizam of Hyderabad
  [see: Hyderabad, Nizam of]
Nobility [see: Aristocracy]
Nolan, Pte Babington, 13
Nootka Sound, 102
North America, 159
Norway, 117

O

Oels, Brunswick-, Duke of
  [see: Brunswick-Oels, Duke of]
Ogle, Lt J G 66,76
Old Pretender [see: Stuart, James Edward]
O'Meara, Barry Edward, 164-165
  *Exposition of affairs at St Helena during the
  captivity of Napoleon*, 165
  Napoleon in exile: a voice from St Helena, 165
Opium, 86
Oporto, 154
Orange (House), 90
Orange, Prince of, 91,141,155,163
  [see also: Frederick William I]
Origins of modern English society 1780-1880, The
  (H Perkins), 18
Ottoman Empire, 145,146
Our American cousin (Tom Taylor), 87
Oxford Movement, 168
Oxford University, 155

Christ Church College, 104,140
Oriel College, 168
    Fellow, 168
    Tutor, 168
    Professor of Poetry, 168

P

Pagan, Lt James, 5,62,143,144
Pagan, Capt S A, 76 [possibly a reference to Lt James Pagan]
Paget, Gen Edward, 154
Paget, Henry [see: Uxbridge, Earl of]
Paget, Henry William [see: Uxbridge, Lord]
Paine, Thomas (Rights of man), 102
Painting, 152
Pakenham family, 7
Palestine, 156,163 [see also: Israel]
Pamela (Samuel Richardson), 6
Pamplona, 124
Papacy, 116,162 [see also: Vatican]
Papal states, 117,163
    [see also: names of individual states; eg Ferrara]
    Inspector General of Fine Arts and Antiquities, 152
Paris, 53,67,69,78,102,107,110,111,112, 126,151,152,155
    Boulevard de l'Observatoire, 111
    Insurrection (1795), 9
    Louvre, 113
    Luxembourg Gardens, 89,111
    Occupation (1815-1818), 139
    Tuilleries, 111,113
Paris, Treaty of [see: Treaty of Paris]
Parkinson, Maj E, 75
Parliament, 17,23,37,106,120,140,162
    House of Commons, 115,124,125, 153,164,168
    Speaker, 124
    House of Lords, 124,146,147
    Peers, 146,147
    Reform, 146,147
Patrols, 54
Pattison, Alexander, 57
Pattison, Frederick Hope, 1,2,4,5,6,7,8,10,11, 15,16,22,26,28,32,33,34,40,42,43,53,73, 74,75,84,88,90,92,93,94,96,100,106,107, 116,119,130,132,134,135,137,142,146, 147,148,150,157,158,162,163,164,165
    Personal recollections of the Waterloo campaign…, 1
Peasantry, 14

Peel, Sir Robert, 147
    Ministry (1841-1846), 88
Peerage [see: Aristocracy]
Pelissier, Aimable, 110
Pembrokeshire, 121
Peninsula [see: Iberian Peninsula]
Perceval, Lord, 115
Percy, Lord, 161
Perevolochna, 145
Persian Gulf, 86
Persians, 156
Perkins, H (The origins of modern English society 1780-1880), 18
Perseus with Medusa's head (Antonio Canova), 151
Personal recollections of the Waterloo campaign…(Frederick Hope Pattison), 1
Perthshire, 104
Peter I ('The Great') (Tsar of Russia, 1696-1725), 145
Philistines, 66,99,155,156
Philoppoteaux, 34
Phoenecians, 120
Pickets, 52,54,118 [see also: Sentries]
    Out pickets, 134
Picasso, Pablo
    Guernica, 73
Picton, Thomas, 121
Picton, Lt Gen Sir Thomas, 39,57,61,70,121-126,141,168
    Monument [see under: Monuments]
    Portrait, 125
Picton, Gen William, 121
Pigot, Maj Gen, 105
Pine, Brig Gen John, 164
Pisani, 151
Pitt, Sir William, 86,114
Pius VI, 162
Pius VII, 162,163
Plague, 146
Plymouth, 154
Poland, 116,117,128,129,130,137,145,146
    [see also: Warsaw, Grand Duchy; specific regions (eg Cracow)]
Poles, 33
Pomerania, 116
Ponsonby, Maj Gen Sir William, 141
Pontiff [see: Pope]
Poole, 153
Pope, 69,151,152,162
    [see also names of individual Popes; eg Clement XIV]

Portland, Duke of, 114
Port of Spain, 122
Portugal, 87,105,140,153,154,157,159,167
   [see also: **Battles, Campaigns, Wars** - Peninsular War]
Posen [see: Warsaw, Grand Duchy]
Postal services, 7
Poyston, 121
Practical treatise on topographical surveying and drawing..., A, (William Siborne), 93
Pride and prejudice (Jane Austen), 19
Prince Bernhard of Sax-Weimar
   [see: Bernhard of Sax-Weimar, Prince]
Prince de la Moskwa
   [see: Moskwa, Prince de la]
Prince of Orange [see: Orange, Prince of]
Prince Regent, 152,157 [see also: George IV]
Prisoners-of-War, 82,94
   Croats, 94
   Danish, 94
   Dutch, 94
   Italians, 94
   Poles, 94
Proby, Lord John, 103,107
Prophets, 120
Prussia/Prussians, 111,112,115,116,117,127
   [see also under: UNITS AND FORMATIONS]
Pugilists, The (Antonio Canova), 151
Pyrenees, 105,124

Q

Quatre Bras (village), 49,57,86
   [see also under: **Battles, Campaigns, Wars**]
Queen Caroline [see: Caroline, Queen]
Queen Victoria [see: Victoria]

R

Raffet, Auguste, 34
Raglan, Lord, 110
Ramsgate, 14
Ramsay, Maj Norman, 119
Ramses II, 160
Razumovsky [adviser to Tsar Alexander I], 116
Rebecque, Constantin de, 92
Recollections of Rifleman Harris, The, 18
Red Indians, 27,102
Reform Bill (1832), 16,88,146,147,153
Regulating Act (1773), 86
Regulations for the Rifle Corps, 19

Restoration (1660), 108
Reid, Capt J, 75
Reille, Marshal Honore-Charles-Michel-Joseph, 152
Rey, Emmanuel, 105
Reynier (French commander), 39
Rhine (River), 89,140
Richardson, Samuel, 6,7
   Clarissa Harlowe, 6
   Pamela, 6
   Sir Charles Grandison, 6
Rights of man (Thomas Paine), 102
Riots, 137
River...
   [see: name of river; eg Don (River)]
Roads/routes, 49
   Brussels-Charleroi, 57
   Nivelle road, 51,155
   Trinidad, 122
   Wavre road, 59,125
Roberts, Field Marshal Lord, 130
Robinson, Maj Gen Sir F, 7
Romagna, 163
Roman Catholics
   [see: Catholics - Church; Catholicism; Irish - Catholics]
Romans, 163
Romantics (movement in English literature), 7,8,10,33
Rome, 151,152,162,163
   Republic (Ancient Rome), 162
   Roman Republic (1798), 162
Ross, Lt Col Sir H Hew, 119
Rostock, 112
Royalists, 119
Royal Military Assylum, Chelsea, 93
Royal Military College, Sandhurst, 96
Royal Military College, Woolwich, 161
Royal Patriotic Fund, 14
Rules and regulations for the field formation exercise of movements of His Majesty's Forces (Gen Sir David Dundas), 28,30
Russell, Lord John, 153
   Ministry (1846), 142
Russia/Russians, 89,110,115,116,117, 128,129,145
   [see also under: **Battles, Campaigns, Wars**]
   Government, 128
   Military colonies, 128
   Tartars, 128

Index

S

Sadducee sect, 163
Saint [*see*: St...]
Salamanca, 105,140
  [*see also under*: **Battles, Campaigns, Wars**]
Salisbury (family), 17
Saltpetre, 86
Sambre (River), 89
Samuel (Old Testament prophet), 99
San Antonio de Cantara (pass), 123
  [*see also under*: **Battles, Campaigns, Wars** - Busaco]
Sandhurst
  [*see*: Royal Military College, Sandhurst]
Sanhedrin, 163
  Priests, 163
Sardinia, 117
Sarre Louis, 111
Saul (King of Israel, 10th Century BC), 3,50, 99,155,156
Savona, 163
Savoy, 115
Saxe, Marshal, 130
Saxe-Coburg (dynasty), 147
Saxe-Coburg Meiningen (dynasty), 146
Saxony, 53,116,117,145,146
Scheldt (River), 144
Schwerin, 112
Scotland, 2,108
  [*see also*: specific place names; eg Glasgow]
  Faculty of Advocates, 102
  Highland and Agricultural Society, 106
Sculpture
  Greek, 151
  Neo-classical school, 151,152
'Sea peoples' [*see*: Dorians]
Seaton, Lord [*see*: Colborne, Sir John]
Secretary at War, 23
Secretary for War, 23
Semites, 156
Sense and sensibility (Jane Austen), 19
Sentinels [*see*: Sentries]
Sentries, 54,57,118 [*see also*: Pickets]
Seringapatam, 2,100,101
  [*see also under*: **Battles, Campaigns, Wars**]
Sermon on the Mount, 113
Shah Sujah, 85
Shakespeare, Arthur, 7
Shakespeare, William, 9
Sharps, Christian, 149
Shaw Kennedy, Gen [*see*: Kennedy, Gen Shaw]

Shee, M A, 125
Shee, Maj, 101
Shelley, Percy Bysshe, 8,116
Shelton, Brig Gen, 85
Sherbrooke, Gen, 105
Shipping/Ships, 102,144
  Andromeda, 146
  Bellerophon, 69,164
  Canada, 98
  Censeur, 98
  Cruisers, 98
  East Indiaman, 84,86
    Dutch, 86
    English, 86
    Portuguese, 86
  English, 102
  French, 99
  Frigates, 98,102
  Men-of-war, 86
  Pegasus, 146
  Prince George, 146
  Privateers, 98
  Revenge, 99
  Santa Brigida, 98
  Spanish, 98,102
  Thetis, 98
  Triton, 98,99
  Victory, 64
  Windsor Castle, 98
Shorncliffe, 27
Shrapnel, Lt Gen Sir Henry Scrope, 143
Siberia, 128
Siborne, Capt Benjamin, 92
Siborne, Maj Gen Herbert Taylor, 93
  Waterloo letters..., 93
Siborne, Capt William, 51,55,61,66,68, 77,92,93
  History of the war in France and Belgium..., 93
  Instructions for civil and military surveyors in topographical plan-drawings..., 93
  A practical treatise on topographical surveying and drawing, containing a simple and easy mode of surveying the detail of any portion of the country...,93
Sicarri, 163
Sicily, 156,159,167 [*see also*: Two Sicilies]
  King, 151
Silesia, 112
Simon, General, 143
Sir Charles Grandison (Samuel Richardson), 6
Skerret, Maj Gen John Byne, 98,157
Slavery, 164

187

Smith, Ensign C, 76
Smith, Lt Col Webber, 119
Snipers, 150
Society of the Friends of the People, 102
    Edinburgh, 102
Soignies, 47
Soldier in time of war, A (John Stevenson), 12
Solomon, 156
Somerset, Lord, 141
Somerset, Maj Gen Lord Edward, 141
Somerset, Fitzroy [*see*: Raglan, Lord]
Soult, Marshal [Nicolas], 89,105,124,154
Sovereign, 107
Spain/Spaniards, 87,89,105,114,115,117, 122,154,167
    [*see also*: individual place names (eg Madrid); **Battles, Campaigns, Wars** - Peninsular War; *see also under*: Trinidad]
    King, 154
Spices, 86
Squares [*see under*: **Tactics**]
Squire, 17,37
St Etienne (royal armoury), 134
St Helena, 69,70,73,164,165
    Governor, 163
St James, 79
St John Bolingbroke, Viscount Henry [*see*: Bolingbroke, Viscount Henry St John]
St Malo, 161
St Paul's Cathedral, 88,98,125
St Philip, 79
St Vincent, 92
Stanhope, Philip Dormer
    [*see*: Chesterfield, Earl of]
Stadtholder (ruler of Holland), 91,117
Staffordshire
    Lord Lieutenant, 142
Stein, Heinrich Friedrich Karl von, 116
Stevenson, John, 12
    A soldier in time of war, 12
Stewart, Brig Gen, 141
Stewart, Lt, 65
Stuart monument (Antonio Canova), 152
Stuart, James Edward, 6
Stewart, Robert, 114
Sutlej (River), 86
Surrealists, 34
Sussex, 83
Sussex, Duke of, 13
Sweden, 117,144,145,146,157,159,167
    [*see also under*: **Battles, Campaigns, Wars**]
    Baltic provinces, 145

Swedish Council, 146
Swedish Pomerania [*see*: Pomerania]
Switzerland, 89,117
    [*see also*: specific regions; eg Geneva]
Swizer, Colour Sgt, 97
Syracuse
    Commandant, 167
Syria, 156

T

Tactics, 11,15,26,28,132,150,151
    Column, 11,24,42,135,151
        Column of attack, 30,39,77,78,79,80, 141,157
        Column of route, 28,29,31,32
            Close column, 29,59,67
            Open column, 29,49
    Line, 11,26,27,28,29,30,31,32,33, 38,42,133,135
    Square, 3,11,15,23,26,28,30,31,32,42, 51,62,64,72,96,97,125,129,130,133,151
Tagus (River), 154
Tale of two cities, A (Charles Dickens), 9
Talleryrand, Prince, 116
Tartars [*see under*: Russia]
Taylor, Tom
    Our American cousin, 87
Tea, 86
Ter la Haye, 125
Test to destruction, A (Henry Williamson), 4
Thain, Adjutant, 66,76,145
Tilsit, Treaty of [*see*: Treaty of Tilsit]
Tipu Sultan, 101,161,162
To all sportsmen (George Hanger), 132
Tope, 162
Tories, 88,100,114
Torquay, 158
Toulouse, 124
    [*see also under*: **Battles, Campaigns, Wars**]
Tower of London, 98
Treasury
    [*see under*: **Great Britain** - Government]
Treaty of Kiel (1814), 117
Treaty of Paris (1814), 115
Treaty of Tilsit (1807), 112
Treaty of Utrecht (1713), 90
Trevor, Capt A H, 62,75
Trinidad, 122
    [*see also*: specific locations; Roads]
    Coloureds, 122
    Commandant, 122

Index

Military Governor, 122
Police force, 122
Rebellion (1797), 122
Spanish inhabitants, 122
Trumpeter, 113
Turkey [*see*: Ionia; *see also*: Ottoman Empire]
Turks, 137
Two Sicilies, Kingdom of, 115
Tyler, Capt, 123,125
Tyrol, 116

U

Ukraine, 145
Ulm, 89
Ulster, 114
Uniform, 22,28,101,113,134
  By rank
    Officers (British), 149,150
  By Unit/formation
    British Army, 150
      5th Regiment, 161
    Brunswick army, 95
    Dragoons
      British, 137
      French, 137
    Dutch forces
      Cavalry, 93
      Infantry, 92
    Foot Guards, 108
    Horse Artillery
      British
        Royal Horse Artillery, 113,118
        Royal Regiment of Artillery (Foot artillery), 118
    Hussars, 129,138
    Infantry
      British
        Light infantry, 149
        Line infantry, 108
    Lancers, 129
    Rifle Corps (British), 150
  By individual item/form
    Camouflage, 27,28,73,74,83,150
    Dolman, 118,138
    Epaulettes, 149,150
    Frock, 149
    Headdress
      Bicorn hat, 137
      Busby, 138
      Czapska, 129
      Fusilier caps, 161

Grenadier caps, 137
Helmet, 95,137
  Foreign service, 150
  Tarleton, 118
Kalpak [*see*: Busby]
Shako, 138
  Belgian, 92
  Dutch, 92
  French, 95
  'Stovepipe', 99,100
  'Waterloo', 100
Home service undress, 150
Khaki, 28,150
  Drill, 150
Mess dress, 150
Patrol jacket, 149,150
Pelisse, 118,138
Rank insignia, 150
Riding breeches, 150
Sabretache, 92,94,138
Sam Browne belt, 150
Sash, 138,149
Shell jacket, 149
Skirts, 149
Tunic, 138
Undress, 150
Uniform Regulations (1797), 149
United Company of Merchants of England, 86
United Irishmen, 102
United Kingdom [*see*: Great Britain]
United Provinces [*see under*: Holland]
United Service Journal, 80
United Services Club (senior), 106
United States, 102
  [*see also*: specific locations; ie New York]
UNITS AND FORMATIONS
  Allied Army of the Netherlands, 88,92,125, 154,155,158,163
    Army Corps, 155
      1st Corps, 154
    Quartermaster General, 163
    Rifle corps, 148,155
  Allied army (Peninsular War), 124
    Army Corps, 154
  America [*see*: United States]
  Archers, 128
  Army of Occupation, 153,155
  Austria-Hungary, 94,129,163
    Army, 95,104,138,149
      Cavalry
        Cuirassiers, 95
        Hussars, 94,137,138

Light cavalry [see: Hussars]
Infantry, 99
Light infantry, 138
Regiments
  Lancers, 130
Belgium [see: Dutch-Belgian forces]
Brunswick, 42,49,94,167
[see also: Great Britain - Army - Brunswick-Oels Corps]
Artillery, 95
Cavalry, 95
Infantry, 95
  Light infantry, 95
Cavalry, 95,130,133,136,141
[see also: individual countries/formations]
Heavy cavalry, 141
Mailed [see: Knights]
Denmark, 149
Cavalry, 159
Dutch-Belgian forces, 42,49,53,90,92,155
Belgian forces, 91
  Cavalry, 91,141
    [see also under: individual regiments]
  Infantry, 91
    [see also under: individual regiments]
  Militia, 91
  Regiments
    Light infantry, 91
      [see also: individual regiments]
    1st Infantry Regiment, 91
    2nd Carabiniers, 91
    2nd Infantry Regiment, 91
    4th Infantry Regiment, 91
    5th Light Dragoons, 91,94
    7th Infantry Regiment, 91
    8th Hussars, 91,94
    29th - 33rd Infantry Regiments, 91
    34th Infantry Regiment, 91
    36th Infantry Regiment, 91
Dutch forces
  Army, 89,90,91,94,158
    Brigades
      Scotch (18th Century), 82,158
    Cavalry, 141
      [see also under: Regiments]
    Militia, 91
    Quartermaster General, 91
    Regiments
      Cavalry, 91,141
        [see also: individual regiments]
      Colonial, 91
        [see also: individual regiments]

East Indies, 91,155
Foot Guards
  1st Battalion (18th Century), 82
  2nd Battalion (18th Century), 82
  Gordon (18th Century), 82
Light infantry, 91
  [see also: individual regiments]
Swiss mercenary, 91
  [see also: individual regiments]
1st Carabiniers, 91,93
3rd Carabiniers, 91,93
4th Light Dragoons, 91,94
5th Infantry Regiment, 91
6th Hussars, 91,94
7th Hussars, 91
10th Infantry Regiment, 91
11th Infantry Regiment, 91
16th-18th Infantry Regiments, 91
19th-26th Infantry Regiments, 91
27th Infantry Regiment, 91
29th-33rd Infantry Regiments, 91
34th Infantry Regiment, 91
Cavalry, 91
  [see also under: Dutch/Belgian forces]
Carabiniers [see: Cuirassiers]
Cuirassiers, 91
Heavy dragoons [see: Cuirassiers]
Light cavalry, 92
Infantry, 91
  Light infantry, 92
Nassau forces, 91
  Regiments, 91
    28th Regiment, 91
Dragoons, 136
[see also under: individual countries]
France, 12,95,147
  Army, 5,56,61,67,69,78,86,89,91,
    95,111,127,129,131,137,138,148,163
    [see also under: **Uniform**]
  Army of the Orient, 152
  Army of the Rhine, 89
  Army of Switzerland, 89
  Artillery, 50,59,61,62,65,123,168
    Horse artillery, 33,119
    [see also: Imperial Guard - Napoleon's Horse Artillery of the Guard]
  Battalion, 30
  Cavalry/cavalrymen, 32,33,49,50,51,
    61,62,72,92,95,96,97,125,129,
    135,137,138,159,168
    [see also under: Imperial Guard]

Index

Brigades, 135
Carabiniers, 135,137
Chasseurs, 135,137,138
Chevaux legers [*see*: Poles]
Companies, 135
Cuirassiers, 8,32,49,54,59,79,95,96, 129,135,136,137,141
   'Sacred Squadron', 96
Divisions, 135
Dragoons, 59,129,137,141
   Heavy Dragoons, 136
   Light Dragoons, 136
Heavy cavalry, 95,96,137
   [*see also*: Carabiniers, Cuirassiers]
Hussars, 88,119,135,137
Lancers, 32,86,125,129,130,135
   [*see also*: individual units]
Light cavalry, 135
   [*see also*: Hussars, Lancers]
Medium cavalry, 135
   [*see also*: Dragoons]
Platoons, 135
Poles, 129,130
   [*see also under*: Imperial Guard]
Regiments, 135
Revolutionary armies, 112
Conscription/conscripts, 127,128
Corps, 114,129
   I Corps (Waterloo), 135,152
   II Corps (Waterloo), 135,152
   III Corps (Waterloo), 135
   IV Corps (Waterloo), 135
   V Corps (Waterloo), 135
   VI Corps (Waterloo), 135
   3rd Corps (Russian campaign, 1812) 89
   6th Corps (1805), 89
Cuirassiers [*see under*: Cavalry]
Divisions
   16th, 114
Dragoons [*see under*: Cavalry]
Garrisons
   Malta
      Valetta, 105
Guardsman, 73,126
Generals, 96
Gunners, 3,10,11,71,73
Hussars [*see under*: Cavalry]
Imperial Guard, 11,39,53,65,66,67,68, 69,70,76,77,78,80,107,127,128,129, 135,155,159
Battalions,129

Cavalry, 128,135
   [*see also under*: Imperial Guard - Regiments]
   Divisions, 135
   Heavy cavalry, 129
   Light cavalry, 135
   Napoleon's Horse Artillery of the Guard, 119
   Old Guard, 128,129,157
   Poles, 128
   Regiments
      Chasseurs-a-Cheval, 128
      Consular Guard
         [*see*: Grenadiers-a-pied]
      Corps of Guides
         [*see*: Chasseurs-a-Cheval]
      Empress's Dragoon Regiment, 128
      Grenadiers-a-cheval, 128
      Grenadiers-a-pied, 128,129
      Horse Grenadiers, 129
      Lancers, 129,130,136
         Penants, 136
      Uhlans [*see*: Lancers]
      1st Chevaliers Lanciers, 128
      Young Guard, 128
Infantry, 33,39,59,61,124,125,141,148
   Light infantry, 95
Lancers [*see under*: Cavalry]
Light troops [*see*: Skirmishers]
Mutiny (World War I), 23
Officers, 79,80,97
Regiments
   [*see also under*: Imperial Guard]
   Beaujolais, 114
   Fusilier, 133
   Grenadier, 133
   1st Polish Lancers of Vistula Region, 33
   2nd Hussars, 33
   21st Cavalry, 152
Skirmishers, 24,39,49,51,68,95,148
Tirailleurs, 24,95 [*see also*: Skirmishers]
Voltigeurs, 24,95 [*see also*: Skirmishers]
Fleet, 63
   Antwerp, 144
   Toulon, 98
Germany [*see also*: Hanover, Prussia]
   Army
      Cavalry, 130
      Regiments
         Lancers, 130
         Uhlans [*see*: Cavalry, Regiments - Lancers]

Mutiny (World War I), 23
Great Britain, 42,94,95
  Army, 11,12,13,14,15,16,17,18,19,20,21, 23,24,25,26,27,29,33,36,37,41,47,56, 59,61,66,67,70,83,84,85,90,95,104, 105,106,107,108,110,112,119,130,132, 135,137,138,140,141,144,156
  [*see also*: **Uniform**]
    Adjutant, 26,31
    Artillery, 23,24,37,52,118,140,155
      [*see also*: Royal Regiment of Artillery; **Weapons and Ammunition** - Artillery]
      Horse, 42,118,141
        [*see also*: Royal Horse Artillery; **Weapons and Ammunition** - Artillery]
        Bombardiers, 113,118
        Carriage smith, 118
        Drivers, 118
        Gunners, 113,118,142
          Foot gunners, 118
          Horse gunners, 118
        Shoeing smith, 118
        Wheelright, 118
    Brevet rank, 109
    Brigades, 24,25,29,31,33,66,77,85, 123,140,153,154,157
      Cavalry, 24,105,140
        Heavy Brigade (Waterloo)
          [*see*: Household Brigade]
        Household Brigade (Waterloo), 61,141,142
        Light Brigade (Crimean War), 12
        Light Brigade (Peninsular War), 157
        Union Brigade (Waterloo), 141
      Guards, 25,80
        [*see also*: individual brigades]
      Household Cavalry Brigade (Waterloo), 119
      Union Brigade (Waterloo), 141
      Infantry, 24,135
      Light Brigade (Waterloo), 66
      Light Infantry, 25
      1st (Guards) Brigade (Peninsular War), 139
      1st (Guards) Brigade (Waterloo), 59, 66,78,103,107,139
      1st Hanoverian Brigade (Waterloo), 59
      2nd (Guards) Brigade (Waterloo), 66, 68,78,103,108,152,153
      3rd Infantry Brigade (Adam's Brigade) (Waterloo), 155
      4th Infantry Brigade (Mitchell's Brigade)(Waterloo), 155
      5th Infantry Brigade (Waterloo), 48, 49,51,59,62,65,71,73,75,83,84,92
    Brigadier, 121
    Brigadier General, 121
    Brunswick-Oels Corps, 28,94
      [*see also*: *Brunswick*]
      Hussars, 94
      Jagers, 25,28,94
      Uniforms, 95
    Captain, 21,26,90,109,113,118
    Cavalry, 23,39,49,52,61,86,95,109, 113,118,119,126,136,137,138,140, 141,143
      [*see also under*: Brigades/Divisions, individual regiments]
      Heavy cavalry, 94,95,137,138
      Hussars, 94,118
        [*see also*: Regiments; individual regiments]
      Light cavalry, 139
      Light dragoons, 94,118
        [*see also under*: Regiments; individual regiments]
    Chasseurs Britanniques, 25
    Chief of the Imperial General Staff, 23
    Colonel, 26
    Colour Sergeant, 12,97
    Commander-in-Chief, 12,20,21,23,24, 88,93,113,130,142,155
    Commandos, 1
    Commissariat, 24,58,94,113,135
      Assistant Commissaries, 135
      Clerks, 135
      Commissary General, 24,135
      Deputy Commissaries, 135
    Commissions, 14,20,38,109,134
      Purchase system, 20,21,109
    Companies, 2,26,29,31,48,51,54,67,75, 113,144
      [*see also under*: Grenadiers]
      Flank [*see*: Light]
      Light, 12,26,27,107,108,167
      Rifle, 26
      Scottish, 108
    Company Sergeant Major, 97
    Cornets, 20,90
    Corporals, 26,90,113,118
    Corps (army corps), 105
    Corps, 21
      Army Ordnance Corps, 21
      Army Service Corps, 21,24,134

Index

Royal Staff Corps, 24
Discipline, 15,16,31
Divisions, 24,66,77,154
   Cavalry, 24,140
   Guards Division, 25,51,52,74
   Household Division, 13,14,25
   [*see also*: individual divisions/ individual units; eg Household Cavalry]
   Light Division (Peninsular War), 24, 25,94,157
   Peninsular War, 24
   1st (Peninsular War), 25,105
   1st (Guards) (Waterloo), 103,107, 152,153
   2nd (France, 1813-1814), 154
   2nd (Peninsular War), 153,154,157
   2nd (Waterloo), 78,155,157
   3rd (Peninsular War), 123,124
   3rd (Waterloo), 167, 168
   4th Division (France, 1813-1814), 154
   4th Division (Waterloo), 155
   5th (Waterloo), 61,124,125,141
   6th (Peninsular War), 105,168
   7th (Peninsular War), 25,83,105
   8th [*see*: Light Division]
Divisions (sub-division within battalion), 29,31,97
Divisions (sub-division within horse artillery troop), 118
Dragoons, 137
   [*see also*: Cavalry - Light Dragoons; *see also under*: Regiments]
Drum Major, 110
Drummer, 26,31,48,68,113
[*see also*: Drums in general section]
Educational standards, 14
[*see also*: Literacy]
Engineers, 23,24,113
Ensign, 20,26,96 [*see also*: Subaltern]
Expeditionary Force (to Holland, 1799), 140
Farrier, 118
Field Marshal, 121
Flogging, 15,16,17,18
Foot Guards, 14,20,21,25,39,53,68, 77,78,79,107,109,110,167
   [*see also*: Commissions, Officers, Officers - Pay; *see also under*: Battalions, Brigades, Divisions, individual regiments]
Garrisons
   Cabul, 85

   [*see also*: Cabul in general section]
   Jellalabad, 85
   [*see also*: Jellalabad in general section]
   Scotland, 108
   Trinidad, 122
General officer, 57,66,121
Grenadiers, 1,108,144
   Battalions, 161
   Companies, 1,3,10,26,42,48,50, 65,161
Guards [*see*: Foot Guards; *see also*: Household Cavalry; under Battalions/ Brigades/Divisions]
Household Cavalry, 13,20,55,136
   [*see also*: individual regiments; ie 1st Life Guards, 2nd Life Guards, Royal Horse Guards]
Hussars, 138
Infantry/infantrymen, 2,11,22,23,26, 30,31,32,61,80,99,129,132,149,150
   [*see also*: Companies; individual units]
   Inspector General, 168
   Light infantry, 25,27,38,39,100, 104,132
   [*see also*: individual units]
   Line infantry, 20,21,24,25,37
   [*see also*: individual units]
   Mounted infantry, 136
in: France, 88
in: Iberian Peninsula, 87,122,124, 153,154,157,159,168
in: Ireland, 153,158
in: Portugal
   [*see*: Iberian Peninsula]
King's German Legion, 25,32,82,83,84, 94,158,159
   [*see also*: Hanover - Army]
   Artillery
      Foot, 83
      Horse, 83
   Brigades, 159
      Cavalry, 83,155
      Infantry, 83
      Light Brigade (Peninsular War), 83,159
      1st Brigade (Du Plat's Brigade) (Waterloo), 155
   Cavalry
      Dragoons, 32,83
      Hussars, 83
   King's German Regiment, 83,158
   1st Light Infantry Battalion, 82, 83,159

2nd Light Infantry Battalion, 83, 158, 159
7th Line Battalion, 159
Line infantry, 83
Lance Corporal, 113
Lieutenant, 26, 75, 109, 118
Lieutenant Colonel, 26
Lieutenant General, 24, 121
Literacy, 14
Major, 21, 26, 31, 109
Major general, 121
Marines, 162
Master General of the Ordnance, 23, 24, 113, 142
Mercenaries, 84
Musicians, 32
Non-Commissioned Officers, 12, 19, 68
Officers, 11, 12, 14, 16, 18, 19, 20, 21, 26, 31, 48, 49, 50, 51, 55, 64, 65, 68, 77, 98, 106, 108, 113, 129, 136, 150
  Company officers, 109
  Mess, 96, 101
  Pay, 109
Parliamentary Army, 20, 108, 120
  Cavalry, 138
  'Ironsides', 96
Pioneers, 31, 90
Platoon, 25, 30
Privates, 26, 90
Quartermaster, 5, 26, 100, 101
Regiments, 20, 21, 41, 66, 77, 101, 106, 109, 110, 126, 140
  Battalions, 21, 24, 26, 29, 31, 32, 33, 97
    Guards, 25, 103
    Line infantry, 103, 109
      [see also: Commissions, Officers - Pay]
    5th Garrison, 157
  Cavalry, 20, 89, 101, 135, 136, 138
    [see also: individual regiments]
    Heavy Cavalry, 138
    Light cavalry, 137, 138
    Squadrons, 90
    Troops, 90
  Coldstream Guards
    [see: 2nd Foot Guards]
  Dragoons, 95, 136, 137
    [see also: individual regiments]
    Dragoon Guards, 95, 136
      [see also: individual regiments]
  Duke of York's Life Guards, 120

Experimental Corps of Riflemen
  [see: 95th Rifles]
General Monck's Troop of Life Guards, 120
Grenadier Guards
  [see: 1st Foot Guards]
Household Cavalry, 96, 120, 141
  [see also: individual regiments]
Infantry, 26, 110, 136
  [see also: individual regiments]
  Light infantry, 15, 25, 104
  [see also: individual regiments]
Hussars, 138
  [see also: Light Dragoons]
Irish Guards, 25, 108
King's Royal Rifle Corps, 28
  [see also: 60th Regiment]
Lancers, 138
  [see also: individual regiments]
Life Guards (pre-Restoration), 120
Life Guards (post-Restoration), 55, 119, 136, 141, 142
  [see also: individual regiments]
Light Dragoons, 137, 138
  [see also: individual regiments]
Monck's Regiment of Foot, 108
  [see also: 2nd Foot Guards]
Perthshire Volunteers
  [see: 90th Regiment]
Prince of Wales's Regiment of Foot
  [see: 75th Regiment]
Rifle, 15, 27, 28
  [see also: individual regiments]
Rifle Brigade, 28, 37
  [see also: 95th Rifles]
Royal Artillery
  [see: Royal Regiment of Artillery]
Royal Fusiliers
  [see: 7th Regiment]
Royal Horse Artillery, 113, 118, 119
  Brigades, 118
    Half-brigades, 118
  A Troop, 119
  D Troop, 119
  E Troop, 119
  F Troop, 119
  G Troop, 118, 119
  H Troop, 119
  I Troop, 119
  O Troop, 110
  2nd Rocket Troop
    [see: O Troop]
Royal Horse Guards, 12, 13, 20, 107, 119, 136, 141, 142

Index

Royal Marines, 1
Royal Regiment of Artillery, 160
    Batteries, 52,113,143
    Brigades, 113
    Field artillery, 113
        Foot artillery, 113,118,119
        Horse artillery, 55,86,113,119
        [see also: Royal Horse Artillery]
    Garrison artillery, 113
    Siege artillery, 113
Scots Greys [see: 2nd Dragoons]
Scots Guards
    [see: 3rd Foot Guards]
Special Air Service, 1
Staffordshire Volunteers, 140
    [see also: 12th Regiment]
Welsh Guards, 25,108
York Infantry Volunteers, 153
1st Dragoons, 141
1st Foot Guards, 1,25,84,107,108, 139,167
    2nd Bn, 103,107,139
    3rd Bn, 68,103,107,139
1st King's Dragoon Guards, 55, 119,141
1st Life Guards, 14,86,95,107, 119,120
1st Regiment (Royal Scots), 15, 18,106,154
2nd Dragoons (Scots Greys), 137, 141
2nd Foot Guards, 12,25,107, 108,109,153
    2nd Bn, 103,107,108,153
2nd Life Guards, 14,95,120,158
2nd West India Regiment, 153
3rd Foot Guards, 12,25,108,153
    2nd Battalion, 153
3rd Regiment, 97,168
    1st Bn, 33
    2nd Bn, 103
4th Foot Guards
    [see : Irish Guards]
5th Foot Guards
    [see: Welsh Guards]
5th Lancers, 130,136
5th Regiment,123,154,161
5th (Royal Irish) Dragoons, 136
6th Dragoons, 141
7th Hussars, 58,86,129,138
7th Light Dragoons, 140,142
    [see also: 7th Hussars]
7th Regiment, 13,26,140

8th Hussars
    [see: 8th Light Dragoons]
8th Light Dragoons, 138
8th West India Regiment, 85
9th Light Dragoons, 130
9th Regiment, 92
10th Hussars, 13,138
10th Light Dragoons, 138
10th West India Regiment, 153
11th Hussars
    [see: 11th Light Dragoons]
11th Light Dragoons, 138
11th Regiment, 167
12th Light Dragoons, 130
12th Regiment, 121
13th Light Dragoons, 13
14th Hussars
    [see: 14th Light Dragoons]
14th Light Dragoons, 138
14th Regiment, 106,154,155
15th Hussars
    [see: 15th Light Dragoons]
15th Light Dragoons, 85,138,140,141
15th Regiment, 167
16th Light Dragoons, 129,130
17th Regiment, 121,139
18th Hussars
    [see: 18th Light Dragoons]
18th Light Dragoons, 138
19th Light Dragoons, 130
20th Hussars
    [see: 20th Light Dragoons]
20th Light Dragoons, 138
21st Lancers, 130
20th Regiment, 156
23rd Light Dragoons, 86
23rd Regiment, 155
26th Regiment, 158
28th Regiment, 30,61
29th Regiment, 153
30th Regiment, 14,47,59,65,71
    2nd Battalion, 75
31st Regiment, 83
32nd Regiment, 61,97,154
33rd Regiment, 2,5,10,21,26,40, 47,50,51,54,57,59,64,65,68,75, 77,84,85,87,88,96,98,100,101, 143,144,148,153,160
    Adjutant, 145
    Officers, 75,144,166-167
    [see also: individual names]
35th Regiment, 83
38th Regiment, 153

40th Regiment, 98
41st Regiment, 26,84
42nd (Highland) Regiment, 17, 32,96
43rd Regiment, 25,27,103
44th Regiment, 97
45th Regiment
  1st Bn, 123
48th Regiment
  2nd Battalion, 33
50th Regiment, 165
51st Regiment, 155
52nd Light Infantry, 11,25,53,67, 68,69,74,77,78,79,157
56th Regiment, 121
58th Regiment, 106
  2nd Bn, 123
60th Regiment, 26,59
  1st Battalion, 168
  5th Battalion, 28,123
61st Regiment, 13
66th Regiment, 167
  2nd Battalion, 33
68th Regiment, 27,121
69th Regiment, 32,47,49,51,65,96
  2nd Battalion, 75
71st Regiment, 14,27,83,155,157
73rd Regiment, 47,59,65,92,162
  2nd Battalion, 75
75th Regiment, 121
76th Regiment, 139,161
77th Regiment, 26
79th Regiment, 61
80th Regiment, 140
83rd Regiment
  2nd Bn, 123
85th Regiment, 27
86th Regiment, 154
87th Regiment, 7,14
88th Regiment, 123
89th Regiment, 26
90th Regiment, 27,104,154
93rd Regiment, 84
95th Rifles, 15,25,28,37,61,94,157
  2nd Battalion, 25,37
  3rd Battalion, 25,37
97th Regiment, 26
98th Regiment, 26
103rd Regiment, 26
Riding master, 101
Riflemen, 24,25,38,39,83,148
Scottish units, 108

Sergeants, 26,31,89,97,98,113,118
  Staff Sergeant, 118
Short service, 14
Skirmishers, 28,30,39,77
  [*see also*: Infantry - Light infantry]
Squadron, 90
Subaltern, 21,97,113,118
  [*see also*: Ensign]
Surgeon, 26,118
Trooper, 90
Troop, 90,118
Trumpeters, 90,118,141
Volunteer, 96
East India Company, 131
[*see also* in general section]
Armies, 86
  Bengal army, 84
    Benares Division, 85
  Bombay army, 101
    Commander-in-Chief, 83,161
  Madras army, 101
    Commander-in-Chief, 161
Navy, 86
Militia, 14,36,37
  Battalions, 36
  Colonial, 27
  Companies, 37
  Officers, 14,36,38
  Regiments, 37
  Staffordshire Militia, 140
Royal Air Force, 21
Royal Navy, 15,24,37,40,94,98,105
  Admiralty, 24
  East Indies station, 99
  Navy Board, 24
Hanover
Army, 42,68,82,83,94,141,158,159
[*see also*: *Great Britain* - Army - King's German Legion]
  Artillery
    Foot batteries, 158
  Battalions
    Field battalions, 158
    Landwehr, 155,158
      Cavalry, 158
      Infantry, 158
  Brigades
    1st, 94,139
    3rd, 159
    4th, 159
    Landwehr (*see*: 3rd, 4th Brigades)
  Corps

Index

10th Army Corps, 159
Landwehr
  [*see under*: Battalions/Brigades]
Levies, 159
Militia [*see*: *Landwehr*]
Regiments
  Hussars, 158
    Duke of Cumberland's Hussars, 40,94
Horse artillery, 119
Hungary [*see*: Austria-Hungary]
Hussars, 130,138
  [*see also under*: individual countries/formations]
Infantry/infantrymen, 129,130,133,134, 136,148
  [*see also*: individual countries/formations]
  Light infantry, 138
  Mechanized infantry, 136
  Motorized infantry, 136
Knights, 95,129,135
Lancers, 130
  [*see also under*: individual countries/formations]
Lithuanians, 129
  Lancers, 129,136
Malta, 105
Men-at-arms, 95,129
Moslems
  Cavalry, 129
Musketeers, 132,134,136
Naples, 105
Netherlands [*see*: Dutch-Belgian forces]
Pikemen, 134
Poland
  Army, 117
    Cavalry, 130
    Polks [*see*: Regiments]
    Regiments, 130
      Lancers, 130
      Uhlan Voluntaires [*see*: Lancers]
Portugal
  Army, 168
    Brigades, 25
    Cacadores, 24,28
    Divisions, 24,154
    Light infantry [*see*: Cacadores]
    Regiments, 123
Prussia, 1,78,125
  Army, 28,67,88,104,106,112,129,130, 138,149,167
    Artillery
      Horse artillery, 119

Cuirassiers, 95
Regiments
  Lancers, 130
  Landwehr
  Militia [*see*: *Landwehr*]
  Uhlans [*see*: Lancers]
Riflemen, 136
  [*see also under*: individual countries]
Rome
  Legions, 162
Russia
  Army
    Cossacks, 89,127,128
      Ataman, 127
      Hetman [*see*: Ataman]
    Mutiny (World War I), 23
    Regiments
      Light cavalry, 128
Sardinia
  Army, 164
Spain, 105,154
Sweden
  Army, 112,145
  Cavalry, 112
Tartars
  Cavalry, 129
Uhlans [*see*: Lancers]
United States
  Sharps Shooter, 149 (American Civil War, 1861-1865)
University of...
  [*see under*: city in which university is located; eg Edinburgh - University]
Upper Canada [*see under*: Canada]
Utrecht, Treaty of [*see*: Treaty of Utrecht]
Uxbridge, Earl of, 140
Uxbridge, Lord, 42,61,86,140-142,154

V

Valence, 162
Vandamme, General Dominique Joseph Rene, 140
Vatican, 162,163 [*see also*: Papacy]
Vaughan, Sir John, 121
Venaissin, 115
Venetia, 116
Venice, 151
  Procurator, 151
Venlo, 82
Venus and Mars (Antonio Canova), 152
Venus Victrix (Antonio Canova), 151

Vera Cruz, 98
Victor, Marshal [Claud], 112
Victoria (Queen of England, 1837-1901), 4,5,40,106,144,146,147
Vienna, 69,127
Vigo, 83
Vittoria, 124
   [see also under: **Battles, Campaigns, Wars**]
Voltaire, 6
Von Bulow
   [see: Bulow, Friedrich Wilhelm von]
Von der Decken, Col Frederick
   [see: Decken, Col Frederick von der]
Von Dreyse, Johann [see: Dreyse, Johann von]
Vyse, Gen, 153

W

Waiters, 14
Wales, 124
Wallis, 117
Walmoden, Count, 159
Walpole, S
   History of England from 1815, 147
War Office, 23
Warre, William, 7
Warsaw, 147
Warsaw, Grand Duchy, 116,117
   [see also: Poland]
Washington, George (Statue) (Antonio Canova), 152
Water, 54
Waterloo (village), 62,72,86,125
   [see also under: **Battles, Campaigns, Wars**]
Waterloo letters... (Herbert Taylor Siborne), 93
Waterloo Roll Call, 1,98,102,166
Watson, Ensign J, 76
Wavell, Lord, 21
Weapons and Ammunition, 101,150
   Ammunition, 78,113,142,143
      Arrows, 129
      Bomb, 113
      Bullet, 148,149
      Cannon-ball, 3,50,62,63,72,107
      Cannister shot [see: Case shot]
      Cannon balls [see: Round shot]
      Cartridge, 8,133
         Combustible, 148
         Rimfire, 149
      Case shot, 107,143
         Heavy case, 107
         Light case, 107

Common shell [see: Shell]
Crossbow bolt, 129
Cylindro-conical projectile [see: Bullet; see also: Minie ball]
Fractured shells [see: Round shot]
Grape shot, 107,143
Minie ball, 148
Musket ball, 10,95,131,132,134,143, 145,148
   British, 148
   French, 148
Powder, 54,130,131,132,133,143
   Smokeless, 149
Rifle ball, 27
Round shot, 142,143
   6 lb, 143
   9 lb, 143
Shell, 65,142,143
   24lb, 143
Shrapnel, 143
Spherical case [see: Shrapnel]
Artillery, 3,11,39,48,59,78,107,113,118, 119,142,143
   [see also: UNITS AND FORMATIONS - Artillery - Horse; Royal Horse Artillery; Royal Regiment of Artillery]
   Breech loading, 130
   Cannon [see: Artillery in this section]
   Field guns, 142
   Gun [see under: Artillery in this section]
   Gun carriages, 8,54,71,78,118
      Drag ropes, 118
   Howitzer, 119,142,143
      5,5", 113,142
   Rifled, 151
   Rockets, 119
      12 pr, 119
      Carts, 119
      Launchers, 119
   Waggons, 113,118
   6 pr, 113,118,119,143
   9 pr, 112,118,119,143
Automatic weapons, 133
Bayonet, 32,133,134
   Plug bayonet, 133
   Socket, 133
Crossbow, 129,131
Dagger, 133
Grenades, 1
Hand grenades, 1
Lance, 127,128,129,130
Longbow, 129

Index

Musket, 8,26,27,28,30,32,42,48,54,58,64, 95,128,148
   Flintlock, 130,131,132,134
      'Brown Bess', 39,58,130,131,132,134, 148,149
         India Pattern musket, 131,132
         Land Pattern musket, 131
            Long Land Pattern, 131
            New Land Service Pattern, 132
            Short Land Pattern, 131
         Sea Service musket, 131,132
         Charleville musket, 134,148
         French [see: Charleville musket]
   Matchlock, 131
      Matches, 133
   Miquelet, 131
   Percussion lock, 131,132,134,148
   Snaphaunce, 131
   Wheel lock, 131
Pike, 97,129
Pistol [see under: Small arms]
Rifle, 27,130,134,148
   Baker rifle, 27,148
   Bolt action, 149
   Breech loading, 149,150
   'Dragon', 136
   Enfield, 148
   Henry, 149
   Lee Enfield, 28
   Martini-Henry, 28,149
   Needle gun, 149
   Percussion cap, 148,149
   Schneider, 28
   Sharps, 149
   Snider-Enfield, 149
   Spencer, 149
   Telescopic sight, 148
   Winchester, 149
      Model 73, 149
Sabre [see: Sword]
Small arms, 148
   [see also: Bayonet, Pistol, Rifle]
   Pistol, 8,54,96,131
      Revolver, 150
   Sword, 54,69,96,127
      Pattern 1796 Light Cavalry Officers', 118
Webb-Carter, B W, 2
Webber Smith, Lt Col
   [see: Smith, Lt Col Webber]
Wellesley, Arthur [see: Wellington, Duke of]
Wellesley, Lord Richard, 87,104,142,162
Wellesley, Marquis of

[see: Wellesley, Lord Richard]
Wellesley, William, 7
Wellington, Duke of, 7,11,12,14,15,16,18,19, 24,29,30,33,37,38,42,49,51,52,55,57,59, 61,64,67,68,70,72,78,83,85,86,87,88,91, 94,100,101,102,105,110,111,112,115,116, 123,124,125,137,141,142,143,147,148, 153,154,155,157,160,163,168
   Command in Peninsula, 115
   Waterloo despatch, 155
Wellington (5th Duke), 88
Wellington (6th Duke), 88
Wellington's army in the Peninsula 1808-1814 (Michael Glover), 16
West Indies [see: Caribbean]
Westminster Abbey, 57,116
Westminster School, 140,161
Westmore, Lt R, 66,76 [referred to as Captain on this page]
Westphalia, 94,116
Whigs, 147
Whinyates, Maj E C, 119
White feather, 87
Whitehill (district of Glasgow), 68
William Frederick I (King of Holland), 89,91
William IV (King of England, 1830-1837), 4,5, 40,63,144,146-147
   [see also: Clarence, Duke of]
Williamson, Henry, 4,5
   Chronicles of ancient sunlight, 4
   Fox under my cloak, 4
   Golden virgin, The, 4
   Love and the loveless, 4
   Test to destruction, A, 4
Winckelmann, Johann, 151
Wolves, 138
Woodville, Richard Caton, 34
Woolwich military academy
   [see: Royal Military College, Woolwich]
Wordsworth, William, 8
Worcestershire, 12
Wurmser, General, 104

Y

Yonge, Sir George, 20
Yonge, William Crawley, 79
York, Duke of, 20,122,140,146,167
Yorkshire, 36

www.ingramcontent.com/pod-product-compliance
Lightning Source LLC
Chambersburg PA
CBHW060519100426
42743CB00009B/1382